GUIDE TO EMPLOYEE STOCK OWNERSHIP PLANS

A Revolutionary Method for Increasing Corporate Profits

GUIDE TO EMPLOYEE STOCK OWNERSHIP PLANS

A Revolutionary Method for Increasing Corporate Profits

Charles A. Scharf

PRENTICE-HALL, INC. Englewood Cliffs, N.J.

Prentice-Hall International, Inc., *London*
Prentice-Hall of Australia, Pty. Ltd., *Sydney*
Prentice-Hall of Canada, Ltd., *Toronto*
Prentice-Hall of India Private Ltd., *New Delhi*
Prentice-Hall of Japan, Inc., *Tokyo*

This publication is designed to provide accurate and authoritative information in regard to the subject matter covered. It is sold with the understanding that the publisher is not engaged in rendering legal, accounting or other professional service. If legal advice or other expert assistance is required, the services of a competent professional should be sought.

—From a Declaration of Principles jointly adopted
by a Committee of the American Bar Association
and a Committee of Publishers and Associations.

Library of Congress Cataloging in Publication Data

Scharf, Charles A
   Guide to employee stock ownership plans.

   Includes index.
   1. Employee ownership--United States.
I. Title.
KF3496.S3   344'.73'01255   76-10365
ISBN 0-13-369447-X

Printed in the United States of America

To Ruthie, Leslie, and Kelley

THE
AUTHOR

Charles A. Scharf is a practicing New York attorney, president of Charles A. Scharf, P.C., a professional corporation. He has been involved for many years in the practice of corporate law, including the preparation of employee benefit plans, Securities and Exchange Commission matters, and acquisitions, mergers and tender offers. The author has spoken on frequent occasions before business and professional organizations, including the Association of Corporate Growth, Corporate Seminars, Inc., Practicing Law Institute and American Management Association. He has also served as a guest lecturer at The New York University School of Continuing Education.

Mr. Scharf is the author of the books *Techniques for Buying, Selling and Merging Businesses,* and *Acquisitions, Mergers, Sales and Takeovers—A Handbook with Forms* published by Prentice-Hall. He is also contributor to *Acquisition and Merger Negotiating Strategy* and *Business of Acquisition and Mergers* published by President's Publishing House, and has numerous articles in a variety of business and legal publications to his credit.

A WORD FROM THE AUTHOR

The Employee Retirement Income Security Act of 1974 ("ERISA"), enacted on September 2, 1974, incorporated a massive overhaul of Federal statutes affecting employee benefit plans. Among its provisions, the Act gives statutory sanction to the use of an Employee Stock Ownership Plan ("ESOP") as a vehicle of corporate finance. Since the enactment of ERISA, ESOP has become a center of debate, and the subject of innumerable articles, both for and against the concept.

An ESOP is an employee benefit plan designed to invest primarily in securities of an employer. It is exempt from income taxes under the same provisions of the Internal Revenue Code as tax-exempt pension and profit-sharing plans. However, an ESOP differs from ordinary employee benefit plans, because an ESOP may legally provide financial assistance to an employer and conduct business transactions prohibited to ordinary plans:

1. An ESOP may borrow to buy employer stock;
2. An ESOP may have its borrowings guaranteed or secured by an employer;
3. An ESOP may borrow and buy stock from a controlling stockholder;
4. An ESOP may invest 100% of its assets in stock of an employer, without regard to fiduciary obligations to diversify investments under ERISA;
5. An employer's contributions to an ESOP may be entirely within the discretion of the Board of Directors, and need not be made under a fixed formula; and
6. Tax-deductible contributions to an ESOP may be made in stock or cash, whether or not an employer has realized profits.

Some proponents of ESOP stress ESOP's fundamental purpose as the political, sociological, economic, and employee benefits of granting the average American wage earner ownership in corporate capital, which in partnership with his efforts, enables him to produce and distribute goods. Other proponents of ESOP point to the corporate benefits it offers as a unique instrument of corporate finance, tax planning, and, often, estate planning.

From any viewpoint, characteristics of an ESOP make it an extraordinarily flexible employee incentive program which provides opportunities to employers for increasing and raising capital, for financial planning, and, in the case of closely-held corporations, for estate planning. This book explains how an ESOP may:

1. Increase working capital of an employer by contributions of stock to the ESOP;

2. Enable an employer to borrow for capital improvements and repay borrowed principal with tax-deductible dollars;

3. Enable an employer to make acquisitions with tax-deductible dollars;

4. Enable an employer to divest, and employees to purchase, a division or subsidiary with tax-deductible dollars;

5. Enable an employer to refinance and repay indebtedness with tax-deductible dollars;

6. Enable controlling stockholders in closely-held corporations to sell stock at capital gains rates and retain control;

7. Enable a public company to avoid an unfriendly takeover;

8. Enable key executives to purchase a closely held business out of earnings on a tax-deductible basis;

9. Enable a controlling stockholder to develop an estate plan and to provide a market and funds for the purchase of his stock from his estate; and

10. Enable employees to receive lump-sum pension payments, on a substantially tax-free basis.

An ESOP can make every one of the above transactions a reality. But to do so, the ESOP must meet complex and detailed requirements for ESOPs contained in the Employee Retirement Income Security Act of 1974, the Internal Revenue Code, the Securities Act of 1933, the Securities Exchange Act of 1934, and the regulations and administrative agency and court decisions construing this interrelated mass of Federal legislation. A failure to comply or to escape the many legal traps set along the path of establishing and administering an ESOP may not only lose expected ESOP benefits, but may cause imposition upon an employer or trustee of penalty taxes as high as 100% of the value of a transaction.

In spite of an ESOP's possibilities as an extraordinarily valuable instrument of corporate finance, no employer should establish an ESOP until it has analyzed possible disadvantages and pitfalls of ESOP, such as possible dilution of earnings. No professional, corporate financial officer, pension administrator, lawyer, or accountant should advise with respect to the adoption of an ESOP until he understands not only the advantages but also possible disadvantages of an ESOP for a particular employer.

This book does three things:

First, it describes the nature of ESOP and its many possible benefits as an instrument of corporate finance and planning, for both public and closely-held corporations.

Second, it cites, explains, and where appropriate quotes the federal laws affecting ESOPs, including pension, tax, and securities laws, and regulations and cases under these laws.

Third, it tells how to set up an ESOP, provides detailed instructions for obtaining an Internal Revenue Service advance determination to qualify an ESOP under the Internal Revenue Code, and provides model ESOP forms for consideration by management and counsel. It also points out and, where feasible, offers solutions to practical and legal pitfalls and problems in forming and maintaining an ESOP.

Often, knowledgeable individuals initially react with skepticism to the revolutionary financial benefits available to a corporation upon installation of an ESOP. The reaction may be "that's impossible," or "that's a gimmick, it won't last."

However, the sociological and financial benefits of making the average American wage earner a stockholder and capitalist, as well as the acknowledged need of American business to meet projected massive capital requirements for plant rehabilitation and growth, provide a solid foundation for the permanence of ESOP. This permanence is reflected in federal legislation incorporating the ESOP concept, in addition to ERISA, such as the Regional Rail Reorganization Act of 1973, the Foreign Trade Act of 1974, the Tax Reduction Act of 1975, and proposed legislation such as the Accelerated Capital Formation Act of 1975.

Businessmen and their financial advisors, lawyers, accountants, investment bankers, controlling stockholders, and anyone involved in corporate finance and planning should not permit traditional thinking to hinder consideration of the ESOP concept with an open and receptive mind. If creative imaginations are applied to the principles of ESOP, and to expanding and building on the examples for its use in this book, sociological and business advantages attainable from ESOP may be extraordinary.

Charles A. Scharf

Acknowledgment

My special gratitude to Kenneth J. Warren, Esq., of The New York Bar, for his valuable assistance in gathering materials for this book, and preparing portions of Chapter 9, "Securities Laws and ESOP."

CONTENTS

15

3 Administering an ESOP—Fiduciary Responsibilities (cont.)

*tion ESOP · Fiduciary Duties · ERISA's Definition of Fiduciary Duties · Exemption from Diversification Requirement · 10% Limitation of Investment in Qualifying Employer Securities · Conference Committee's Rationale · **Fiduciary Duties Under the Internal Revenue Code** · Exclusive Benefit Rule · IRS "Exclusive Benefit" Requirements—Impossibility of Diversion · Incidental Benefits Permissable · Investment Requisites · Dealings at Fair Market Value · **Prohibited Transactions** · Prohibited Transactions · Limitation on Ownership of Employer Securities · Exemptions for ESOP · ESOP Loan Transactions · Party-in-Interest · Exempt ESOP Loan Transactions—IRS Ruling and Committee Report · Penalties · Summary*

PART II: ESOP AS A VEHICLE OF
CORPORATE FINANCE AND MANAGEMENT TOOL

Financing Vehicle · ESOP's Privileges · Employer's Privileges · Some Illustrations · Contribution of Stock · Pension Plan vs. ESOP · Profit-Sharing Plan vs. ESOP · The Leveraged ESOP · Maximum Permissible Tax Deduction · Carryover of Unused Deductions · Summary

Acquisitions *· Capital Transactions · Asset Acquisition · Stock Acquisition · Acquisition Fact Pattern · Cash Purchase Use of ESOP · Cash Purchase by Employer · Note Purchase Use of ESOP · Leveraged ESOP Purchase · Requirements for ESOP Acquisitions · **Dispositions** · Disposition Through an ESOP · Disposition from Lender's Viewpoint · Disposition from Employees' Viewpoint · Disposition from Seller's Viewpoint · Example of ESOP Disposition · **Debt Refinance Device** · Example · Same Creditor · Accounting Treatment · **ESOP—Special Situations** · Banks · Takeover Bids · Avoiding S.E.C. Registration · Summary*

PART III: SPECIAL APPLICATIONS OF AN
ESOP TO CLOSELY-HELD CORPORATIONS

*Opposing Fundamental Principles · Closely-Held Corporation Fact Pattern · Key Employees or Closely-Held Corp. as Purchasers · Redemption Equivalent to Dividend · Use of an ESOP · Sale from ESOP's Viewpoint · Sale from Founder's Viewpoint · Sale from Closely-Held Corp.'s Viewpoint · Installment Sale by Founder · **Employer Stock Valuation** · Appraisal · Possible Penalties · Adequate Consideration—Definitions · Valuation Problems—OTC Stocks · No Generally Recognized Market · Tax Reduction Act of 1975—Valuation · **IRS Valuation Guidelines** · Rev. Rule 59-60—Value a Question of Fact · Scarcity of Market Quotations · Willing Buyer and Seller · Prophecy of Future · Eight Fundamental Factors · Weighting the Factors · Stock Subject to Restriction · Summary*

*Purchase by Closely-Held Corp. · Section 318 of the Code · Redemption to Pay Death Taxes—Section 303 · Problems in Section 303 Redemptions · General Effect of ESOP Purchase · Valuation Conflicts · **Sale to ESOP vs. Corporate Redemption** · Income*

PART IV: TAX TREATMENT OF BENEFICIARIES, SECURITIES LAWS, AND GENERAL COMMENTARY

GUIDE TO EMPLOYEE STOCK OWNERSHIP PLANS

A Revolutionary Method for Increasing Corporate Profits

PART I

The Nature, Formation
and Administration of ESOP

DESCRIPTION OF ESOP

An Employee Stock Ownership Plan, often referred to by its acronym "ESOP," is difficult to describe accurately—if the person giving the description attempts to reflect a single viewpoint of such a plan. ESOP has different meanings for different persons.

To a corporate financial planner, ESOP may mean a tool to raise capital, an instrument of corporate finance. To an employee, ESOP may mean an employee benefit plan which may make him a part owner of the capital of his employer. To management of a publicly-held corporation, ESOP may mean a management tool to oppose a raider's takeover bid. To management or controlling stockholders of a closely-held corporation, ESOP may mean a market for stock where no market exists, or it may mean a device for estate planning. To the economist or social planner, ESOP may mean an instrument to help supply the anticipated vast capital requirements of United States industry or to spread the ownership of that capital among the average wage earners in the United States. Each of these different meanings of ESOP may be accurate.

This chapter contains a description of the different elements of an ESOP as described in Federal legislation incorporating the ESOP concept, and in the Congressional committee reports which reflect the legislative intent in enacting the statutes. The chapter describes how the ESOP concept was incorporated in four Federal statutes including the Employee Retirement Income Security Act of 1974. This Act, enacted on September 2, 1974, is generally referred to by the acronym "ERISA" which, for the sake of brevity, will be used to describe the Employee Retirement Income Security Act of 1974 in this book. ERISA sets Employee Stock Ownership Plans (ESOPs) within the general framework of tax-exempt employee benefit plans such as pension, profit sharing, and stock bonus plans. ERISA also provides the fundamental legislative sanctions which permit use of ESOP as a vehicle of corporate finance, as an instrument to spread capital ownership to wage earners, and as an instrument for estate planning. Although this chapter makes brief reference to other Federal legislation involving ESOPs to place the concept in perspective, the basic subject matter of this book is ESOP within the meaning of ERISA and uses of ESOP as sanctioned under ERISA.

GENERAL NATURE OF ESOP

ESOP–Relationship to Other Plans. Simply defined, an ESOP is an employee benefit plan designed to invest primarily in employer securities. Before analyzing details of the ERISA statutory definition of ESOP, a description of ESOP's relationship to other employee benefit plans helps place ESOP in perspective within the general statutory scheme of such plans. Traditionally, employee benefit plans have been either (1) stock bonus, (2) pension, or (3) profit sharing plans of an employer established and administered for the exclusive benefit of the employees or their beneficiaries. All three types of employee benefit plans have received special tax treatment for half a century. Assets in such plans are normally held in trusts which are "qualified" for special tax treatment by meeting the requirements of Section 401 of the Internal Revenue Code of 1954 ("Code"). Trusts qualified under Section 401 are exempt from income taxation under Section 501 of the Code, and, subject to limitations in amount, contributions to such trusts are tax deductible by an employer and not taxable to employee participants until distributed or made available by the trust to the participants.

Within this general framework of employee benefit plans, an ESOP, as we will use the term, is a qualified stock bonus plan. As a qualified stock bonus plan, the ESOP must be created and administered for the "exclusive benefit" of employees or their beneficiaries, in the same manner as all qualified employee benefit plans. To qualify under Section 401 of the Code a trust created under an ESOP must also meet other detailed requirements of that section. The ESOP Trust must benefit employees in general and may not discriminate in favor of employees who are officers or highly compensated. ESOPs must also meet the same participation and vesting requirements imposed by ERISA on all stock bonus, pension, and profit sharing plans to qualify under Section 401 of the Code. An ESOP, then, is one of the general group of qualified employee benefit plans known as stock bonus, pension or profit sharing plans.

Employee Benefit Plans–Retirement Benefits. An acknowledged general purpose of pension and profit sharing plans is to provide retirement benefits for employees. Indeed, one of the basic findings by Congress which motivated the adoption of ERISA involved the loss of retirement benefits by employees who were participants in pension and profit sharing plans. In this connection Congress found as follows:

> That despite the enormous growth in such plans many employees with long years of employment are losing anticipated retirement benefits owing to the lack of vesting provisions in such plans.

Based on these findings, Congress adopted a comprehensive reform act which was originally known as the Pension Reform Act of 1974. It is a complete overhaul of the system of employee pension and benefit plans. The pension reform legislation contains few direct references to ESOP, but the most significant reference, contained in that part of the legislation which deals with fiduciary responsibility, permits investment and borrowing techniques, and dealings between ESOPs and parties in interest, which differentiate ESOPs from other employee benefit plans. The Congressional legislation is officially entitled "Employee Retirement Income Security Act of 1974," but for the sake of brevity, as mentioned above, will be generally called ERISA in this book.

ESOP–Employee Capital Ownership. Although an ESOP is an employee benefit plan within the meaning of Section 401 of the Code, as are pension and profit-sharing plans, the primary purpose of an ESOP differs from the purpose of other employee benefit plans to provide retirement benefits to employees. In the case of an ESOP, the emphasis on the benefits for employees and their beneficiaries, shifts away from retirement benefits, to granting the average American wage earner equity ownership in American corporations. In addition, ESOPs are generally recognized as vehicles for corporate finance, which is not the case with other employee benefit plans, such as pension and profit sharing plans. Therefore, an ESOP differs from the ordinary qualified pension and profit-sharing plan in two fundamental respects. It differs in that (1) its primary purpose is not to provide retirement benefits for employees but to increase the equity ownership of employees in American corporations and (2) it is a recognized vehicle of corporate finance.

Federal Legislation Incorporating ESOPs. Enough Congressmen have been influenced to support ESOP legislation of varying kinds to permit enactment of a number of significant Federal statutes. Some Congressmen have been favorably influenced by the concept that ESOPs may be vehicles of corporate finance which may provide much needed capital to American business in the future. Others have been influenced by the concept that ESOPs will help spread the ownership of corporate capital among average wage earners in America. Regardless of the rationale causing favorable legislative treatment of ESOPs, Congress has incorporated the ESOP concept, not only in ERISA, but in important pieces of legislation enacted both before and after the enactment of ERISA. In addition to the special legislation involving ESOPs which has been enacted, other legislation has been introduced in Congress which would strengthen the use of ESOPs as vehicles for capital formation, and provide ESOPs with additional tax and related advantages. This Federal legislation indicates that ESOPs have become an integral part of our national social and economic policy, and tax structure. A review of ESOP legislation enacted by Congress and the Committee reports concerning this legislation gives a good deal of insight into the nature of an ESOP as viewed by our Congressmen.

Regional Rail Reorganization Act of 1973. The Regional Rail Reorganization Act of 1973 was adopted on January 2, 1974, eight months before the adoption of ERISA. This act clearly embraced the concept of an ESOP as a technique of corporate finance and as a means of spreading capital ownership among employees. In Section 102(5) of the Act, the Act defines an ESOP as follows:

> [An] "employee stock ownership plan" means a technique of corporate finance that uses a stock bonus trust or a company stock money purchase pension trust which qualifies under section 401(a) of the Internal Revenue Code of 1954 (26 U.S.C. 401(a)) in connection with the financing of corporate improvements, transfers in the owner-

ship of corporate assets, and other capital requirements of a corporation and which is designed to build beneficial equity ownership of shares in the employer corporation into its employees substantially in proportion to their relative incomes, without requiring any cash outlay, any reduction in pay or other employee benefits, or the surrender of any other rights on the part of such employees.

The above quotation indicates that under the Regional Rail Reorganization Act Congress viewed an ESOP as a technique of corporate finance to meet capital requirements of a corporation, and to build equity ownership in employee participants. The Act required the formation of a new corporation, to be known as the Consolidated Rail Corporation, to rehabilitate the railroad system of the Northeastern United States. Although the Act did not require this corporation to establish an ESOP, the Act recognized that the plan to create a financially self-sustaining railway system should consider the use of ESOPs. In this connection the Act provides that the plan should give consideration to the following:

[T]he manner in which employee stock ownership plans may, to the extent practicable, be utilized for meeting the capitalization requirements of the Corporation, taking into account (A) the relative cost savings compared to conventional methods of corporate finance; (B) the labor cost savings; (C) the potential for minimizing strikes and producing more harmonious relations between labor organizations and railway management; (D) the projected employee dividend incomes; (E) the impact on quality of service and prices to railway users; and (F) the promotion of the objectives of this Act of creating a financially self-sustaining railway system in the region which also meets the service needs of the region and the Nation.

As quoted, the Regional Rail Reorganization Act describes some of the financial advantages which theoretically may be realized from the utilization of an ESOP in connection with the railroad reorganization. As set forth in the act, these could include cost savings in borrowing compared to conventional methods of corporate finance, possible labor cost savings, and the potential for minimizing strikes and producing more harmonious relations between labor organizations and management.

Special Treatment of ESOP in ERISA. As is set forth in greater detail throughout different sections of this book, ERISA extends special treatment to employee benefit plans which qualify as ESOPs not extended to other employee benefit plans. First, 100% of the assets of an ESOP may be invested in the securities of an employer, and an ESOP fiduciary is under no obligation to diversify the investments of an ESOP Trust. Secondly, an ESOP Trust may borrow money to buy securities of an employer, and the employer may guarantee the repayment of the borrowing. Thirdly, an ESOP Trust may enter into transactions with the employer corporation and the controlling stockholders, who could otherwise be parties in interest not permitted to deal with a qualified employee trust. The transactions between the ESOP Trust and parties who could otherwise be disqualified parties in interest, may include purchases and sales of employer securities, and the borrowing from and lending to the ESOP Trust. ERISA's special treatment of ESOPs also appears to reflect congressional belief that ESOPs may provide a technique of corporate finance to help provide American industry with the anticipated vast amounts of future capital it will require, and may enable the ownership of capital to be shared with the average worker in America. ERISA's recognition of these aspects of ESOP is implicit in the possible uses of ESOP developed in this book.

Trade Act of 1974. On January 3, 1975, approximately four months after the enactment of ERISA, the Trade Act of 1974 became law. Among the purposes of this Act is to provide procedures to safeguard American industry and labor against unfair or injurious import competition and to assist industries, firms, workers and communities to adjust to changes in international trade flows. As one method of providing such assistance to industry, in the trade impacted areas, the Secretary of Commerce is authorized to guarantee loans for working capital made to private borrowers by private lending institutions. Section 273(f)(1) of the Trade Act recognizes the special status of ESOP by providing that the Secretary of Commerce give preference to a corporation which agrees (1) to have 25% of the principal of the loan paid by the lender to a trust established by the corporation under an ESOP which meets the requirements of the Act, and (2) by contract with the lender and the trust, to make sufficient contributions to the trust to repay both principal and interest of the loan. Under the Trade Act, the definition of ESOP is the same as the definition used in ERISA, with the very important differences that only common stock (with voting power and dividends no less favorable than the voting power and dividend rights on other common stock) will qualify as "a qualified employer security," and that the voting power of the stock acquired by the ESOP Trust be exercisable by the employee participants after the stock is allocated to their plan accounts. The requirement contained in this Act and in other legislation that employees be authorized to vote the stock allocated to their accounts is not required under ERISA. Furthermore, under ERISA preferred stock which is nonvoting may be a qualified employer security. Among sections of the Trade Act relating to ESOPs Section 273(f)(4) provides a description of a method for allocating stock to employees' accounts as follows:

> (4) At the close of each plan year, an employee stock ownership plan shall allocate to the accounts of participating employees that portion of the qualified employer securities the cost of which bears substantially the same ratio to the cost of all the qualified employer securities purchased under paragraph (2)(A) of this subsection as the amount of the loan principal and interest repaid by the qualified trust during that year bears to the total amount of the loan principal and interest payable by such trust during the term of such loan. Qualified employer securities allocated to the individual account of a participant during one plan year must bear substantially the same proportion to the amount of all such securities allocated to all participants in the plan as the amount of compensation paid to such participant bears to the total amount of compensation paid to all such participants during that year.

And Section 273(f)(5)(C) describes the type of stock which constitutes a qualified employer security for a Trade Act ESOP in the following manner:

> (C) "qualified employer securities" means common stock issued by the recipient corporation or by a parent or subsidiary of such corporation with voting power and dividend rights no less favorable than the voting power and dividend rights on other common stock issued by the issuing corporation and with voting power being exer-

cised by the participants in the employee stock ownership plan after it is allocated to their plan accounts.

Whether the employees' right to vote stock held in their ESOP accounts is a valid requirement to fulfill the fundamental purposes of ESOP is discussed in detail in the commentary in the last chapter of this book.

Legislative History of 1974 Trade Act. The legislative history of the Trade Act of 1974, in the Congressional Committee Reports, contains a detailed analysis of reasoning and rationale underlying many aspects of the ESOP concept. Quotations from the Committee Reports help provide an understanding of the nature of ESOP, and help provide laws to the future of ESOP in the economic system of the United States.

Reflecting upon the projected need for capital and for new capital ownership in the United States over the next decade, the Joint Congressional Committee Report provides as follows:

> Over 95 percent of investment finance is based on either the reinvestment of current profits or borrowings repaid with future profits; only a tiny fraction is based on the sale of new equities for cash to the small segment of the public who can afford such a cash transaction. But conventional techniques of investment finance are expanding the productive power of U.S. corporations by annual increments of over $100 billion of newly fabricated capital formation. Some industry spokesmen are projecting U.S. capital needs over the next decade at $4.5 trillion. If industry continues to rely almost exclusively on conventional methods of finance, we may achieve that estimate, but we will create virtually no new capital owners in the process.

The Committee Report also recognizes that almost 100% of privately owned United States capital is concentrated in less than 10% of United States households, and that the top 1% of wealthholders own over 50% of all stock of United States corporations. Removal of barriers between capital owners and workers, accomplished within principles of private property, can, in the opinion of Congress, only strengthen our national well-being. In this connection, the Committee Report states as follows:

> Qualitative studies of the U.S. capital ownership base show that almost 100 percent of privately owned U.S. capital assets are concentrated in less than 10 percent of U.S. households. Although 30 million Americans own at least one share of corporate stock, the top 1 percent of U.S. wealthholders own 50 percent of all U.S. corporate stock. Few workers, including most corporate executives, own capital of any appreciable income significance. Hence, few working Americans have any effective means of participating as stockholder-constituents of our free enterprise system, even in the corporations for which they work. A removal of any institutional barriers between capital owners and workers, if accomplished wholly within the principles of private property and free market economics, could only strengthen our national well-being and our capacity to remain competitive in world trade.

Congress also recognized that expanded productivity must be accompanied by expanded capital formation:

> In recognizing the critical role that our financial system must play in pumping new sources of investment credit into areas suffering from international trade forces

over which they have little or no control, the Committee has provided an attractive incentive to potential lenders in the form of loan guarantees not available under conventional finance. In turn, this could generate $1 billion of new income-producing assets in companies that establish or expand their facilities in these areas. Expanded productivity and expanded capital formation go naturally hand-in-hand. New and more efficient tools of production are main ingredients of any well-conceived strategy to encourage economic growth and revitalization and for the expansion of unsubsidized private sector payrolls within enterprises that can meet the challenge of fair world competition.

The foregoing quotations indicate that Congress recognizes its responsibility to help create the vast amount of new capital required by American business, but it also feels that it is responsible to determine who should own that new capital and share in the profits it generates. In this connection, the Committee Report states:

> This Committee, while anxious to help create the vast amounts of new capital formation which we need within our corporate sector today, cannot ignore the central issue of who will own that capital and share in its profits.
> The key to corporate ownership is access to corporate credit. Credit is generally available to well-managed corporations for investing under conditions where the investment is expected to pay for itself. The effect of this policy, however, has been to deny access to more fair and more effective participation in corporate ownership among middle-income and low-income American workers.

In a specific reference to ESOPs, the Committee Report provides that ESOPs make it possible for workers to share in the ownership of corporate capital without any redistribution of property belonging to existing stockholders, and act as vehicles of corporate finance which have tax incentives and cost reductions available which are not available under conventional methods of corporate finance:

> Employee stock ownership plans make it possible for workers in the private sector of our economy to share in the ownership of corporate capital without redistributing the property or profits from existing assets belonging to existing stockholders.
> Since its first application as a financing tool in 1957, employee stock ownership plans have been implemented by a growing number of successful U.S. corporations. Through the vehicle of a specially designed tax-exempt trust, this method of finance offers corporations certain tax incentives and cost reductions not available under conventional methods of corporate finance. The employee stock ownership plan also allows workers to accumulate significant holdings of capital in a tax-free manner during their working careers, while being taxed only on second incomes received in the form of dividend checks or on their assets when removed from their trust accounts.

The Committee Report also defines a Trade Act ESOP as a technique of corporate finance which utilizes a qualified stock bonus plan and is designed to invest primarily in qualifying employer securities. It also sets forth certain design requirements for a Trade Act ESOP as follows:

As defined in this bill, an "employee stock ownership plan" is a technique of corporate finance which utilizes a stock bonus plan which is qualified, or a stock bonus and a money purchase pension plan both of which are qualified, under section 401 of the Internal Revenue Code of 1954, and which is designed to invest primarily in qualifying employer securities. The employee stock ownership plan and the qualified trust forming a part of the plan must also be designed: (i) to meet general financing requirements of the corporation, including capital growth and transfers in the ownership of corporate stock; (ii) to build into employees beneficial ownership of stock of their employer or its affiliated corporations, substantially in proportion to their relative incomes, without requiring any cash outlay, any reduction in pay or other employee benefits, or the surrender of any other rights on the part of such employees; and (iii) to receive loans or other forms of credit to acquire stock of the employer corporation or its affiliated corporations, with such loans and credit secured primarily by a legally binding commitment by the employer to make future payments to the trust in amounts sufficient to enable such loans to be repaid.

Tax Reduction Act of 1975. The Tax Reduction Act of 1975 was signed by the President on March 29, 1975, almost seven months after the enactment of ERISA. Among its many provisions relating to the reduction of individual income taxes and changes in business taxes, this Act also gives special recognition to the ESOP concept. Under this Act a corporation may elect an 11% investment credit, rather than a statutory 10% credit, if the corporation establishes an ESOP to which it transfers its own securities with an aggregate value of 1% of the amount of the investment which qualifies for the investment credit. An ESOP which qualifies an employer for the additional 1% investment credit is subject to special restrictions in that it must provide (1) that each participant has a non-forfeitable right to the stock allocated to his account and (2) each participant is entitled to direct the plan as to the manner of voting any employer securities allocated to his account. These special requirements for an ESOP under the Tax Reduction Act of 1975 may limit the number of employers willing to comply with these special ESOP provisions in order to obtain the additional 1% investment credit.

Accelerated Capital Formation Act of 1975. On March 26, 1975 William Frenzel, Republican Representative from Minnesota, introduced the Accelerated Capital Formation Act of 1975. This Act contains additional tax advantages for ESOPs and their participants as well as some basic provisions which would permit greater certainty in the administration of ESOPs. This proposed legislation clearly recognizes ESOP as a technique of corporate finance. It proposes to increase the amounts contributed by employers to ESOPs which may be deducted for tax purposes by eliminating the ceilings based on 15% or 25% of employee compensation. The proposed legislation would allow as a deduction to an employer the amounts of any dividends paid by the employer on employer securities held by an ESOP Trust. It would make lump sum distributions to participants from ESOPs, in the form of employer securities or otherwise essentially tax free. Perhaps most significant of all of its provisions is one which would permit an application to be made to the Secretary of the Treasury for an advance opinion whether a proposed transaction involving an ESOP will satisfy the requirements of ERISA. The enactment of such a provision would greatly benefit any corporation or fiduciary of an ESOP, where the employer corporation is a closely-held corporation and faces the uncertainty of establishing a fair market value for its stock. The serious nature of the valuation problem as it affects closely held corporations is discussed in detail in Chapter 6.

ERISA STATUTORY DEFINITION OF ESOP

ESOP–Statutory Definition. The statutory definition of an Employee Stock Ownership Plan is contained in Section 407(d)(6) of ERISA:

> The term "employee stock ownership plan" means an individual account plan—
> (A) which is a stock bonus plan which is qualified, or a stock bonus plan and money purchase plan both of which are qualified, under section 401 of the Internal Revenue Code of 1954, and which is designed to invest primarily in qualifying employer securities, and
> (B) which meets such other requirements as the Secretary of the Treasury may prescribe by regulation.

Although the Secretary of the Treasury has not yet promulgated regulations for ESOP under the authority contained in sub-paragraph (B) above, most authorities believe that the Congressional intent is so clearly set forth in the committee reports made public with ERISA, that regulations promulgated by the Secretary will closely follow the Congressional intent as well as prior regulations and rulings of the Internal Revenue Service respecting stock bonus plans, and will not contain unexpected restrictions on ESOPs.

The statutory definition of an ESOP contains four fundamental elements. An ESOP must be: (1) a stock bonus plan (or a stock bonus and money purchase plan); (2) an individual account plan; (3) qualified under Section 401 of the Internal Revenue Code of 1954; and (4) designed to invest primarily in qualifying employer securities.

Benefits Distributable in Stock. Definitions developed in the regulations under the Internal Revenue Code of 1954, prior to the enactment of ERISA, Reg. §1.401-1(b), define a stock bonus plan, and since ESOP is a stock bonus plan, the definitions are applicable to ESOP. These regulations define a stock bonus plan as a plan of an employer to provide employees or their beneficiaries with "benefits similar to those of a profit-sharing plan," except that in a stock bonus plan the "benefits are distributable in stock of the employer company," and contributions by the employer are "not necessarily dependent upon profits." A stock bonus plan, however, "must provide a definite predetermined formula for allocating the contributions made to the plan among the participants and for distributing the funds accumulated under the plan."

Individual Account Plan. The second fundamental element of an ESOP in the statutory definition requires that it be an "individual account plan." The reference in the definition to an individual account plan involves methods for computing benefits to which participants are entitled. Pursuant to ERISA Section 3(34), an individual account plan is a "plan which provides for an individual account for each participant and for benefits based solely upon the amount contributed to the participant's account, and any income, expenses, gains and losses, and any forfeitures of accounts of other participants which may be allocated to such participant's account." Rather than benefits based upon a formula, then, an individual account plan provides benefits based solely upon the amount contributed to a participant's account and any additions to that account, in the form of income, gains, or forfeitures, and any subtractions from the account in the form of expenses or losses.

Qualified Trust. Generally, assets of an employee benefit plan must be held in trust by one or more trustees. In this connection, Section 403(a) of ERISA provides:

> Sec. 403.(a) Except as provided in subsection (b) [not applicable to ESOP], all assets of an employee benefit plan shall be held in trust by one or more trustees. Such trustee or trustees shall be either named in the trust instrument or in the plan instrument described in section 402(a) or appointed by a person who is a named fiduciary . . .

The third element of the ERISA definition of ESOP requires that the Trust under the plan be "qualified" under Section 401 of the Internal Revenue Code of 1954. Under Regulation 1.401-1(a) to be "qualified" an ESOP must be a "written program and arrangement which is communicated to the employees and which is established and maintained by the employer. . . ." In addition, the regulations under Code Section 401 require the trust to meet the following tests:

(1) It must be created or organized in the United States and it must be maintained at all times as a domestic trust in the United States;

(2) It must be part of a pension, profit-sharing, or stock bonus plan established by an employer for the exclusive benefit of its employees or their beneficiaries;

(3) It must be impossible under the trust instrument at any time before the satisfaction of all liabilities with respect to employees and their beneficiaries under the trust, for any part of the corpus or income to be used for, or diverted to, purposes other than for the exclusive benefit of the employees or their beneficiaries;

(4) It must be part of a plan which benefits prescribed percentages of the employees, or which benefits such employees as qualify under a classification set up by the employer and found by the Commissioner not to be discriminatory in favor of certain specified classes of employees;

(5) It must be part of a plan under which contributions or benefits do not discriminate in favor of certain specified classes of employees; and

(6) It must be part of a plan which provides the nonforfeitable rights described in Section 411 of the Code which are described below.

ESOP–Investment Requirement. The fourth element contained in ERISA's definition of an ESOP requires that such plan be "designed to invest primarily in qualifying employer securities." This requirement for an ESOP, as is developed further in Chapter 3, underlies the ESOP's exemption from a trustee's fiduciary duty to diversify investments which would otherwise apply to an ESOP as a qualified employee benefit plan. Since an ESOP must be designed to invest primarily in qualifying employer securities, a trustee administering such a plan is not required to diversify investments and may invest substantially all of the assets of an ESOP Trust in qualifying securities of an employer.

Qualifying Employer Security. ERISA Section 407(d)(5) defines the term "qualifying employer security" for purposes of ERISA's definition of an ESOP. This Section provides as follows:

> The term "qualifying employer security" means an employer security which is stock or a marketable obligation (as defined in subsection (e)).

Note that the definition of a qualifying employer security in ERISA includes the general term "stock." The definition is not limited to common stock, nor to voting stock. Therefore, preferred stock which is nonvoting may, under ERISA, constitute a "qualifying employer security." The fact that preferred stock may constitute a qualifying employer security under ERISA is one element which distinguishes an ESOP formed under ERISA from ESOPs formed to comply with other Federal legislation, discussed above, which requires that employer stock eligible for ownership by an ESOP Trust be limited to voting common stock.

Marketable Obligation. Also included within the term qualified employer security is a "marketable obligation." Under ERISA a marketable obligation means a bond, debenture, note, certificate, or other evidence of indebtedness which meets certain requirements. These requirements relating to such debt securities will generally restrict the use of marketable obligations as ESOP investments to marketable obligations which may be publicly traded or which may be capable of private placement, without consideration to the ESOP. Immediately after the acquisition of any such obligation by the ESOP Trust, under the ERISA requirements, the Trust must hold not more than 25% of the obligations constituting the issue of such obligations outstanding at the time of acquisition by the trust, and, at that time, at least 50% of the aggregate amount of the issue must be held by persons independent of the employer or issuer. The ERISA definition of a "marketable obligation" is as follows:

> (e) For purposes of subsection (d)(5), the term "marketable obligation" means a bond, debenture, note, or certificate, or other evidence of indebtedness (hereinafter in this subsection referred to as "obligation") if—
>
> (1) such obligation is acquired—
>
>   (A) on the market, either (i) at the price of the obligation prevailing on a national securities exchange which is registered with the Securities and Exchange Commission, or (ii) if the obligation is not traded on such a national securities exchange, at a price not less favorable to the plan than the offering price for the obligation as established by current bid and asked prices quoted by persons independent of the issuer;
>
>   (B) from an underwriter, at a price (i) not in excess of the public offering price for the obligation as set forth in a prospectus or offering circular filed with the Securities and Exchange Commission, and (ii) at which a substantial portion of the same issue is acquired by persons independent of the issuer; or
>
>   (C) directly from the issuer, at a price not less favorable to the plan than the price paid currently for a substantial portion of the same issue by persons independent of the issuer;
>
> (2) immediately following acquisition of such obligation—
>
>   (A) not more than 25 percent of the aggregate amount of obligations issued in such issue and outstanding at the time of acquisition is held by the plan, and

(B) at least 50 percent of the aggregate amount referred to in sub-paragraph (A) is held by persons independent of the issuer; and

(3) immediately following acquisition of the obligation, not more than 25 percent of the assets of the plan is invested in obligations of the employer or an affiliate of the employer.

ESOP COMPARED TO PENSION PLAN

An ESOP must meet many requirements imposed upon both pension plans and profit-sharing plans to qualify for tax exemption, as set forth above. Yet, due to differences between an ESOP on the one hand and a pension plan or profit-sharing plan on the other hand, an ESOP may provide many incidental and valuable advantages to an employer prohibited to an employer with a pension or profit sharing plan. The different characteristics of an ESOP which make special incidental benefits available to an employer exist both in the terms of ESOPs and in their administration. To highlight some of these differences, first, compare an ESOP with a pension plan, in the following respects:

(1) Contributions Not Actuarially Determined. Under a pension plan the contributions must be capable of determination actuarially, on the basis of definitively determinable benefits, or, as in the case of money purchase pension plans, such contributions must be fixed in amount, and contributed each year without in any way being related to profits. In an ESOP, the contributions are not determined actuarially, and are not required to be made annually in any fixed or other amount. Contributions to an ESOP are within the discretion of the Board of Directors, and may be withheld or paid, regardless of whether or not an employer has profits. All qualified plans must, however, be "permanent" as that term is used in the income tax regulations. To meet this requirement, contributions to an ESOP should be "recurring and substantial" as required under a profit-sharing plan by I.R.S. Reg. §1.401-1(b)(2).

(2) Contributions in Stock. Contributions to pension plans are made in cash. On the other hand, contributions to an ESOP may be made in either cash or stock. In practice, contributions to an ESOP are often made in employer stock, whether newly issued or treasury stock.

(3) Limit on Contributions. The Internal Revenue Code provides certain limits on amounts of contributions by an employer to a pension plan or an ESOP beyond which contributions are not deductible for income tax purposes. With respect to pension plans, deductions by an employer are limited by various formulae, the net effect of which is to permit an employer to deduct contributions to a pension plan for income tax purposes to the extent necessary to actuarially fund the pensions due to participants in the plan, without any other effective overall ceiling. On the other hand, deductible contributions by an employer to an ESOP are limited to 15 percent of the compensation paid to employees under the plan. Under the Code, if less than 15 percent is contributed to the ESOP in any one taxable year, the employer may carry forward the deficiency, and subject to certain restrictions, deduct as much as 25 percent of covered compensation of employees in one taxable year with the addition of the carry-overs to the deductible amount.

(4) Fiduciary Transactions. Certain basic differences exist in restrictions imposed upon a trustee in administering a trust fund for a pension plan on the one hand and an

ESOP on the other. The differences involve (a) the type of property in which a trustee may invest, (b) diversification requirements for investments, (c) methods by which the trustee may make purchases or sales of property, and (d) persons with whom the trustee may transact business. Under ERISA, a trust under a pension plan may not engage in certain prohibited transactions permitted to an ESOP Trust. A pension plan may not, except in limited amounts, buy and own stock of an employer, and it may not borrow, lend money, or engage in transactions with parties in interest, including employers and certain controlling stockholders. An ESOP, on the other hand, may invest 100% of its assets in employer stock, and may borrow from, lend to, and buy and sell employer stock with employers and controlling stockholders. Prohibited transactions, and the exemptions of ESOPs from the restrictions of prohibited transactions, are dealt with in greater detail in Chapter 3 which describes requirements for administering an ESOP.

(5) Benefits–Not Actuarially Determined. A pension plan provides for the payment of actuarially determinable benefits to participants, generally measured by such factors as years of service and compensation. An ESOP provides for benefits based solely upon the amount contributed to the participant's account and any income, expenses gains and losses, and any forfeitures of other participants which may be allocated to such a participant's account.

(6) Benefits–Form of Distribution. Under a pension plan a distribution to a participant upon retirement or otherwise is made in cash or in the form of an annuity contract. On the other hand, an ESOP may make distributions to participants only in the form of employer stock.

ESOP COMPARED TO PROFIT-SHARING PLAN

Although more closely related to a profit-sharing plan than a pension plan in some ways, an ESOP differs from a profit-sharing plan in the following respects:

(1) Contributions Not Dependent on Profits. Under a profit-sharing plan contributions are generally made each year where profits exist and are related to profits. Contributions to an ESOP are generally within the discretion of the Board of Directors, and may be withheld or paid, regardless of whether or not an employer has profits. As mentioned in comparing an ESOP to a pension plan, however, to meet the requirement of permanence, contributions to an ESOP should be "recurring and substantial."

(2) Contributions in Stock. Contributions to profit-sharing plans are for the most part made in cash. On the other hand, contributions to an ESOP may be made in either cash or stock. In practice, contributions to an ESOP are often made in employer stock, whether newly issued or treasury stock.

(3) Fiduciary Transactions. Certain basic differences exist in restrictions imposed upon a trustee in administering a trust fund for a profit-sharing plan on the one hand and an ESOP on the other. As in the case of pension plans, the differences involve (a) the type of property in which a trustee may invest, (b) diversification requirements for investments, (c) methods by which the trustee may make purchases or sales of property, and (d) persons with whom the trustee may transact business. Under ERISA a trust under a profit-sharing plan may not engage in certain prohibited transactions permitted to an ESOP Trust. A profit-sharing trust may not borrow, lend money, or engage in transactions with parties in interest or disqualified persons, including employers and

certain controlling stockholders. An ESOP, on the other hand, may borrow from, lend to, and buy and sell employer stock with employers and controlling stockholders. As mentioned above, prohibited transactions, and the exemptions of ESOPs from the restrictions of prohibited transactions, are dealt with in greater detail in Chapter 3.

(4) Benefits–Form of Distribution. Under a profit-sharing plan a distribution to a participant upon retirement or otherwise is normally made in cash or in the form of an annuity contract. On the other hand, an ESOP may make distributions to participants only in the form of employer stock.

ESOP INCENTIVE COMPENSATION
FROM EMPLOYEES' VIEWPOINT

Employee Attitude. It has been demonstrated that the basic objective of an ESOP is to give an employee a stock or equity interest in his employer, not to provide the employee with retirement benefits. This objective differs from the basic objective of pension plans and profit-sharing plans to provide the employee with financial security in retirement. From an employee's point of view, this fundamentally different purpose of an ESOP should cause a different attitude on the employee's part to the ESOP as opposed to a pension plan or profit-sharing plan. Other differences in the operation of an ESOP also affect employees directly.

Differences in Contributions. From the employee's point of view, the ESOP differs from pension and profit-sharing plans in the nature of the contributions made by the employer. Under a pension plan, an employer is required to contribute to the plan regardless of whether or not it realizes profits. Under a profit-sharing plan, customarily an employer is required to make contributions and only makes contributions if the employer realizes profits. The ESOP differs from both plans in that no fixed amount of contributions is required to be made by the employer, and contributions to the ESOP may be made whether or not the employer realizes any profits.

Since no formula exists for the amount to be contributed to an ESOP by an employer, and since the contribution is solely at the discretion of the Board of Directors of an employer, the employee may have the attitude that he has less assurance that contributions will be made to the ESOP by the employer than to a pension or profit-sharing plan.

However, in order to remain qualified as an ESOP under the tax laws, the employer must make recurring and substantial contributions to the ESOP and must annually contribute sufficient amounts to the ESOP to pay its current expenses. Where an ESOP has borrowed money and purchased stock of an employer, the agreement on the part of the employer to contribute funds to the ESOP to amortize the loan and pay current expenses of the ESOP may itself bind the employer to make annual contributions. In this sense, an employee may have greater assurance of contributions than under a profit-sharing plan, and essentially equivalent assurance that contributions will be made as under a pension plan.

Differences in Benefits. Under a pension plan an employee is relatively certain of the amount of retirement benefits he may expect to receive in the future, if he continues in employment and plan contributions are made. Under a defined benefit pension plan, an employee may expect to receive a pension based upon a formula which takes into account the employee's earnings and years of employment. Under a defined contribution pension plan, he may expect to receive a pension based upon fixed annual contributions by the employer. Under a profit-sharing plan, an employee may expect his account to be credited with profits each year the employer operates on a profitable basis, although, if there are no profits, normally no contribution is made to the plan to add to the employee's account to increase future retirement benefits. Under an ESOP, the amount which an employee may expect to receive upon retirement is not fixed as a dollar amount, but the employee may have expectations of a minimum number of shares of employer stock he will receive upon retirement, should his interest vest in accordance with the terms of the plan.

For example, if an ESOP borrows money and makes a purchase of employer stock, the employer stock becomes an asset of the ESOP Trust and is allocated to each employee's individual account as the loan is repaid. Under these circumstances, the employee's account is credited with a number of shares of employer stock as the indebtedness is repaid. How valuable this stock is at the time of retirement depends to a substantial degree upon the efforts of the employee and his fellow participating employees. In this sense, the employee covered by an ESOP has an initial interest in his employer's stock, and has more of an opportunity to add to the value of his retirement asset than under a pension plan (where the value of the pension fund has no effect on what the employee is entitled to receive) or under a profit-sharing plan (where a trustee will invest in securities which for the most part are totally unrelated to the employee or his productive efforts).

Special ESOP Benefits. Where the ESOP is introduced as a new employee incentive plan, the ESOP should be explained in detail to the employee participants. The expenditure of time and careful effort on the education of employees in the elements of an ESOP is advisable for two reasons. First, to be fully effective as an employee incentive compensation plan, the employees should understand the general workings of the ESOP, and secondly, where the employees already participate in either a pension or profit-sharing plan, the ESOP should be fully explained to allay any fears on the part of the employees of losing vested benefits in the existing plans. In educating the employees as to the workings of an ESOP, some advantages of the ESOP to the employees which may be mentioned as possibilities are the following:

1. The additional cash flow and increased working capital advantages to the employer provided by the ESOP will enable the employer to contribute more in stock to the ESOP annually, than it would be able to contribute in cash to a pension plan or a profit-sharing plan.

2. The ESOP, to avoid Securities and Exchange Commission problems, is a non-contributory plan, i.e., the employees need not contribute any of their pay to the plan.

3. Although contributions to the ESOP are discretionary with the Board of Directors of the employer, such discretionary contributions may actually insure an employee a continuation of the incentive plan, rather than a cessation of contributions. For example, a pension plan may require such huge contributions annually during years when an employer's business suffers reverses, that an employer is forced to terminate the plan rather than continue it with its fixed annual obligation of contributions. In a profit-sharing plan, during years of no profits, no contributions are made to the plan. Under an ESOP if a corporation has a non-profitable year, the directors may, in their discretion, still contribute stock to the ESOP. Depending on circumstances, such a contribution to the ESOP may recover cash for the corporation in the form of tax refunds. Furthermore, because of the discretionary nature of the contributions, if a corporation has no earnings or low earnings for a number of years, the directors may eliminate contributions for those years, but make contributions of a greater amount through carryover rights in subsequent years.

4. The investment of the assets of the ESOP primarily in employer's stock assures the employee that funds allocated to his account are being invested in assets of which he has knowledge. If he has faith in his employer, he will be happy that the investment is made in his employer's stock and that he, through his efforts, may increase the value of the asset in his account. Good employee morale and employee concerted effort to improve the business of the employer may be the single most important factor in improving profits of the employer.

5. The plan may grant a right to a retired employee to sell the stock to either the ESOP or the employer, at the employee's option. Therefore, if the price of the stock on the market is low at the time it is distributed to the employee, the employee is not in a position of forced sale, but may hold the stock with the hope that it will increase in value.

Summary. An ESOP is an employee benefit plan designed to invest primarily in employer securities. It forms part of the general category of employee benefit plans qualified under Section 401(a) of the Internal Revenue Code of 1954, such as employee pension and profit-sharing plans. However, an ESOP differs from other employee benefit plans in that (1) the basic purpose of an ESOP is to grant employees an equity interest in their employer, rather than to provide retirement benefits, and (2) an ESOP is also a vehicle of corporate finance, which other employee benefit plans are not. An ESOP also differs from pension and profit-sharing plans since (1) its contributions are not actuarially determined, (2) contributions may be made regardless of profits, (3) the contributions may be made in stock, (4) tax deductions of contributions are limited in amount to 15% of compensation paid to employees covered by the plan, subject to increase of carry-overs, (5) distributions of benefits must be made solely in employer stock, and (6) fiduciaries of ESOPs may invest total trust assets in employer company stock without regard for diversification requirements, and may engage in purchases or sales of property with an employer, or with other parties with whom dealings are normally prohibited to employee trusts. Although an ESOP normally does not require an employer to make annual contributions of a fixed or formula amount, where an ESOP has borrowed money which an employer has contracted or guaranteed to repay, annual contributions must be made by the employer over the period of the loan to amortize the principal and interest. Finally, to avoid Securities and Exchange Commission problems, an ESOP is normally non-contributory on the part of employees.

2

IRS REQUIREMENTS AND
PROCEDURES TO QUALIFY AN ESOP

EMPLOYEE BENEFIT PLANS GENERALLY

Income Tax Benefits. The Internal Revenue Code provides valuable income tax benefits for employee pension, profit-sharing and stock bonus plans which meet the Code requirements set forth in Section 401(a). These special tax benefits include (1) the right by an employer to deduct contributions to the plan as made, (2) non-taxablility of contributions for employees until contributions are distributed or made available to employees or beneficiaries, (3) tax-free accumulation of earnings on a plan's invested capital, and (4) special favorable tax treatment of distributions from the plan to employees and their beneficiaries, in the form of non-taxability of portions of distributions, capital gains treatment, or averaging tax treatment of other portions. To qualify for this special tax treatment an employee incentive plan and its trust must comply with special rules set forth in Section 401(a) of the Code and the regulations and administrative rulings under it. For income tax purposes, normally a trust is treated as a separate taxable entity subject to special income tax rules which determine the taxability of its income. Section 501(a) of the Code exempts a trust which forms part of a qualified pension, profit-sharing, or stock bonus plan from such income taxation.

Exclusive Benefit Rule. Every plan, whether a pension, profit-sharing or stock bonus plan, must meet one fundamental requirement of the Internal Revenue Code to qualify under Section 401(a) of the Code: The plan must be for the *exclusive benefit of employees or their beneficiaries.* This fundamental requirement for qualification requires not only that the trust be created exclusively for the employees or their beneficiaries, but also that it be maintained for this purpose. From time to time, during our

39

discussion of ESOPs, we will return to this fundamental requirement that the plan be for the exclusive benefit of the employees or their beneficiaries. Since employers may realize substantial incidental benefits from maintaining an ESOP, care should be exercised in the use of an ESOP to avoid benefits to an employer which would violate the "exclusive benefit" requirement. The Internal Revenue Service has traditionally held that although a plan may provide incidental benefits to an employer, it is not from this fact alone that the plan violates the requirement that it be for the exclusive benefit of its employees or their beneficiaries. It is axiomatic that by providing fringe benefits in the form of a pension, profit-sharing, or stock bonus plan, an employer hopes to realize, and should realize, benefits from increased employee loyalty and increased employee incentive.

Detailed Requirements of Section 401(a). Section 401(a) of the Code lists 19 specific detailed requirements which a trust created under a stock bonus, pension, or profit-sharing plan must meet to qualify under the Section. In addition, the trust must meet the requirements set forth in voluminous regulations and guidelines promulgated by the IRS, as the regulations and guidelines are supplemented and amended from time to time due to changes in court interpretations and IRS thinking. This chapter discusses highlights for qualifying a trust, but an employer establishing an employee benefit plan should require his advisors, lawyers, and accountants to check the plan against the existing requirements at the time the plan is drafted. All qualified plans must meet three basic principles. Each plan must (1) be a definite written program and arrangement, (2) be communicated to the employees, and (3) be established and maintained by an employer to provide benefits to employees or their beneficiaries. The purpose of benefits under a pension plan is to provide for the livelihood of employees after retirement whereas benefits under a profit-sharing or stock bonus plan are to enable employees to participate in profits. Profit-sharing plans and stock bonus plans, including ESOPs, must provide definite formulae for allocating contributions and for distributing the accumulated benefits under the plan to employees. In the case of an ESOP, contributions need not be dependent upon profits, but benefits under the plan may be distributed only in stock of the employer.

Trust Requirements. Under the Code and the IRS Regulations, the trust which forms part of a pension, profit-sharing, or stock bonus plan, must meet eight fundamental requirements to qualify for special tax treatment as a qualified trust under the Code:

(1) *Domestic Trust.* The trust must be created or organized in the United States and it must be maintained at all times as a domestic trust within the United States;

(2) *Employees' Exclusive Benefit.* The trust must form a part of a pension, profit-sharing, or stock bonus plan established for the exclusive benefit of employees or their beneficiaries;

(3) *Distribution of Trust Assets.* The trust must be formed or availed of, for purposes of distributing to employees or their beneficiaries the corpus and income of the fund accumulated by the trust in accordance with the plan;

(4) *Non-Diversion of Assets.* The trust instrument must provide that it be impossible, at any time prior to satisfaction of all liabilities to employees and their beneficiaries, for any part of the corpus or income of the trust to be used for, or

diverted to, purposes other than for the exclusive benefit of the employees or their beneficiaries;

(5) *Prescribed Employee Coverage.* The trust must form part of a plan which benefits prescribed percentages of employees, or benefits a classification of employees set up by the employer and found by the Commissioner of Internal Revenue not to be discriminatory. The prescribed percentages of employees required to be benefited under the plan are set forth in Section 410(b) of the Code as follows:

(a) 70 percent or more of all employees, or

(b) 80 percent of all eligible employees if 70 percent or more of all employees are eligible under the plan, excluding employees who have not satisfied the minimum age and service requirements prescribed by the plan.

(6) *Non-Discrimination.* The trust must be part of a plan under which contributions or benefits do not discriminate in favor of officers, shareholders, or other highly compensated employees, compared with other employees both within or without the plan.

(7) *Non-Forfeitable Employee Rights.* The trust must be part of a plan which expressly provides that upon termination of the plan or complete discontinuance of contributions under the plan, the rights of each employee to benefits accrued to the date of such termination or discontinuance, to the extent then funded, or the rights of each employee to the amounts credited to his account at such time, are non-forfeitable.

(8) *Pension Plan Forfeitures.* The trust must be part of a plan, if the plan is a pension plan, which provides that forfeitures may not be applied to increase the benefits of the employees which would otherwise be payable under the plan.

Plan Permanence. In addition to the foregoing eight requirements, the plan must be permanent. In this sense, the concept of a "plan" implies a permanent as distinguished from a temporary program. The Internal Revenue Service, therefore, takes the position that the abandonment of any employee benefit plan for any reason other than business necessity within a few years after it has taken effect is evidence that the plan, from its inception, was not a bona fide program for the exclusive benefit of employees in general. For a profit-sharing plan to meet the test of permanence, the employer need not contribute every year, nor must he contribute the same amount, or contribute in accordance with the same formula every year. However, merely making a single or occasional contribution out of profits for employees does not establish a plan of profit-sharing. To constitute a profit-sharing plan, recurring and substantial contributions for employees must be made. ESOPs must also meet the requirement of recurring and substantial contributions.

General Benefit of Employees. A plan is not for the exclusive benefit of employees in general, if by any device whatever, it discriminates either in eligibility requirements, contributions, or benefits in favor of employees who are officers, shareholders, or highly compensated employees. Similarly, a stock bonus or profit-sharing plan is not a plan for the exclusive benefit of employees in general if its assets may be used to relieve the employer from contributing to a pension plan operating concurrently and covering the same employees. These restrictions are contained in IRS Regulation §1.401-1(b)(3) as follows:

> If the plan is so designed as to amount to a subterfuge for the distribution of profits to shareholders, it will not qualify as a plan for the exclusive benefit of employees even though other employees who are not shareholders are also included under the plan. The plan must benefit the employees in general, although it need not provide benefits for all of the employees. Among the employees to be benefited may be persons who are officers and shareholders. However, a plan is not for the exclusive benefit of employees in general if, by any device whatever, it discriminates either in eligibility requirements, contributions, or benefits in favor of employees who are officers, share-holders, . . . or the highly compensated employees. . . . Similarly, a stock bonus or profit-sharing plan is not a plan for the exclusive benefit of employees in general if the funds therein may be used to relieve the employer from contributing to a pension plan operating concurrently and covering the same employees.

Allocation Formulae. In the case of an ESOP and other stock bonus plans, as mentioned above, the plan must provide a definite predetermined formula for allocating contributions among the participants, and for distributing the assets accumulated under the plan after a fixed number of years, the attainment of a stated age, or upon the prior occurrence of some event such as layoff, illness, disability, retirement, death, or severance of employment. The benefits under an ESOP, of course, are distributable in stock of the employer company. IRS Regulation §1.401-1(b)(1)(iii) provides the following:

> A stock bonus plan is a plan established and maintained by an employer to provide benefits similar to those of a profit-sharing plan, except that the contributions by the employer are not necessarily dependent upon profits and the benefits are distributable in stock of the employer company. For the purpose of allocating and distributing the stock of the employer which is to be shared among his employees or their beneficiaries, such a plan is subject to the same requirements as a profit-sharing plan.*

Minimum Participation Standards. ERISA established minimum participation standards for an employee benefit plan to qualify under Section 401(a). Under these standards, as set forth in Section 410(a) of the Code, generally, the plan may not require as a condition of participation by an employee that the employee complete a period of service beyond the later of the date on which he (1) reaches the age of 25 or (2) completes one year of service. Section 410(a) of the Code also limits the right of a plan to exclude employees from participation because of age. The pertinent provisions of the Section are as follows:

(a) PARTICIPATION.—
    (1) MINIMUM AGE AND SERVICE CONDITIONS.—
        (A) GENERAL RULE.—A trust shall not constitute a qualified trust under section 401(a) if the plan of which it is a part requires, as a condition of participation in the plan, that an employee complete a period of service

---

*For a complete discussion of the special problems involved when choosing an ESOP allocation formula, see ¶1043 of the Prentice-Hall *Pension and Profit Sharing Service.*

with the employer or employers maintaining the plan extending beyond the later of the following dates—

(i) the date on which the employee attains the age of 25; or

(ii) the date on which he completes 1 year of service.

(B) SPECIAL RULES FOR CERTAIN PLANS.—

(i) In the case of any plan which provides that after not more than 3 years of service each participant has a right to 100 percent of his accrued benefit under the plan which is nonforfeitable (within the meaning of section 411) at the time such benefit accrues, clause (ii) of subparagraph (A) shall be applied by substituting "3 years of service" for "1 year of service."

(ii) In the case of any plan maintained exclusively for employees of an educational institution (as defined in section 170(b)(1)(A)(ii)) by an employer which is exempt from tax under section 501(a) which provides that each participant having at least 1 year of service has a right to 100 percent of his accrued benefit under the plan which is nonforfeitable (within the meaning of section 411) at the time such benefit accrues, clause (i) of subparagraph (A) shall be applied by substituting "30" for "25." This clause shall not apply to any plan to which clause (i) applies.

(2) MAXIMUM AGE CONDITIONS.—A trust shall not constitute a qualified trust under section 401(a) if the plan of which it is a part excludes from participation (on the basis of age) employees who have attained a specified age, unless—

(A) the plan is a—

(i) defined benefit plan, or

(ii) target benefit plan (as defined under regulations prescribed by the Secretary or his delegate), and

(B) such employees begin employment with the employer after they have attained a specified age which is not more than 5 years before the normal retirement age under the plan.

Employees' Nonforfeitable Rights. ERISA amended the Code by adding a new section, Section 411, setting forth minimum vesting standards which apply to all employees' trusts qualified under Section 401. Section 411 provides that a trust may not qualify under Section 401 unless the plan provides that an employee's right to benefits derived from employer contributions is nonforfeitable under any one of three alternative vesting schedules:

(A) 10-Year Vesting.—A plan satisfies the requirements of this subparagraph if an employee who has at least 10 years of service has a nonforfeitable right to 100 percent of his accrued benefit derived from employer contributions.

(B) 5- to 15-Year Vesting.—A plan satisfies the requirements of this subparagraph if an employee who has completed at least 5 years of service has a nonforfeitable right to a percentage of his accrued benefit derived from employer contributions which percentage is not less than the percentage determined under the following table:

Years of service:	Nonforfeitable percentage
5	25
6	30
7	35
8	40
9	45
10	50
11	60
12	70
13	80
14	90
15 or more	100.

(C) Rule of 45.—

(i) A plan satisfies the requirements of this subparagraph if an employee who is not separated from the service, who has completed at least 5 years of service, and with respect to whom the sum of his age and years of service equals or exceeds 45, has a nonforfeitable right to a percentage of his accrued benefit derived from employer contributions determined under the following table:

If years of service equal or exceed–	*and sum of age and service equals or exceeds–*	*then the nonforfeitable percentage is–*
5	45	50
6	47	60
7	49	70
8	51	80
9	53	90
10	55	100.

(ii) Notwithstanding clause (i), a plan shall not be treated as satisfying the requirements of this subparagraph unless any employee who has completed at least 10 years of service has a nonforfeitable right to not less than 50 percent of his accrued benefit derived from employer contributions and to not less than an additional 10 percent for each additional year of service thereafter.

SPECIAL ESOP REQUIREMENTS

The foregoing portions of this chapter have set forth in a general way the requirements for pension and profit-sharing plans and ESOPs to qualify under the Internal Revenue Code. In addition to these general requirements, an ESOP must meet certain requirements specially applicable to it:

Individual Account Plan. As set forth in Chapter 1, ESOP, as well as a profit-sharing or stock bonus plan, must be an "individual account plan." To meet this requirement, an individual account plan normally contains detailed provisions setting forth methods for allocating employer contributions and purchases by the trust under the plan to individual employee accounts. In addition, if the plan provides for a committee to administer the plan, such committee is often vested with authority to provide detailed accounting procedures pursuant to which contributions by the employer, both in cash and stock, and income, gains, losses, and forfeitures by other participants, are added to and subtracted from the individual accounts of each participant. A form of such accounting procedures is set forth in the Appendix at the end of this book.

Investment in Employer Securities. A second special requirement to qualify an ESOP, different from the requirements for a pension or profit-sharing plan, provides that the ESOP be designed to invest "primarily in qualifying employer securities." To meet this requirement the written plan itself, in that section of the plan which provides for investment of trust assets, should contain a provision that the investment policy of the plan requires investment primarily in qualified employer securities. The effect of the fundamental investment policy of an ESOP upon trustees is discussed in detail in the following chapter which deals with the general administration of the plan and the trust.

Adequate Consideration on Purchase or Sale. From an employer's viewpoint, the most valuable incidental benefits of an ESOP flow from the exemption of the ESOP from certain "prohibited" transactions and from the limitation of investment in employer securities to 10% of plan assets set forth in ERISA Sections 406 and 407. To qualify for the exemptions, any acquisition or sale of employer securities by an ESOP must be for "adequate consideration." These basic and crucial exemptions permitting an ESOP to buy and sell with a party in interest are contained in Section 408(e) of ERISA which provides as follows:

> (e) Sections 406 and 407 shall not apply to the acquisition or sale by a plan of qualifying employer securities (as defined in section 407(d)(5)) or acquisition, sale or lease by a plan of qualifying employer real property (as defined in section 407(d)(4))—
>
> (1) if such acquisition, sale, or lease is for adequate consideration (or in the case of a marketable obligation, at a price not less favorable to the plan than the price determined under Section 407(e)(1)),
>
> (2) if no commission is charged with respect thereto, and
>
> (3) if—
>
> > (A) the plan is an eligible individual account plan (as defined in section 407(d)(3)), or
> >
> > (B) in the case of an acquisition or lease of qualifying employer real property by a plan which is not an eligible individual account plan, or of an acquisition of qualifying employer securities by such a plan, the lease or acquisition is not prohibited by section 407(a).

The term "adequate consideration" as used in ERISA has three different meanings depending on whether a security has a generally recognized market in (1) a national securities exchange, (2) the over-the-counter market or (3) is not traded in a generally recognized market. Section 3(18) of ERISA which defines "adequate consideration" provides as follows:

> (18) The term "adequate consideration" when used in part 4 of subtitle B means (A) in the case of a security for which there is a generally recognized market, either (i) the price of the security prevailing on a national securities exchange which is registered under section 6 of the Securities Exchange Act of 1934, or (ii) if the security is

not traded on such a national securities exchange, a price not less favorable to the plan than the offering price for the security as established by the current bid and asked prices quoted by persons independent of the issuer and of any party in interest; and (B) in the case of an asset other than a security for which there is a generally recognized market, the fair market value of the asset as determined in good faith by the trustee or named fiduciary pursuant to the terms of the plan and in accordance with regulations promulgated by the Secretary.

The requirements that purchases and sales of employer securities be made for adequate consideration and that no commission is charged are normally incorporated as specific provisions in the investment portion of an ESOP.

Distributions Solely in Stock. A special limitation imposed upon an ESOP to qualify for income tax exemption requires that distributions to participants and beneficiaries be limited to distributions solely in the form of employer stock. ESOPs qualify for tax benefits as stock bonus plans under Section 401(a) of the Code. Historically, and as provided in the IRS Regulations, a stock bonus plan is a plan providing for benefits distributable in the form of stock of the employer. This requirement is clearly set forth in the regulations under Section 401 of the Code, Regulation Section 1.401-1(a)(2)(iii), quoted above. Furthermore, revenue rulings issued prior to the 1974 pension legislation also clearly require that distributions to beneficiaries under a stock bonus plan or an ESOP must be made in stock of the employer. In Rev. Rule 71-256, Cumulative Bulletin 1971-1, p. 118, the Commissioner of Internal Revenue was requested to rule whether a plan could qualify as a stock bonus plan if it permitted distributions in the form of annuity contracts. The plan provided that any participant could direct the trustee to sell the stock that would otherwise be distributed to him and apply the proceeds to the purchase of a single premium annuity contract. Accordingly, it was held that the plan did not qualify as a stock bonus plan within the meaning of Section 401. The Internal Revenue Service stated as follows:

> In order for a plan to be a stock bonus plan within the meaning of Section 1.401-1(b)(iii) of the Regulations, the entire distribution (except for the value of a fractional part of a share) must be in stock of the employer corporation. This plan does not require distributions in stock of the employer corporation but permits distributions of annuity contracts.

The above requirement that distributions to participants and beneficiaries under the plan be made solely in employer stock should, therefore, be explicitly set forth in the plan. The only distribution which may be made in a form other than stock of the employer should be limited to the value of a fractional part of a share of stock held in a participant's account for his benefit at the time of distribution.

PROCEDURES FOR IRS RULINGS

The balance of this chapter sets forth in some detail the procedures to obtain an advance IRS determination that a plan qualifies under Section 401(a) of the Code, and the procedures to appeal from an adverse ruling. The procedures are contained in IRS regulations which are amended from time to time, and which should be checked before any application for an IRS advance determination is filed. An employer who adopts an employee benefit plan should be aware that an advance determination by the IRS that the plan qualifies is not a requirement for tax exemption. A plan may qualify under Section 401(a) of the Code if the plan meets all the applicable requirements of that Section, without any ruling from the IRS to that effect. Under some circumstances, it may be impractical to supply all the data required for an advance IRS determination, and an employer may have to decide whether to adopt a plan without an advance determination. For example, Technical Information Release No. 1411 of the IRS requires submission with a request for determination of data involving the rate of turnover for rank and file employees. Where this information is not readily available to an employer, the employer may not wish to apply for an advance determination that the plan qualifies.

Letter of Determination Desirable. Although advance rulings with respect to qualification of pension, profit-sharing, or stock bonus plans are not required under the Internal Revenue Code, in view of the substantial funds involved in employee benefit plans and the need of employers for certainty in the tax treatment of the plans, it is desirable, and customary practice, to obtain rulings with respect to the tax qualification of such plans. For ESOPs the ruling is requested by filing an Application for Determination with a District Director of Internal Revenue on Form 5301. The purpose of the application is to have the District Director issue a so-called "letter of determination." The details of the IRS procedure to obtain a determination letter are contained in Regulation Section 601.201(o). This regulation was amended after the passage of ERISA to reflect changes brought about by ERISA, and contains complete detailed instructions for applying to the IRS for determination letters.

Contents of Regulations. The regulations provide procedures relating to the issuance of determination letters with respect to the qualification of retirement plans. They set forth (1) the authority of key district directors to issue determination letters, and (2) instructions to applicants, including which forms to file, where such forms must be filed, and requirements for giving notice to interested parties, as well as the administrative remedies available to interested parties and the Pension Benefit Guaranty Corporation. The regulations also describe the administrative appeal rights available to applicants and provide for the issuance of notice of final determination. They describe the documents which will make up the administrative record, and notice of final determination. In addition, the regulations set forth the actions necessary on the part of applicants, interested parties, and the Pension Benefit Guaranty Corporation for each to exhaust the administrative remedies within the meaning of the Code, when appealing from an adverse determination.

The procedures set forth in the regulation are discussed below in general terms and some sections of the regulations deemed of particular interest are quoted. However, counsel faced with drafting an ESOP and filing an application for a determination letter should familiarize himself with the regulations in detail.

Place of Filing. The application for determination should be filed by an employer with the Key District Director of Internal Revenue set forth in the regulation. Normally, this is the Director for the district in which the place of business of the employer is located. A parent company and each of its subsidiaries that adopt a single plan will file with the Key District Director for the district in which the principal place of business of the parent is located, whether or not separate or consolidated income tax returns are filed. Where multiple employers are involved, other than parent and subsidiaries, the adopting employer must file with the Key District Director in which the principal place of business of the Trustee or Plan Supervisor is located. The key district officers which are authorized to issue determination letters are set forth in the regulations as follows:

Key District Offices. Following are the 19 key district offices that issue determination letters and the areas covered:

Key District(s)	IRS Districts Covered
Central Region	
Cincinnati	Cincinnati, Louisville, Indianapolis
Cleveland	Cleveland, Parkersburg
Detroit	Detroit
Mid-Atlantic Region	
Baltimore	Baltimore (which includes the District of Columbia and Office of International Operations), Pittsburgh, Richmond
Philadelphia	Philadelphia, Wilmington
Newark	Newark
Midwest Region	
Chicago	Chicago
St. Paul	St. Paul, Fargo, Aberdeen, Milwaukee
St. Louis	St. Louis, Springfield, Des Moines, Omaha
North-Atlantic Region	
Boston	Boston, Augusta, Burlington, Providence, Hartford, Portsmouth
Manhattan	Manhattan
Brooklyn	Brooklyn, Albany, Buffalo
Southeast Region	
Atlanta	Atlanta, Greensboro, Columbia, Nashville
Jacksonville	Jacksonville, Jackson, Birmingham
Southwest Region	
Austin	Austin, New Orleans, Albuquerque, Denver, Cheyenne
Dallas	Dallas, Oklahoma City, Little Rock, Wichita
Western Region	
Los Angeles	Los Angeles, Phoenix, Honolulu
San Francisco	San Francisco, Salt Lake City, Reno
Seattle	Seattle, Portland, Anchorage, Boise, Helena

Application Form 5301. A separate form of application, Form 5301, is required for defined contribution plans such as stock bonus and profit-sharing plans. Since ESOPs, as defined in Chapter 1, are stock bonus plans the application for the determination should be made on Form 5301 as prescribed by the Commissioner of Internal Revenue with respect to such plans.

Form 5301 requires data on twenty-six categories of information concerning the subject plan, each category in turn broken down into many specific items including the identity of the employer and the trustee, and a general statement of the type of plan involved. In addition to such items, the form requires a brief description of some of the fundamental provisions in the plan, such as (1) eligibility requirements, (2) the employer contribution formula, (3) the allocation formula, (4) the employee contribution formula, if any, (5) the benefit formula indicating benefits upon normal retirement, early retirement or disability retirement or death, and (6) vesting provisions.

In addition, Form 5301 requires an identification by article or section of important provisions of the plan or trust such as definitions of compensation and net profit, and other sections required by statute such as (1) disposition of forfeitures, (2) non-transferability of benefits, (3) vesting upon termination or discontinuance of contributions, (4) prohibitions against reversion, (5) annual valuation of assets, and (6) if a stock bonus plan, the requirement that distributions be made solely in employer stock.

The form also requires such information as (1) a summary of employees employed by the employer and an indication of the number of employees eligible and ineligible under the plan, (2) whether contributions are based on a definite formula, and (3) whether the plan is integrated with social security.

Supplementary Documents and Information. In addition to filing the application form itself, an employer seeking a determination from the District Director must also file copies of all documents which constitute the plan, including the trust indenture, Form 5302, an Employee Census form, and specimen copies of the formal announcement to employees containing a comprehensive detailed description of the plan, with all amendments to any such instruments or documents. Finally, financial statements in the form of a balance sheet and statement of receipts and disbursements of the trust should be submitted with the application. Form 5301, Application for Determination for Defined Contribution Plan, Schedule A to Form 5301, and Form 5302, an Employee Census form, are reproduced in the Appendix of Forms at the end of this book. Note that Form 5302, the Employee Census, is not open to public inspection pursuant to Section 6104(a)(1)(C) of the Code.

Notice Requirements. When an employer wishes to file an application for determination, it must give notice to all interested parties as defined in the regulations not less than 7 days nor more than 21 days prior to making application, where notice is posted or given in person, and not less than 10 days nor more than 24 days prior to making application where notice is given by mail. The notice must be in writing and contain the following information, in addition to procedures for requesting participation by the Department of Labor:

> (a) a brief description identifying the class or classes of interested parties to whom the notice is addressed (e.g., all present employees of the employer, all present employees eligible to participate);
>
> (b) the name of the plan, the plan identification number, and the name of the plan administrator;
>
> (c) the name and taxpayer identification number of the applicant;
>
> (d) that an application for a determination as to the qualified status of the plan is to be made to the Internal Revenue Service, stating whether the application relates to an initial qualification, a plan amendment or a plan termination,

and the address of the district director to whom the application will be submitted;

(e) a description of the class of employees eligible to participate under the plan;

(f) whether or not the Service has issued a previous determination as to the qualified status of the plan. . . .

Interested Parties. The regulations under Section 7476 of the Code set forth in detail the persons who are "interested parties" for notice requirements. The persons who must receive notice as interested parties differ with the purpose of the application for determination. Where the application for determination is with respect to an initial qualification all present employees of the employer are interested parties, and where the application relates to a plan amendment affecting contributions or benefits of former employees, all former employees who have nonforfeitable rights to accrued benefits are included as interested parties. Under certain circumstances employees who are covered by collective bargaining agreements and nonresident aliens are not interested parties. Before filing an application for determination, an employer should carefully determine the interested parties, because failure to notify all interested parties may cause a rejection of the application.

Notice Materials. In additon to the notice, generally a copy of the plan and trust and the application for determination must be made available to interested parties, as well as additional documents dealing with the application submitted to the Internal Revenue Service. Where less than 26 participants are involved in the plan, a description of the plan rather than the copies of documents provides sufficient notice to a category of interested parties who are not participants.

Internal Revenue Service Administrative Remedies. Interested parties have a right to make written comments to the Key District Director concerning the application within forty-five days after the application is received by the District Director. Such parties may also request the Department of Labor to file a comment with the District Director, and where the Department of Labor declines to do so, the comment by the interested party must be made by the later of the forty-fifth day after the application is received by the District Director or the fifteenth day after which the Department of Labor notifies such party that it declines to submit a comment. But in no event, may the comment be made later than the sixtieth day after the application for determination is received by the District Director.

If after consideration, the Key District Director issues a notice of a proposed adverse determination, the applicant may notify the District Director that it requests a Regional Office consideration, by submitting a request in writing to the District Director within thirty days after the issuance of the District Director's notice. After receipt of the administrative record in the Regional Office, if the applicant has requested a conference, it is afforded the opportunity of such a conference. The Assistant Regional Commissioner notifies an applicant in writing of the proposed decision and his reasons therefor.

If the applicant disagrees with the proposed decision of the Regional Office, the applicant is entitled to request National Office consideration of any disagreed issue, by submitting a request in writing to the Regional Commissioner within thirty days of the date of notice of the proposed decision of the Regional Office.

Grounds for appeal to the National Office are the following:

(1) that the position of the Regional Office is contrary to law or regulations; or

(2) that the position of the Regional Office is contrary to published precedent; or

(3) that the position of the Regional Office is contrary to a court decision followed by the service; or

(4) that the contemplated Regional Office action is in conflict with a determination made in a similar case in the same or another region; or

(5) that the issues arise because of unique or novel facts that have not previously been passed upon in any published precedent.

After consideration by the National Office, the National Office will notify the applicant of its decision and the administrative record is returned to the Key District Director Office for issuance of a notice of final determination.

Exhaustion of Administrative Remedies. Under Section 7476 of the Internal Revenue Code, prior to appealing to the Tax Court, a petitioner must have exhausted the administrative remedies available to it within the Internal Revenue Service as set forth above. If a final determination is not issued by the District Director, the petitioner may not be deemed to have exhausted its administrative remedies with respect to the failure of the Internal Revenue Service to make a determination before the expiration of 270 days after the request for determination is made.

TAX COURT DECLARATORY JUDGMENT

Code Section 7476. Section 1041(a) of ERISA added Section 7476 to the Internal Revenue Code, providing petitioners with a declaratory judgment remedy respecting determinations by the Internal Revenue Service involving qualification of employee benefit plans. This new section of the Code provides an interested party, whether the employer, a plan administrator, an employee, or the Pension Benefit Guaranty Corporation, with a procedure to appeal to the Tax Court, after a determination by the District Director or if the District Director does not issue his determination after 270 days have elapsed from the filing of the request for determination with the District Director. Pursuant to Section 7476 an interested party may file a petition with the Tax Court requesting a declaratory judgment, with respect to either an initial qualification of a plan or a continuing qualification. The declaratory judgment has the same force and effect as a decision of the Tax Court and is reviewable as such.

Premature Petition. The filing of the petition by the petitioner may, however, be held to be premature unless the petitioner establishes to the satisfaction of the Tax Court that it has complied with notice requirements to all interested parties prior to filing the request for determination of the qualification of the plan with the District Director. In addition, the petitioner must have (1) exhausted the administrative remedies available to the petitioner within the Internal Revenue Service, and (2) placed its pension, profit-sharing or employee stock ownership plan into effect. As mentioned above, where the Internal Revenue Service does not rule, an employer is not deemed to have exhausted its administrative remedies before the expiration of 270 days after the employer made the request for the determination. In other words, approximately nine months may pass after an application for determination is made by an employer before the employer may appeal to the Tax Court for a declaratory judgment determining whether the plan qualifies under Section 401 of the Internal Revenue Code. The employer is also prohibited from filing its petition to the Tax Court unless the plan for which the employer has made an application for determination has been put into effect before the pleading with the Tax Court is filed. In this respect, however, the plan is not treated as not being in effect solely because, under the terms of the plan, the funds contributed to the plan may be refunded to the employer if the plan is found not to be qualified.

Timely Filing of Petition. Not only must the foregoing prerequisites be met by an employer or petitioner, but if the District Director sends his notice of determination with respect to qualification of the plan to the employer, the employer may not initiate any proceeding for a declaratory judgment unless it files its pleading before the 91st day after the day after such notice is mailed to the employer.

Employer Protection Against Adverse Determination. To guard against the eventuality that the ultimate decision of the Commissioner of the Internal Revenue, or the Tax Court, may be adverse to the initial qualification of the plan under Section 401 of the Code, it is recommended that both the plan and the trust agreement provide that upon such an adverse determination, all funds in the plan, including contributions by the employer, be returned to the employer. Such a provision for the return of an employer's contribution will also not prevent qualification of a plan or the exemption of the trust under the Internal Revenue Code. In this connection, the guides established by the Internal Revenue Service for the qualification of an employee pension, profit-sharing, or stock bonus plan, as those guides were in existence prior to the enactment of ERISA, have historically condoned such provisions:

> Conditional Payments—A provision in a newly established plan for the return of employer contributions only in the event that the Commissioner of Internal Revenue rules that the plan is not qualified does not, of itself, prevent qualification of the plan and exemption of the trust. The plan must be in full force and effect, and the non reversionary provisions must otherwise prevent the non exempt use of the funds. It is only by the Commissioner's determination that the plan does not qualify that a recovery of employer contributions made prior to such determination is possible. Under such circumstances, the conditional payment, and the provision therefor, are held not to prevent qualification of the plan and exemption of the trust. See Rev. Rule 60-276, 1960-2 Cumulative Bulletin, page 150.

Summary. An ESOP shares in the tax benefits of qualified employee benefit plans including (1) deductibility of contributions by an employer, (2) non-taxability of contributions to employees until benefits are distributed, (3) tax-free accumulation of earnings on a plan's vested capital, and (4) special favorable tax treatment for distributions by the ESOP to employees and their beneficiaries. To qualify for the tax benefits, an ESOP must meet the requirements of Section 401(a) of the Internal Revenue Code of 1954. Some of the major requirements of Section 401(a) are (1) qualified plans must be for the exclusive benefit of employees or their beneficiaries, (2) qualified trusts must be maintained to distribute trust corpus and income to employees or their beneficiaries, (3) it must be impossible at any time prior to the satisfaction of all liabilities to employees and their beneficiaries for any part of trust assets to be used for purposes other than the exclusive benefit of the employees, (4) qualified trusts must benefit prescribed percentages of employees, *ie.*, 70% or more of all employees, or 80% of all eligible employees if at least 70% of all employees are eligible, and may not discriminate in favor of officers, shareholders or other highly compensated employees, (5) profit-sharing and stock bonus plans must provide definite predetermined formulae for allocating contributions among participants and for distributing trust assets, and (6) the minimum participation and vesting standards provided under the Code for all qualified plans must be met. Special requirements for ESOPs to qualify for special tax benefits include that the ESOP (1) be an individual account plan, (2) be formed to invest primarily in employer securities and (3) purchase and sell qualifying employer securities only for adequate consideration, (4) pay no commission for such purchases and sales, and (5) make distributions solely in employer stock. An ESOP may apply for an advance ruling with respect to qualification under Code Section 401(a) by filing an Application for Determination, Form 5301, with the key district director of Internal Revenue specified in the Regulations. Upon failure to obtain a favorable Letter of Determination from the Internal Revenue Service, the ESOP may appeal to the Tax Court for a declaratory judgment.

3

ADMINISTERING AN ESOP— FIDUCIARY RESPONSIBILITIES

FIDUCIARY DUTIES UNDER ERISA

Administration. An ESOP, like all qualified pension, profit-sharing, and stock bonus plans, must be administered for the "exclusive benefit" of employees or their beneficiaries. An ESOP must also be administered to invest "primarily" in employer securities, and to make distributions solely in employer stock to the employees or their beneficiaries. As in the case of other employee benefit plans, under the ESOP Trust instrument it must be impossible, at any time prior to the satisfaction of all liabilities to employees and their beneficiaries under the trust, for any part of the corpus or income of the trust to be used for or diverted to purposes other than for the exclusive benefit of the employees or their beneficiaries.

Named Fiduciary. Under Section 402 of ERISA every employee benefit plan must be established and maintained pursuant to a written instrument. The written plan must provide "for one or more named fiduciaries" who, jointly or severally, have the authority to control and manage the operation of the plan. The named fiduciary under the plan is the person who is named in the plan instrument as the fiduciary, or is a person identified as a fiduciary by the employer, or, where applicable, an employee organization, or both, in accordance with procedures specified in the plan. The named fiduciaries, then, are the persons who have the authority to control and manage the operation and administration of the plan.

Single Transaction ESOP. An ESOP may engage in a single transaction involving employer securities. For example, the sole transaction of the ESOP could be to borrow a substantial amount, assume $1,000,000, to purchase $1,000,000 of an employer's stock. The employer may utilize the $1,000,000 received from the sale of its stock for any purpose in the employer's business, perhaps to satisfy outstanding indebtedness. After the refinancing is completed, the function of the trustee of the ESOP Trust, the named fiduciary, could be limited to the collection of annual cash contributions by the employer, and the transfer of the cash received to amortize the principal and interest of the $1,000,000 indebtedness of the trust. As participants in the ESOP retire, the trustee would make distributions of the employer's stock to the participants. Where an ESOP's use is limited to one sizeable transaction with an employer, the fiduciary obligations of the named fiduciary under ERISA are minimal.

Fiduciary Duties. Rather than single transaction ESOPs, an ESOP maintained as a continuing active employee incentive program under which the employer makes periodic contributions in the form of cash or stock, affords the most opportunities to benefit employees and also incidentally benefit employers with financing opportunities. Where the ESOP continues to engage in transactions, occasionally with the employer and on other occasions with third parties, the fiduciary assumes a greater burden in administering the plan. Every fiduciary is under a duty to administer the plan in accordance with rules set forth in ERISA and under the Internal Revenue Code. Failure to comply with legal requirements may result in the imposition of penalties against a fiduciary, or other parties in interest, and may result in the imposition of substantial excise taxes, possibly as high as 100% of the amount of a prohibited transaction, against an employer or other party-in-interest.

ERISA sets forth general guidelines applicable to fiduciaries of pension, profit-sharing and stock-bonus plans for fulfillment of fiduciary obligations. ERISA also lists and specifies certain types of prohibited transactions which a fiduciary should not permit a plan to undertake. The fiduciary of an ESOP, however, is exempted from some of the obligations imposed upon fiduciaries of other types of qualified plans, and the ESOP fiduciary may legally engage in specified transactions with parties in interest which would be so-called prohibited transactions to other fiduciaries. These exemptions from general fiduciary duties and prohibited transactions available to the ESOP fiduciary permit ESOP transactions of substantial incidental benefit to employers, although the ESOP continues to be operated and maintained exclusively for the benefit of the employees or their beneficiaries as required by law.

ERISA's Definition of Fiduciary Duties. ERISA defines duties of a fiduciary in Sections 404(a)(1) and (2) as follows:

> Sec. 404.(a)(1) Subject to sections 403(c) and (d), 4042, and 4044, a fiduciary shall discharge his duties with respect to a plan solely in the interest of the participants and beneficiaries and—
>
> (A) for the exclusive purpose of:
>   (i) providing benefits to participants and their beneficiaries; and
>   (ii)defraying reasonable expenses of administering the plan;
> (B) with the care, skill, prudence, and diligence under the circumstances then prevailing that a prudent man acting in a like capacity and familiar with such matters would use in the conduct of an enterprise of a like character and with like aims;

(C) by diversifying the investments of the plan so as to minimize the risk of large losses, unless under the circumstances it is clearly prudent not to do so; and

(D) in accordance with the documents and instruments governing the plan insofar as such documents and instruments are consistent with the provisions of this title.

(2) In the case of an eligible individual account plan (as defined in section 407(d)(3)), the diversification requirement of paragraph (1)(C) and the prudence requirement (only to the extent that it requires diversification) of paragraph (1)(B) is not violated by acquisition or holding of qualifying employer real property or qualifying employer securities (as defined in section 407(d)(4) and (5)).

Exemption From Diversification Requirement. The above quoted portion of ERISA relating to the discharge of his duties by a fiduciary requires that a fiduciary act solely in the interest of plan participants, and exclusively (1) to provide benefits to participants and beneficiaries and (2) to defray reasonable expenses of the plan. In administering the funds under its control, the fiduciary must act as a "prudent man" and must diversify the investments of the plan to minimize risk of large losses. But with respect to an ESOP, Sec. 404(a)(2) provides that the prudent man and diversification requirements imposed on other fiduciaries, are not violated by acquisition and holding of qualifying employer securities.

10% Limitation of Investment in Qualifying Employer Securities. Section 407(a) of ERISA further restricts a fiduciary of an employee benefit plan from investing in employer securities which are not qualifying securities and limits the amount a fiduciary may invest in qualifying employer securities to 10 percent of the fair market value of the assets of the plan. In this connection, Sections 407(a)(1) and (2) provide as follows:

Sec. 407.(a) Except as otherwise provided in this section and section 414:
(1) A plan may not acquire or hold—
(A) any employer security which is not a qualifying employer security, or
(B) any employer real property which is not qualifying employer property.
(2) A plan may not acquire any qualifying employer security or qualifying employer real property, if immediately after such acquisition the aggregate fair market value of employer securities and employer real property held by the plan exceeds 10 percent of the fair market value of the assets of the plan.

Conference Committee's Rationale. The Joint Statement of the Conference Committee also sets forth the committee's rationale for exempting individual account plans from the diversification requirements. The committee report states as follows:

Employer securities and employer real property.—
Eligible individual account plans.—The labor provisions of the substitute generally limit the acquisition and holding by a plan of employer securities and of employer real property (combined) to 10 percent of plan assets. (Employer securities are securities issued by an employer with employees covered by the plan or its affiliates. Employer real property is real property which is leased by a plan to an employer (or its affiliates) with employees covered by the plan.)

However, a special rule is provided for individual account plans which are profit-sharing plans, stock bonus plans, employee stock ownership plans, or thrift or savings plans, since these plans commonly provide for substantial investments in employer securities or real property. Also, money purchase plans which were in existence on the date of enactment, and which invested primarily in employer securities on that date are to be treated the same way as profit-sharing, etc., plans. (However, employer-established individual retirement accounts are not to be eligible individual account plans.)

In recognition of the special purpose of these individual account plans, the 10 percent limitation with respect to the acquisition or holding of employer securities or employer real property does not apply to such plans if they explicitly provide for greater investment in these assets. In addition, the diversification requirements of the substitute and any diversification principle that may develop in the application of the prudent man rule is not to restrict investments by eligible individual account plans in qualifying employer securities or qualifying employer real property.

These exceptions apply only if the plan explicitly provides for the relevant amount of acquisition or holding of qualifying employer securities or qualifying real property. For example, if a profit-sharing plan is to be able to invest half of its assets in qualifying employer securities, the plan must specifically provide that up to 50 percent of plan assets may be so invested. In this way, the persons responsible for asset management, as well as participants and beneficiaries, will clearly know the extent to which the plan can acquire and hold these assets. Plans in existence on the date of enactment will have one year from January 1, 1975, to be amended to comply with this requirement. If the plan does not comply within one year (but, e.g., complies 2 years after January 1, 1975), then during the interim period, the plan will be subject to the 10 percent rule as well as the diversification requirement. This means, generally, that the plan will not be able to acquire any additional employer securities or employer real property during this period (and preparation should be made for divestiture of half of the excess of employer securities and real property by January 1, 1980).

The above quotation from the Conference Committee's joint explanation to Sec. 407 of ERISA indicates the Committee's clear intent that individual account plans such as profit-sharing plans, stock bonus plans, ESOPs, and thrift or savings plans should receive special leeway to invest in employer securities and not be limited to a maximum investment of 10 percent of plan assets in such securities nor by fiduciary diversification requirements. To permit individual account plans to invest in employer securities beyond the normal 10% limitation, however, the plans must "explicitly" provide for the relevant amount of acquisition or holding of qualifying employer securities. For example, if a profit-sharing plan is to be able to invest half its assets in such securities, it must specifically provide that up to 50 percent of plan assets may be so invested.

The Committee rationale for permitting profit-sharing, stock bonus, ESOP, and thrift or savings plans to invest a greater portion of their assets in employer securities is simply that "these plans commonly provide for substantial investments in employer securities or real property."

FIDUCIARY DUTIES UNDER THE INTERNAL REVENUE CODE

Exclusive Benefit Rule. To qualify under Section 401(a) of the Internal Revenue Code the trust created under an ESOP must be for the "exclusive benefit of (the) employees or their beneficiaries. . . ." This requirement that the trust be for the "exclusive benefit" of the employees or their beneficiaries is not violated even though an employer realizes incidental benefits from transactions with the trust. Prior to the codification of the types or ordinarily prohibited transactions permitted to an ESOP, Revenue rulings made it clear that incidental benefits to an employer from dealings with an exempt ESOP Trust, would not affect the tax exemption of the trust under the Code. Furthermore, if a fiduciary meets the "prudent man" fiduciary requirements of ERISA, Congress intended that meeting these requirements would also, with nothing further, meet the "exclusive benefit" requirements of the Internal Revenue Code.

The Joint Explanation of the Conference Committee on ERISA indicates the conferees' intention that to the extent a fiduciary meets the prudent man rule of the labor provisions, he will also be deemed to meet the Internal Revenue Service rules governing the investment of plan assets under the "exclusive benefit" requirements of the Internal Revenue Code; and, as a consequence, investment of ESOP assets in qualifying employer securities without diversification, may also meet the Internal Revenue Service fiduciary requirements. In this connection, the Conference Committee states the following:

> Basic fiduciary rules—Prudent man standard—The substitute requires that each fiduciary of a plan act with the care, skill, prudence, and diligence under the circumstances then prevailing that a prudent man acting in a like capacity and familiar with such matters would use in conducting an enterprise of like character and with like aims. The conferees expect that the courts will interpret this prudent man rule (and the other fiduciary standards) bearing in mind the special nature and purpose of employee benefit plans.
>
> Under the Internal Revenue Code, qualified retirement plans must be for the exclusive benefit of the employees and their beneficiaries. Following this requirement, the Internal Revenue Service has developed general rules that govern the investment of plan assets, including a requirement that cost must not exceed fair market value at the time of purchase, there must be a fair return commensurate with the prevailing rate, sufficient liquidity must be maintained to permit distributions, and the safeguards and diversity that a prudent investor would adhere to must be present. *The conferees intend that to the extent that a fiduciary meets the prudent man rule of the labor provisions, he will be deemed to meet these aspects of the exclusive benefit requirements under the Internal Revenue Code.* (Emphasis added.)

IRS "Exclusive Benefit" Requirements—Impossibility of Diversion. The general requirement under Section 401 of the Code that an employee benefit plan be established and administered "exclusively for the benefit of employees or their beneficiaries" contains the basic element that the trust funds may not be diverted for any use other than for the benefit of the employees or their beneficiaries. The regulations promulgated by the Internal Revenue Service expand on this concept that no diversion of trust assets may occur, and provide that the trust instrument itself must make such diversion impossible, as stated in Regulation Section 1.401-2(a) paragraphs (1), (2), and (3):

> §1.401-2. Impossibility of diversion under the trust instrument.—(a) In general. (1) Under section 401(a)(2) a trust is not qualified unless under the trust instrument it is impossible (in the taxable year and at any time thereafter before the satisfaction of

all liabilities to employees or their beneficiaries covered by the trust) for any part of the trust corpus or income to be used for, or diverted to, purposes other than for the exclusive benefit of such employees or their beneficiaries. . . .

(2) As used in Section 401(a)(2), the phrase "if under the trust instrument it is impossible" means that the trust instrument must definitely and affirmatively make it impossible for the nonexempt diversion or use to occur, whether by operation or natural termination of the trust, by power of revocation or amendment, by the happening of a contingency, by collateral arrangement, or by any other means. Although it is not essential that the employer relinquish all power to modify or terminate the rights of certain employees covered by the trust, it must be impossible for the trust funds to be used or diverted for purposes other than for the exclusive benefit of his employees or their beneficiaries.

(3) As used in section 401(a)(2), the phrase "purposes other than for the exclusive benefit of his employees or their beneficiaries" includes all objects or aims not solely designed for the proper satisfaction of all liabilities to employees or their beneficiaries covered by the trust.

Incidental Benefits Permissible. The rule requiring that a plan be operated for the exclusive benefit of employees or their beneficiaries, as provided in the Code, has historically been interpreted by the Internal Revenue Service not to prevent others from also deriving some benefit from transactions with the plan or trust. Prior rulings as well as the Internal Revenue Service qualification guides for employee benefit plans in effect prior to ERISA make clear that such incidental benefits are permitted. In this connection, IRS Qualification Guides, Part 2(K)(1), provide as follows:

(1) *Exclusive Benefit Requirement*—The primary purpose of benefiting employees or their beneficiaries must be maintained with respect to investments of the trust funds as well as with respect to other activities of the trust. This requirement, however, does not prevent others from also deriving some benefit from a transaction with the trust. For example, a sale of securities at a profit benefits the seller, but if the purchase price is not in excess of the fair market value of the securities at the time of sale and the applicable investment requisites set forth below have been met, the investment is consistent with the exclusive-benefit-of-employees requirement.

From the foregoing quotation from the IRS Guidelines the realization of a profit by an employer from the sale of securities to an ESOP Trust will not violate the exclusive benefit rule if the purchase price for the securities is not in excess of fair market value.

Investment Requisites. The IRS Guidelines in effect prior to ERISA also set forth the requisites which must normally be met by trustees in investing in trust assets as follows:

The requisites are: (1) The cost must not exceed fair market value at time of purchase; (2) a fair return commensurate with the prevailing rate must be provided; (3) sufficient liquidity must be maintained to permit distributions in accordance with the terms of the plan; and (4) the safeguards and diversity that a prudent investor would adhere to must be present. However, the requirement set forth in item (2) with respect to a fair return is not applicable to obligatory investments in employer securities in the case of a stock bonus plan. . . . Upon compliance with these requisites, if the trust instrument and local law permit investments in the stock or securities of the employer, such investments are not deemed to be inconsistent with the purpose of section 401(a) of the Code. The Internal Revenue Service however is to be notified if trust funds are invested in stock or securities of, or loaned to, the employer or related or controlled interests so that a determination may be made whether the trust serves any purpose other than constituting part of a plan for the exclusive benefit of employees.

Of the four requisites for trust investments contained in the portion of the Guidelines quoted above, the first, the requirement for dealings at "fair market value" are carried over into the ERISA requirement for dealings for "adequate consideration" between an ESOP Trust and parties in interest. Note that the second requirement, a fair return on investment "is not applicable to obligatory investments in employer securities in the case of a stock bonus plan." Note, however, that sufficient liquidity must be maintained by the trust to permit distributions in accordance with the terms of the plan, and the Internal Revenue Service must be notified of investments in securities of the employer, or loans to the employer.

Dealings at Fair Market Value. The tax law has required for many years that purchases and sales of securities between an ESOP and the employer corporation be at "fair market value." This concept was carried into current law by ERISA's requirement that dealings between an ESOP Trust and parties in interest be for "adequate consideration." The requirement that purchases and sales be made at "fair market value" may not cause difficulty where the securities of an employer are listed on a national securities exchange and are heavily traded, but in the case of a closely-held corporation the requirement for dealing at "adequate consideration" may cause great difficulty. This problem is considered in detail in Chapter 6.

PROHIBITED TRANSACTIONS

Prohibited Transactions. In addition to the general duties imposed upon a fiduciary to invest with prudence, ERISA sets forth specific transactions generally prohibited to fiduciaries of employee benefit trusts in Sections 406(a), (b) and (c) of ERISA. Of these prohibited transactions, two are of special importance in the discussion of ESOPs. Qualified trusts under employee benefit plans may generally not engage in transactions which constitute (1) a sale or exchange or leasing of any property between such trusts and an employer and (2) the lending of money or other extension of credit between such trusts and an employer. Subject to certain restrictions, ESOP trusts are generally exempt from restrictions imposed on such dealings with employers. If these two types of prohibited transactions were construed to apply to ESOPs, many of the incidental benefits available to employers through the maintenance and operation of such plans would be denied to the employers. Section 406 of ERISA sets forth prohibited transactions as follows:

> SEC. 406. (a) Except as provided in section 408:
> (1) A fiduciary with respect to a plan shall not cause the plan to engage in a transaction, if he knows or should know that such transaction constitutes a direct or indirect—
>> (A) sale or exchange, or leasing, of any property between the plan and a party in interest;

      (B) lending of money or other extension of credit between the plan and a party in interest;

      (C) furnishing of goods, services, or facilities between the plan and a party in interest;

      (D) transfer to, or use by or for the benefit of, a party in interest, of any assets of the plan; or

      (E) acquisition, on behalf of the plan, of any employer security or employer real property in violation of section 407(a).

  (2) No fiduciary who has authority or discretion to control or manage the assets of a plan shall permit the plan to hold any employer security or employer real property if he knows or should know that holding such security or real property violates section 407(a).

(b) A fiduciary with respect to a plan shall not—

  (1) deal with the assets of the plan in his own interest or for his own account.

  (2) in his individual or in any other capacity act in any transaction involving the plan on behalf of a party (or represent a party) whose interests are adverse to the interests of the plan or the interests of its participants or beneficiaries, or

  (3) receive any consideration for his own personal account from any party dealing with such plan in connection with a transaction involving the assets of the plan.

(c) A transfer of real property by a party in interest to a plan shall be treated as a sale or exchange if the property is subject to a mortgage or similar lien which the plan assumes or if it is subject to a mortgage or similar lien which a party in interest placed on the property within the 10-year period ending on the date of the transfer.

Limitation on Ownership of Employer Securities. In addition to the prohibited transactions set fort in Section 406, Section 407 of ERISA, as discussed above, limits the amount of qualified employer securities in which a fiduciary may invest. Section 407(a) of ERISA provides that a plan may not acquire any qualifying employer security, or qualifying employer real property, if immediately after such acquisition the fair market value of employer securities and employer real property held by the plan exceeds 10% of the fair market value of the plan's assets. Under Section 407(b)(1) of ERISA the 10% limitation on the holding or acquisition of qualifying employer securities and qualifying employer real estate is made inapplicable to ESOPs. This section provides that the 10% limitation "shall not apply to any acquisition or holding of qualifying employer securities or qualifying employer real property by an eligible individual account plan," which includes an ESOP. This exemption from the 10% limitation on investments in qualifying employer securities permits the fiduciary of an ESOP to invest as much as 100% of the plan's assets in eligible securities of an employer.

Exemptions for ESOP. The basic exemption which is granted to ESOP from the prohibited transactions outlined in Section 406 of ERISA (as well as a repetitious exemption from the 10% limitation on ownership of qualifying employer securities contained in Section 407 of ERISA) is set forth in Section 408(e) of ERISA. Section 408(e) provides that sections 406 and 407 "shall not apply" to the acquisition or sale by a plan of qualifying employer securities if the acquisition or sale is (1) for adequate consideration, (2) no commission is charged in the transaction, and (3) the plan is an eligible individual account plan. Section 408(e) of ERISA provides as follows:

(e) Sections 406 and 407 shall not apply to the acquisition or sale by a plan of qualifying employer securities (as defined in section 407(d)(5)) or acquisition, sale or lease by a plan of qualifying employer real property (as defined in section 407(d)(4))—

   (1) if such acquisition, sale, or lease is for adequate consideration (or in the case of a marketable obligation, at a price not less favorable to the plan than the price determined under Section 407(e)(1)),

   (2) if no commission is charged with respect thereto, and

   (3) if—

      (A) the plan is an eligible individual account plan (as defined in section 407(d)(3)), or

      (B) in the case of an acquisition or lease of qualifying employer real property by a plan which is not an eligible individual account plan, or of an acquisition of qualifying employer securities by such a plan, the lease or acquisition is not prohibited by section 407(a).

ESOP Loan Transactions. In addition to permitting an ESOP to purchase and hold qualifying employer securities and qualifying employer real estate without limitation as to amount, ERISA also provides special exemptions for debt financing on the part of ESOPs. Generally, any qualified plan is permitted to make loans to "parties in interest who are participants or beneficiaries of the plan" if the loans (1) are available to all participants and beneficiaries on an equivalent basis, (2) are not made available to highly compensated employees, officers, or shareholders in amounts greater than the amounts made available to other employees, (3) are in accordance with specific provisions regarding such loans set forth in the plan, (4) bear a reasonable rate of interest, and (5) are adequately secured.

In addition to loans permitted to be made to a participant or beneficiary, an employee stock ownership plan may borrow money from a party in interest and in this regard is exempt from the prohibitions set forth in Section 406. The loan must be primarily for the benefit of participants and beneficiaries to the plan and at a rate of interest not in excess of a reasonable rate. If the plan gives collateral to a party in interest for such a loan, such collateral may consist only of qualifying employer securities. This exemption for loans to an ESOP is set forth in section 408(b)(3) of ERISA:

   (3) A loan to an employee stock ownership plan (as defined in section 407(d)(6)), if—

      (A) such loan is primarily for the benefit of participants and beneficiaries of the plan, and

      (B) such loan is at an interest rate which is not in excess of a reasonable rate.

   If the plan gives collateral to a party in interest for such loan, such collateral may consist only of qualifying employer securities (as defined in section 407(d)(5)).

Party In Interest. As defined in section 3, paragraph (14) of ERISA the term party in interest means any fiduciary, counsel, or employee of a plan; a person providing services to the plan; an employer of employees covered by the plan; and a 50% owner of an employer. The definition of a "party in interest" as contained in Section 3(14) of ERISA provides in part as follows:

   (14) The term "party in interest" means, as to an employee benefit plan—

      (A) any fiduciary (including, but not limited to, any administrator, officer, trus-

tee or custodian), counsel, or employee of such employee benefit plan;
(B) a person providing services to such plan;
(C) an employer any of whose employees are covered by such plan;
(D) an employee organization any of whose members are covered by such plan;
(E) an owner, direct or indirect, of 50 percent or more of—
    (i) the combined voting power of all classes of stock entitled to vote or the
        total value of shares of all classes of stock of (an employer) . . .

The above definition of a party in interest, includes an owner who is the direct or indirect owner of 50 percent or more of the stock of an employer. Any "relative" of such owner, is also considered to be a party in interest, although for the purpose of construing the act, relative means "a spouse, ancestor, lineal descendent, or spouse of a lineal descendent."

Exempt ESOP Loan Transactions–IRS Ruling and Committee Report. In a pre-ERISA Revenue ruling a question was raised whether the borrowing of funds by a qualified trust and purchase of employer stock with the borrowed funds affected the tax exemption of the trust. With respect to this question in Rev. Rule 71-311, 1971-2, C.B. 184, the IRS stated the following:

> The purpose of this Revenue Ruling is to update and restate, under the current statute and regulations, the position set forth in Revenue Ruling 46, CB 1953-1, 287. The question presented is whether the qualification of an employees' trust is affected if such trust borrows capital and invests it in the securities of, or enters into transactions with, the employer by which it was established and from whom it has received or does receive contributions, or with an entity closely related to the employer.
>
> Section 401(a) of the Internal Revenue Code of 1954 provides that a trust forming part of a stock bonus, pension, or profit-sharing plan of an employer for the exclusive benefit of his employees or their beneficiaries shall constitute a qualified trust if certain requirements are met. Section 501(a) of the Code provides that a trust decribed in 401(a) shall be exempt from taxation unless such exemption is denied because the trust entered into a prohibited transaction or operated as a feeder organization.
>
> There is no prohibition in the Code or in the regulations promulgated thereunder against a trust borrowing funds to purchase investments. The borrowing of funds by a trust and investing them in the securities of, or entering into transactions with, the employer or an entity closely related to the employer does not disqualify a trust as one for the exclusive benefit of employees unless the borrowing is undertaken for the purpose of benefiting the employer as, for example, borrowing in order to furnish capital or property for use in the employer's business at a time when the employer's financial condition is such that it is unable to borrow money from usual financial sources.

The foregoing Revenue Ruling permits the borrowing unless the borrowing is undertaken for the purpose of benefiting the employer as, for example, borrowing to furnish capital for the employer when the employer's financial condition prohibits it from borrowing from usual financial sources.

ESOPs' special position in borrowing to buy stock under tax rulings prior to the adoption of ERISA, was recognized by the Joint Committee of Congress on the ERISA legislation. In this connection, the Conference Committee Report to Section 408 of ERISA provides in part as follows:

> Furthermore, it is understood that a frequent characteristic of some employee stock ownership plans is that they leverage their purchase of qualifying employer securities as a way to achieve transfers in the ownership of corporate stock and other capital requirements of a corporation and that such a plan is designed to build equity ownership of shares of the employer corporation for its employees in a nondiscriminatory manner.
>
> The conferees intend that the exemption from the prohibited transaction rules with respect to loans to employee stock ownership plans is to apply only in the case of loans (and guarantees) used to leverage the purchase of qualifying employer securities (and related business interests).

Note that ESOP's exemption from prohibited transaction rules which permits an ESOP to borrow with the guarantee of the employer is limited to such borrowing solely to leverage the purchase of qualifying employer securities.

Penalties. If a named fiduciary violates any of his fiduciary responsibilities as set forth in this chapter he may be required to reimburse the ESOP for any losses incurred, or if the violation is willful, he may be subject to criminal penalties. In addition, a party in interest such as an employer or controlling shareholder may be liable for a tax ranging from 5% to 100% of the amount involved in a prohibited transaction. The matter of possible penalties which may be incurred for violations of ERISA by fiduciaries or parties in interest is discussed in detail in Chapter 10.

Summary. Under ERISA, the fiduciary of an ESOP is the fiduciary named as such under the plan. An ESOP fiduciary must administer the trust for the exclusive benefit of employees or their beneficiaries, to invest primarily in employer securities, and to make distributions solely in employer stock. ESOP fiduciaries are exempt from normal duties of a fiduciary to diversify trust assets, and ESOP fiduciaries may invest 100% of trust assets in qualified employer securities. An ESOP fiduciary also need not realize a fair return on employer securities held by the fiduciary. In any acquisition or sale of qualifying employer securities, an ESOP fiduciary is exempt from prohibitions against dealing with parties in interest, such as controlling stockholders or employers, dealings prohibited to other fiduciaries. ESOPs may also engage in the lending of money between the plan and a party in interest, provided the transactions are (1) for adequate consideration, (2) no commission is charged. Finally, an ESOP fiduciary may borrow money from a third party to purchase qualifying employer securities and may permit the employer to guarantee the ESOP loan. An ESOP's ability to engage in transactions with disqualified persons, to invest 100% of its assets in employer securities, and to borrow money guaranteed by its employer, all types of transactions prohibited to other employee benefit plans, makes it possible for an employer to utilize an ESOP as a vehicle of corporate finance.

PART II

ESOP As a Vehicle
of Corporate Finance
and Management Tool

4

ESOP AS A VEHICLE
OF CORPORATE FINANCE

Legislating special privileges for ESOP reflects two fundamental objectives of Congressional policy. One objective is to distribute ownership of capital to the average American wage earner, to give him a stake in the capital employed by American business. To the extent that ESOPs provide employees with an interest in employer stock and distribute such stock to the employees, the employees acquire a stake in the business of the employer, and ownership of a portion of the capital which enables the employees to be productive. The second objective for legislating special privileges for ESOPs is to sanction continued use of an established financing vehicle to assist American industry to raise the additional substantial capital it will require to refurbish its plant, and to continue the growth of the national economy to assure future prosperity.

Although an ESOP presents an employer with a number of ways of increasing an employer's working capital, the issuance of additional stock by an employer to increase working capital may dilute reported earnings per share. In corporations where reported earnings per share are important to management, generally publicly-held companies, employers should determine the extent to which dilution in earnings per share may occur, in light of the use the employer intends to make of the additional working capital. This subject is treated in greater detail in Chapter 10, which sets forth some of the pitfalls and possible disadvantages of an ESOP.

Financing Vehicle. As a vehicle for corporate finance, the ESOP provides a means for creating, conserving, and raising capital. This chapter discusses the ESOP as an instrument which makes capital available to an employer which would not be available without an ESOP. What elements of an ESOP enable an employer to conserve or raise capital which would otherwise not ordinarily be available to the employer? Consider this question first from the point of view of the ESOP and its trust.

ESOP's Privileges. From the plan's point of view, the four privileges outlined below, permit the ESOP, as an incidental benefit to the employer, to assist the employer in increasing working capital:

(1) The ESOP may receive and accept contributions from the employer in the form of employer stock.

(2) The ESOP may buy employer stock, from the employer and others, and may invest 100% of its trust's assets in such stock.

(3) The ESOP may borrow funds to invest in employer securities; such funds may be borrowed from the employer or from a third party.

(4) The ESOP may accept a guaranty of the employer on any borrowings of the ESOP to purchase employer stock, or, alternatively, an undertaking of the employer to periodically make sufficient contributions to the ESOP Trust to amortize principal and interest of the loan.

Employer's Privileges. From the viewpoint of the employer, two fundamental privileges legally available to an employer with an ESOP permit the employer to increase and conserve working capital, as an incident to the operation of the ESOP:

(1) The employer may make contributions to the ESOP in the form of newly issued or treasury stock, and for income tax purposes, may deduct an amount equal to the fair market value of the stock contributed to the ESOP, subject to the limitation on deductible amounts in Section 404(a), discussed below.

(2) The employer may sell stock (newly issued or treasury stock) to the ESOP. The basic legal restriction ERISA and the Internal Revenue Code impose on such sales requires that the purchase price paid by the ESOP not exceed the fair market value of the stock.

Some Illustrations. The illustrations set forth below indicate how various transactions between an employer and an ESOP may affect the working capital of the employer. Tax computations in the illustrations assume an effective combined corporate income tax rate, Federal and local, of fifty percent, and that contributions are within maximum deductible limits. The actual effective rate in individual cases will vary, and in some instances the combined rates will exceed the fifty percent used in the illustrations. However, for the sake of simplicity, illustrations in this book assume an effective combined Federal and local corporate income tax rate of fifty percent, and in spite of different rates in specific situations, the principles set forth in the illustrations will apply generally.

Contribution of Stock. A contribution of stock illustrates how an ESOP may increase working capital for an employer. Assume a situation of an employer which has no employee benefit plan. As an incentive for its employees, the employer establishes and qualifies an ESOP. The employer then contributes $100,000 in fair market value of newly issued employer common stock to the ESOP. Upon making the contribution, the employer becomes entitled to a $100,000 income tax deduction; and, assuming an effective combined Federal and local income tax rate of 50%, the employer pays $50,000 less in income taxes than it would have paid had it not established the ESOP and made the stock contribution. The reduction of $50,000 in income taxes due to the stock contribution by the employer to the ESOP, adds $50,000 to the working capital of the employer. This principle is set forth in the simple illustration below:

	Employer Without ESOP	Employer With ESOP
1. Working Capital:	$1,000,000.	$1,000,000.
2. Taxable Income, Prior to Contribution to ESOP:	250,000.	250,000.
3. Contribution of Stock Valued at $100,000 to ESOP:	00.	100,000.
4. Net Taxable Income:	$ 250,000.	$ 150,000.
5. Combined Federal and Local Income Taxes (Assumed 50% Rate):	125,000.	75,000.
6. Net After Tax Income of Employer (Item 2 Minus Item 5):	125,000.	175,000.
7. Total Working Capital Available to Employer After Payment of Income Taxes (Item 1 plus Item 6):	$1,125,000.	$1,175,000.

The above illustration indicates how an employer may increase working capital by establishing an ESOP and making contributions to it in stock. It indicates that a contribution of $100,000 in stock may increase an employer's working capital by $50,000. In the illustration the employer increases its working capital from $1,125,000 to $1,175,000 by forming an ESOP and contributing $100,000 of stock to the ESOP Trust.

Pension Plan vs. ESOP. The next illustration, based on the same financial assumptions set forth in the preceding illustration, compares an employer with a pension plan to an employer with an ESOP. Contributions by the employer to the pension plan are made in cash, and contributions by the employer to the ESOP are made in stock. The net working capital available to each of these employers may be illustrated as follows:

	Employer With Pension Plan	Employer With ESOP
1. Working Capital:	$1,000,000.	$1,000,000.
2. Taxable Income, Prior to Contributions to Pension Plan or ESOP:	250,000.	250,000.
3. Contribution of $100,000 Cash to Pension Plan:	100,000.	00.

	Employer With Pension Plan	Employer With ESOP
4. Contributions of $100,000 in Stock to ESOP:	00.	100,000.
5. Net Taxable Income:	$ 150,000.	$ 150,000.
6. Combined Federal and Local Income Taxes (Assumed 50% Combined Rate):	75,000.	75,000.
7. Net After-Tax Income of Employer (Item 2 Minus Item 6):	175,000.	175,000.
8. Increase in Cash Flow After Deducting Cash Contributions to Plan (Item 7 minus Item 3):	75,000.	175,000.
9. Total Working Capital Available to Employer After Payment of Income Taxes (Item 1 Plus Item 8):	$1,075,000.	$1,175,000.

The above illustration compares an employer's available working capital after making contributions in stock to an ESOP, on the one hand, and in cash to a pension plan on the other hand. The comparison indicates that, all other things being equal, an employer which contributes $100,000 in stock to an ESOP has $100,000 more in working capital available than an employer which contributes $100,000 in cash to a pension plan. In each instance, the contribution of $100,000 reduces the income tax bill of the employer by $50,000. However, since the contribution to the pension plan is made in cash, the effect of the $100,000 cash contribution, partially offset by the $50,000 tax saving, is a *net decrease* of $50,000 in working capital; whereas the $50,000 tax saving by the employer with the ESOP, represents a *net increase* of $50,000 in that employer's working capital.

Profit-Sharing Plan vs. ESOP. The difference in the working capital of an employer of making cash contributions to a profit-sharing plan, compared to stock contributions to an ESOP, is identical to the difference of making cash contributions to a pension plan, compared to stock contributions to an ESOP, as set forth in the foregoing illustration. However, since a profit-sharing plan is also an individual account plan, contributions to a profit-sharing plan may, depending upon the terms of the plan, also be made substantially in the form of stock.

The Leveraged ESOP. The foregoing illustrations indicate how an ESOP may increase working capital of an employer through income tax deductions for stock contributions. This basic incidental benefit of an ESOP to an employer may be leveraged where the ESOP borrows money. To illustrate this principle of leverage, assume an employer plans to borrow $1,000,000 for a capital improvement program. The terms negotiated with the lender provide for the repayment of the $1,000,000 in 10 equal annual installments of principal of $100,000 each, with interest at the rate of ten per cent per annum on unpaid balances. If the employer itself borrows the $1,000,000 from the lender and repays the loan in accordance with its terms, the employer is required to pay the lender a total of $1,275,000 in after-tax dollars to repay the principal and interest on the loan; i.e., the employer reduces its cash flow by $1,275,000 to repay the $1,000,000 loan. Interest payments by the employer are tax deductible, but principal payments are not.

Assume the same employer has established an ESOP for the benefit of its employees. The administrative committee under the ESOP determines to purchase $1,000,000 worth of the employer's newly issued stock. Under these circumstances, the ESOP may borrow the $1,000,000 from the lender. This borrowing may be guaranteed by the employer, or the employer may contract with the ESOP Trust to make future annual contributions to the Trust in an amount sufficient to amortize loan principal and interest. Either approach is acceptable under ERISA and the Internal Revenue Code, with the ultimate form of the transaction fixed to satisfy the wishes of the lender. Assume further that the ESOP borrows $1,000,000 from the lender, and purchases $1,000,000 of newly issued stock from the employer. The ESOP will repay the loan through annual contributions to the ESOP Trust by the employer in amounts sufficient to amortize the principal and interest payments on the loan. Under the assumed facts, the annual contributions by the employer to the ESOP are fully tax deductible. As a result, the employer incurs a total cost in after-tax dollars of $775,000 for contributions to the ESOP to repay the principal of $1,000,000, plus interest, in accordance with the terms of the loan.

The following illustrations compare the effect upon an employer's cash flow of borrowing funds directly on the one hand, and through an ESOP on the other. The illustrations assume a $1,000,000 loan on identical terms set forth above and each annual payment of principal and interest is made on an anniversary date of the date of the loan. Where an employer borrows directly, only the interest portion of the annual loan payment is tax deductible, but where an ESOP borrows and repayment is made through annual employer contributions to the ESOP, the entire contribution is tax-deductible, including the portion which represents principal.

EMPLOYER BORROWING VS ESOP BORROWING
Borrowing of Employer
Directly and No Contributions
to ESOP to Repay Loan

Loan Anniversary Dates	Principal and Interest Payment	Interest Deduction	After-Tax Cost
1st	$200,000	$100,000	$150,000
2nd	190,000	90,000	145,000
3rd	180,000	80,000	140,000
4th	170,000	70,000	135,000

Loan Anniversary Dates	Principal and Interest Payment	Interest Deduction	After-Tax Cost
5th	160,000	60,000	130,000
6th	150,000	50,000	125,000
7th	140,000	40,000	120,000
8th	130,000	30,000	115,000
9th	120,000	20,000	110,000
10th	110,000	10,000	105,000
Total After-Tax Cost to Employer of Repayment of Borrowing:			$1,275,000

Borrowing by ESOP with Repayment of Loan from Annual Contributions by Employer to ESOP

Loan Anniversary Dates	Principal and Interest Payment	Interest Deduction	After-Tax Cost
1st	$200,000	$200,000	$100,000
2nd	190,000	190,000	95,000
3rd	180,000	180,000	90,000
4th	170,000	170,000	85,000
5th	160,000	160,000	80,000
6th	150,000	150,000	75,000
7th	140,000	140,000	70,000
8th	130,000	130,000	65,000
9th	120,000	120,000	60,000
10th	110,000	110,000	55,000
Total After-Tax Cost to Employer of Repayment of Borrowing:			$775,000

The above illustrations indicate that the employer conserves a total of $500,000 in capital by indirectly repaying the loan of $1,000,000 through annual contributions to the ESOP. Direct repayment by the employer costs $1,275,000 in after-tax funds, whereas repayment through ESOP costs $775,000.

The employer may achieve a similar $500,000 saving of working capital, by borrowing the $1,000,000 directly from a lender and itself repaying principal and interest to the lender directly, provided the employer makes annual contributions to the ESOP in stock of a value of $100,000 on each anniversary date of the loan. Each annual contribution of $100,000 in stock, equal to the annual principal payment on the loan, increases the cash flow of the employer by $50,000, or a total of $500,000 saving in working capital over the ten year period of the loan. Where the employer does the borrowing and repays the loan itself, the employer must, of course, also pay the interest on the loan. Such interest payments are separately deductible, like interest on any other indebtedness of the employer. Direct borrowing by an employer may be the preferred approach where annual contribution by the employer to the ESOP to repay loan principal and interest would exceed the maximum tax-deductible contribution of 15% of covered compensation, discussed at the end of this chapter. This principle is illustrated in the series of computations set forth below:

DIRECT BORROWING BY EMPLOYER, AND ANNUAL STOCK CONTRIBUTIONS TO ESOP

	Employer Cash Payment			**Employer Stock Contributions to ESOP**	
Loan Anniversary Dates	*Total Payment*	*Tax Deductible Interest*	*After-Tax Cost*	*Annual Stock Contribution (Equal to Principal Payment)*	*Increased Working Capital (Tax Saving)*
1st	$200,000	$100,000	$150,000	$100,000	$ 50,000
2nd	190,000	90,000	145,000	100,000	50,000
3rd	180,000	80,000	140,000	100,000	50,000
4th	170,000	70,000	135,000	100,000	50,000
5th	160,000	60,000	130,000	100,000	50,000
6th	150,000	50,000	125,000	100,000	50,000
7th	140,000	40,000	120,000	100,000	50,000
8th	130,000	30,000	115,000	100,000	50,000
9th	120,000	20,000	110,000	100,000	50,000
10th	110,000	10,000	105,000	100,000	50,000

Total After-Tax Cost to Employer of Cash Repayment of Borrowing: $1,275,000

Total 10-year Tax Savings From Stock Contributions to ESOP: $500,000

The above illustration demonstrates how annual stock contributions to an ESOP, each in the amount of annual principal repayments of $100,000, result in an aggregate $500,000 increase in available working capital over the period of the loan. By offsetting the total after-tax cost to the employer of repaying principal and interest; i.e., $1,275,000, by the $500,000 increase in cash flow, the net cost to the employer of repayment of principal and interest on the loan where annual offsetting stock contributions are made to the ESOP, equals $775,000, or the same after-tax cost as where the borrowing is done by the ESOP, and repayment of the loan is made indirectly by the employer through contributions to the ESOP.

The effect on an employer's working capital is identical where, on the one hand, the ESOP borrows funds and repays the loan with employer contributions of cash, and, on the other hand, the employer borrows and repays the loan directly, making annual contributions of stock to the ESOP equal in value to annual principal payments on the loan. However, in addition to the possible effect of the 15% contribution ceiling, a fundamental difference exists in the two alternative methods of financing the transaction.

Where the ESOP borrows the funds and buys $1,000,000 of newly issued stock from an employer, the stock is outstanding on the employer's books from the moment of issuance and purchase, and the additional outstanding stock has the effect of diluting earnings per share on the financial statements of the employer issued thereafter. Where new shares are issued and contributed annually, dilution of earnings per share is delayed until such time as shares are actually issued. Furthermore, the number of shares which an employer issues is fixed where an ESOP borrows the $1,000,000 and purchases that amount of stock from the employer. If the fair market value of the stock increases with the passage of time, the employer will have issued more shares of stock by the one-time sale to the ESOP than if the employer makes annual contributions of stock valued at $100,000 at the time of each contribution.

Maximum Permissible Tax Deductions. Contributions by employers to qualified employee benefit plans are deductible for income tax purposes under Section 404(a) of the Code. This Section sets forth maximum amounts of such contributions which are deductible by employers. The maximum deductions for income tax purposes differ with the type of plan to which the employer makes contributions. Section 404(a)(1) provides the maximum deductions allowable to pension trusts, in respect to which deductions are generally limited to amounts actuarially necessary to fund the pensions set forth in the applicable pension plan.

Section 404(a)(3) sets forth the maximum deductions allowable to both stock bonus plans (including ESOPs) and profit-sharing plans. Under this section, an employer's contributions are limited to 15% of compensation paid to employees covered under such a plan, subject to possible increase by carry-overs of additional deductible amounts from prior years. With regard to the 15% limitation, Section 404(a)(3) provides as follows:

(a) General Rule—If contributions are paid by an employer to or under a stock bonus, pension, profit-sharing, or annuity plan . . . they shall be deductible under this section, subject, however, to the following limitations as to the amounts deductible in any year:

*   *   *

(3) Stock Bonus and Profit-Sharing Trusts—
(A) Limits on Deductible Contributions—In the taxable year when paid, stock bonus or profit-sharing trust . . . in an amount not in excess of 15 percent of the compensation otherwise paid or accrued during the taxable year to all employees under the stock bonus or profit-sharing plan.

Carryover of Unused Deductions. If in any taxable year an employer pays into an ESOP less than the 15% of compensation permitted to be deducted, the difference may be carried forward and added to future deductible contributions, subject to a maximum deductible limit of 25% of compensation. In this connection, Section 404(a)(3) of the Code provides as follows:

> If in any taxable year there is paid into the trust, or a similar trust then in effect, amounts less than [15% of compensation], the excess, or if no amount is paid, the amount deductible, shall be carried forward and be deductible when paid in the succeeding taxable years in order of time, but the amount so deductible under this sentence in any such succeeding taxable year shall not exceed 15 percent of the compensation otherwise paid or accrued during such succeeding taxable year to the beneficiaries under the plan, but the amount so deductible under this sentence in any one succeeding taxable year together with the . . . [15% of compensation] shall not exceed 25 percent of the compensation otherwise paid or accrued during such taxable year to the beneficiaries under the plan.

Any time an employer intends to utilize an ESOP as a vehicle of corporate finance, the 15% and 25% of compensation limitations on the deductible amounts of contributions must be considered. Borrowings by an ESOP Trust should not be made in such amounts that the employer is unable to deduct the full amounts contributed to the ESOP to amortize indebtedness. The limitations on the deductible amounts of contributions to an ESOP pose a more fundamental problem in that an ESOP may not be a feasible financial vehicle for an employer whose covered compensation is too small to permit meaningful deductions. This matter is discussed in greater detail in Chapter 10.

Summary. As a vehicle of corporate finance, an ESOP provides a means for creating, conserving and raising capital for an employer. An ESOP's uses as a vehicle of corporate finance include (1) receipt of stock contributions from an employer which result in tax savings or tax refunds and additional cash flow to an employer, (2) purchases of stock by an ESOP from an employer, newly issued or treasury stock, to provide increased capital to an employer, (3) borrowing of funds by the ESOP from a third party to buy employer securities, and repayment of the loan from tax deductible contributions received from an employer, enabling the employer indirectly to repay the principal of indebtedness with tax-deductible dollars. On a borrowing of $1,000,000, an employer may conserve $500,000 in working capital by indirect repayment of the $1,000,000 loan made by the ESOP, rather than a direct repayment of a loan made by the employer itself. The deductibility of contributions by an employer to an ESOP are, however, limited to 15% of compensation of covered employees, subject to a maximum deductible limit of 25% where carry-overs of unused deductible amounts exist.

5

ESOP AS A VEHICLE FOR ACQUISITIONS, DISPOSITIONS OR DEBT REFINANCE

ACQUISITIONS

Capital Transactions. From an income tax point of view, an acquisition is a capital transaction. Payments made to acquire the stock or assets of a business are not deductible for income tax purposes as expense items, and, unless the acquisition is tax-free, the payments must be allocated to the properties purchased as the cost of such properties.

Asset Acquisition. Where the assets of a business are acquired in a taxable transaction, for cash for example, the purchase price paid by the buyer is allocated among the assets acquired for income tax purposes as provided in the acquisition contract; or if the contract is silent, first to tangible assets such as inventories, plant and equipment, and land and buildings, then to intangibles such as accounts receivable and prepayments, and finally to the extent not allocable to other assets such as the foregoing assets, the balance is treated as goodwill. Income tax deductions are available to the buyer as the inventory is sold off, as accounts receivable are collected, and as depreciable items such as buildings, machinery, and furniture and fixtures are depreciated over their useful lives. To the extent, however, that portions of the purchase price are allocable to land and goodwill, non-depreciable items, income tax benefits in the form of tax deductions are not realizable by the buyer on its income tax returns.

Stock Acquisition. Where the buyer buys stock in a taxable transaction, the net effect from an income tax point of view is substantially similar to that described above. The cash purchase price is not deductible as an expense upon the purchase of the stock, but is a capital expenditure. If the purchased corporation continues to conduct its business and file separate tax returns, no change occurs in the basic income tax position of the acquired corporation. Where it is treated as a separate entity and its business is conducted in the same corporate form, the acquired corporation, after the acquisition, realizes the same basic income from the sale of its inventories and deduction of expense items, and same rates and methods of depreciation of depreciable items continue to apply, as before the acquisition. Or in the alternative, if the buyer liquidates the acquired corporation and meets the requirements of Section 334(b) of the Internal Revenue Code, the assets of the acquired company in the hands of the buyer take on a tax basis equal to the cost or adjusted basis of the stock in the hands of the buyer. Upon liquidation an allocation of purchase price is made to the assets of the acquired corporation in the hands of the buyer, as in the foregoing paragraph when the buyer acquires the assets of a going business directly.

In either of the above events, whether a buyer buys assets or stock in a taxable transaction, no part of the purchase price, as such, is deductible as an expense item for income tax purposes. To the extent that a buyer so structures an acquisition that the payment of the purchase price is deductible for income tax purposes, the cost of the acquisition to the buyer in after-tax dollars is less; and in the case of a buyer subject to a 50% combined federal and local tax rate, such an acquisition would cost only one-half the purchase price in after-tax dollars, compared to the same acquisition treated as a capital transaction for income tax purposes.

Acquisition Fact Pattern. Assume that buyer and seller have agreed in principle that an acquisition of the seller by the buyer would be mutually advantageous and have agreed on price. In discussing the method of payment, the seller reiterates its willingness to sell, but will not accept stock of the buyer in payment of the price. The seller or the selling shareholders, as the case may be, will sell only for cash, or for cash and notes. Such a situation is not uncommon. It may arise where the buyer's stock is not marketable, where the seller believes that the buyer's stock is due to decline in value, where the seller needs cash which would necessitate immediate sale of the buyer's stock and the buyer is unwilling to register the stock with the Securities and Exchange Commission, or for tax or any other of many valid reasons of a seller to require payment in other than a seller's stock. Assume the purchase price for the seller's business is $1,000,000, and that the seller, or its shareholders, require payment in cash, or as an alternative will accept a $200,000 cash down payment, with the balance of $800,000 represented by notes, payable in four equal annual installments plus interest on the first, second, third and fourth anniversaries of the acquisition date.

Under these circumstances, if the buyer is an employer which has established and maintains an ESOP, the ESOP may participate in the transaction to permit payment of a substantial portion of the purchase price with pre-tax dollars, indirectly resulting in deductions of purchase payments for income tax purposes.

Cash Purchase Use of ESOP. If a contribution of $1,000,000 to the ESOP is deductible by the employer and does not exceed the maximum income tax deduction of

15% of covered compensation, plus carry-overs, the employer may contribute $1,000,000 to the ESOP. The ESOP, as part of an integrated transaction may buy the stock of the seller for $1,000,000, and, as a last step in the transaction, the employer may acquire the stock of the seller from the ESOP in exchange for $1,000,000 fair market value of the employer's stock. The net effect upon the employer is a purchase of the seller's business for $1,000,000 which is tax deductible, plus $1,000,000 in newly issued stock transferred to the ESOP for the benefit of covered employees. Although the transaction, viewed in its entirety, involves payment by the employer of $1,000,000 in cash and $1,000,000 in employer stock for the stock of the seller, the final step in the transaction may give rise to a tax problem. If the employer stock exchanged for the seller's stock is solely voting stock, will the final step of the transaction qualify as a tax-free "reorganization" under Section 368(a)(1)(B) of the Code? This section provides that the term "reorganization" means the acquisition by one corporation (the employer) in exchange solely for all or a part of its voting stock (employer stock) of stock of another corporation (the seller) if immediately after the acquisition, the acquiring corporation (the employer) has control of the other corporation (the seller). Control for the purposes of this section is satisfied if the acquirer obtains 80% of the voting power of the selling corporation's stock. This requirement is met in the subject illustration, because the employer acquires 100% of the outstanding stock of the seller. The employer's tax counsel should not only consider whether the exchange may qualify as a tax-free reorganization, but should give thought to whether (in a situation which could have adverse tax consequences to the employer) the Internal Revenue Service may take the position that the substance of the transaction, viewed as the final step in the transaction, is a tax-free exchange. In our illustration, the net income tax effect to the employer is the same, whether or not the transaction is treated as a tax-free exchange. In either event, the employer acquires 100% of the stock of the seller which has a tax basis, or tax cost, to the employer of a total of $1,000,000.

Cash Purchase by Employer. The same acquisition with an identical ultimate effect upon the employer may be cast in a different mechanical mold. As an alternative to making a cash contribution to the ESOP which in turn is utilized to buy the seller's stock, the employer may itself purchase the seller's stock for $1,000,000 and subsequent to the purchase of the stock, or simultaneously with the purchase, the employer may make contributions of employer stock to the ESOP aggregating $1,000,000 to increase the employer's cash flow by $500,000. The ultimate effect of this transaction upon the employer is identical to an original purchase of the seller's stock by the ESOP, and an exchange of the seller's stock for employer's stock. A direct purchase by the employer, however, with subsequent contributions of employer stock to the ESOP, may avoid one element of the problem of valuing employer stock where it is exchanged for seller's stock. Where the transaction does not involve an exchange, the employer does not face the added risk of proving the fair market value of employer stock to meet the "adequate consideration" requirements of ERISA, but solely to determine the tax deduction as a contribution to the ESOP. The valuation problem is discussed in Chapter 6.

Note Purchase Use of ESOP. If as an alternative to a cash transaction, the employer decides to make the acquisition for $200,000 cash and $800,000 in notes, in accordance with the terms mentioned above, the employer may itself directly purchase the Seller's stock for $200,000 in cash and $800,000 in the employer's notes, due in equal annual installments of $200,000 on the first, second, third and fourth anniversaries of the closing date. To replenish working capital as it makes its annual $200,000 note payments, the employer may simultaneously contribute $200,000 in newly issued stock to the ESOP. As a net effect of such an arrangement, the employer replenishes $100,000 of its working capital by income tax reductions of that amount for each $200,000 stock contribution to the ESOP, which offsets by half each $200,000 payment of principal on its notes.

Leveraged ESOP Purchase. Where a seller negotiates payment of the $1,000,000 purchase price in cash and the employer must borrow the funds from an outside source, the employer may itself borrow the funds for the acquisition and repay the loan without making any contributions to an ESOP. Or, on the other hand, the employer may borrow the funds to make the acquisition and contemplate use of contributions to an ESOP to offset partially the after-tax cost of the borrowing. The employer, further, may cause the ESOP to borrow money to purchase employer stock to provide the employer with the necessary cash to complete the transaction. Assume that the lender is willing to make the $1,000,000 loan on the same basis as that set forth above in Chapter 4, i.e., the $1,000,000 loan is to be repaid in 10 equal annual installments of principal of $100,000 each, bearing interest at the rate of 10% per annum on unpaid balances. If the employer borrows the funds directly and makes repayment to the lender without in any way taking into account contributions to an ESOP, the total cost to the employer in after-tax dollars to repay the principal and interest on the loan will amount to $1,275,000. On the other hand, if the employer utilizes tax deductible contributions to the ESOP to repay the loan, either directly or indirectly, the total cost in after-tax dollars of the repayment of the borrowing to the employer will amount to $775,000. This $500,000 savings in working capital to the employer is illustrated by the table set forth in Chapter 4 as follows:

EMPLOYER BORROWING ESOP VS. BORROWING

**Borrowing of Employer
Directly and No Contributions
to ESOP to Repay Loan**

Loan Anniversary Dates	Principal and Interest Payment	Interest Deduction	After-Tax Cost
1st	$200,000	$100,000	$150,000
2nd	190,000	90,000	145,000
3rd	180,000	80,000	140,000
4th	170,000	70,000	135,000
5th	160,000	60,000	130,000
6th	150,000	50,000	125,000
7th	140,000	40,000	120,000
8th	130,000	30,000	115,000
9th	120,000	20,000	110,000

Loan Anniversary Dates	Principal and Interest Payment	Interest Deduction	After-Tax Cost
10th	110,000	10,000	105,000
Total After-Tax Cost to Employer of Repayment of Borrowing:			$,1,275,000

Borrowing by ESOP with Repayment of Loan from Annual Contributions by Employer to ESOP

Loan Anniversary Dates	Principal and Interest Payment	Interest Deduction	After-Tax Cost
1st	$200,000	$200,000	$100,000
2nd	190,000	190,000	95,000
3rd	180,000	180,000	90,000
4th	170,000	170,000	85,000
5th	160,000	160,000	80,000
6th	150,000	150,000	75,000
7th	140,000	140,000	70,000
8th	130,000	130,000	65,000
9th	120,000	120,000	60,000
10th	110,000	110,000	55,000
Total After-Tax Cost to Employer of Repayment of Borrowing:			$775,000

The above illustration demonstrates how the employer may conserve a total of $500,000 in working capital by indirectly repaying the loan of $1,000,000 to make the acquisition through annual contributions to the ESOP. In addition to the saving of working capital, as demonstrated in Chapter 4, deductions by the employer for contributions to an ESOP are limited to the amount of 15% of covered employee compensation annually. After the acquisition, the compensation of the employees of the seller may be added to the tax deductible compensation base if the seller's employees are covered by the employer's ESOP. Increased contributions to the ESOP may be tax deductible as a result of the increased employee's payroll. Possible increased tax deductible amounts, may make the borrowing of greater sums to make acquisitions feasible, where the 15% of compensation limitation would otherwise limit the amount of borrowing.

Requirements for ESOP Acquisitions. The foregoing illustrations of possible uses of ESOP to make acquisitions illustrate methods of making acquisitions and using the ESOP to permit the employer to deduct a portion of the purchase price. Other uses of an ESOP may be available to a particular employer to make acquisitions. For example, acquisitions may incorporate sale of preferred stock to the ESOP, where the circumstances of an acquisition makes use of preferred stock desirable to an employer, but not a feasible method of direct payment to a seller. Regardless of the mechanical means chosen to consummate any particular acquisition, where an ESOP is involved, the employer and the fiduciaries of the ESOP Trust should bear in mind that the transaction must meet the legal requirements for ESOP dealings to avoid penalties.

As set forth in Chapters 1, 2, and 3, the fundamental requirements are that the ESOP must (1) be maintained exclusively for the benefit of its employees or their beneficiaries, (2) invest primarily in employer securities, and (3) borrow money only to purchase employer securities. The body of legal precedents involving ESOPs will grow, through the promulgation of regulations and guidelines by the Commissioner of Internal Revenue and the Secretary of Labor, and through IRS rulings and decisions of the United States Tax Court and other Federal courts. Lawyers and other advisors to fiduciaries and employers involved with ESOPs should carefully scrutinize each proposed transaction which involves the ESOP and its employer, including participation in the purchase or sale of stock or assets of a selling corporation, to ascertain whether the particular transaction is permissible and meets the requirements of the statutes, regulations, and case law.

DISPOSITIONS

Disposition Through an ESOP. During the 1950's and 1960's many corporations grew through acquisitions of other businesses. In the process, acquisition-minded corporations found they had become conglomerates or mini-conglomerates with, in some instances, divisions which either did not fit the general corporate objectives of the acquirer or were not economically viable as part of the larger corporate structure. Assume such a situation, where a parent corporation wishes to sell a subsidiary for $1,000,000.

Where it is difficult to find a purchaser for the subsidiary, sometimes the employees of the subsidiary may be its most likely buyers. Under these circumstances, if the parent company and the employees of the subsidiary agree upon a sale, an ESOP may be formed to enable the employees to purchase the subsidiary with tax-deductible dollars. The mechanics for closing the sale may be structured to include the formation of a new employee owned corporation ("Employee Corp.") which forms an ESOP ("Employee ESOP"). Key employees of the subsidiary may contribute the initial capital, assume $100,000, to Employee Corp. as working capital in exchange for 100% of the stock of the corporation. Employee Corp. then forms and qualifies an ESOP.

The ESOP borrows $1,000,000, guaranteed by Employee Corp. and further secured as indicated below, and buys $1,000,000 of newly issued stock from Employee Corp. This transaction leaves the ESOP with approximately 91% of the outstanding stock of Employee Corp., and the key employees with approximately 9% of the stock. The ESOP and the key employees together own 100% of the stock of Employee Corp., although the key employees may control the management of Employee Corp. By control of the Board of Directors and the ESOP Committee, the key employees may control the vote of the stock by the trustee of the ESOP Trust.

Employee Corp. utilizes $1,000,000 of its $1,100,000 of capital to buy the stock, or the assets, as a going business, of the subsidiary which the parent organization wishes to sell. Employee Corporation contemplates repayment of $1,000,000 of indebtedness to the lender through annual contributions of Employee Corp. to the ESOP. As demonstrated in Chapter 4, the indirect repayment of the $1,000,000 loan by Employee Corp. through contributions to the ESOP, assuming a combined federal and local income tax rate of 50%, costs Employee Corp. only $500,000 in after-tax dollars.

Disposition from Lender's Viewpoint. From the lender's viewpoint, the transaction must, of course, be viable. Fundamentally, the disposition to the employees depends upon the earning capacity and assets of the subsidiary being sold by the parent company. As is true in any situation where an ESOP's funds are invested in the stock of an employer corporation, the employer should be a profitable organization with reasonable hopes for future growth and continued profitability. Assuming that Employee Corp. meets this basic requirement, the lender may receive any or all of the following security for the repayment of its loan:

(1) The ESOP and the key employees may pledge 100% of the stock of Employee Corp. to secure repayment of the loan;

(2) In addition, Employee Corp. may pledge its assets as security;

(3) Under the proper circumstances, the selling parent corporation may guaranty the repayment of the loan.

Not only may the lender obtain security for the loan as set forth above, but since repayment of principal will be tax deductible and only cost Employee Corp. $500,000 in after-tax dollars, a shorter repayment period or higher interest rate may be financially feasible. In any event, since Employee Corp. will be able to repay the $1,000,000 loan with pre-tax dollars, at a cost of only $500,000 in working capital, less after-tax working capital is required for repayment. Possibility of repayment of the loan from earnings is greatly improved.

Disposition from Employees' Viewpoint. From the viewpoint of the employees, they become 100% owners of the business rather than solely employees. This change in the relationship between the employees and their employer should have a substantial effect on employee morale, and on the profitability of Employee Corp. in the future. From the viewpoint of the key employees, they become owners and are in control of the business and they are responsible for their own business' destiny. As employees of Employee Corp., they will share in contributions made to the ESOP, and as participants in the ESOP will ultimately receive additional stock as the net asset position of the ESOP Trust increases.

Disposition from Seller's Viewpoint. From the viewpoint of the original parent-seller of the business, it has not only successfully sold its subsidiary for the price it desired, but at the same time has countered possible unpleasantness associated with the sale of a business unit and termination of a substantial number of its employees. Employees of a sold business unit who leave with resentments against any employer may adversely affect the morale of employees who remain and who have the continuing responsibility of carrying on the parent-employer's business. Sale of a division or a subsidiary to employees requires that the employees be able to raise sufficient capital to pay the seller a fair price for its business. Often employees are the most logical buyers for a subsidiary or a division which a corporation wishes to sell. Since use of an ESOP may provide a unique cash flow advantage, permitting repayment of money borrowed to buy the business with tax-deductible dollars, any corporation desiring to sell a subsidiary or a division should consider the possibility of sale to its employees through the use of an ESOP, to take advantage of the additional capital available to pay the purchase price.

Example of ESOP Disposition. An example of the use of an ESOP by employees to purchase their employer's business, was reported in the Wall Street Journal. The article illustrates that purchase of a relatively large business by employees through use of an ESOP is feasible. The article describes the purchase by employees of the business of South Bend Lathe Co. from Amsted Industries Inc. for approximately $10,000,000 in cash. Because the transaction is such an outstanding example of a sale of a business unit to its employees through use of an ESOP, the article is quoted in its entirety:

> CHICAGO—Under an unusual method of financing, the 500 employes of South Bend Lathe Co., South Bend, Ind., purchased the company from Amsted Industries Inc. for about $10 million in cash.
>
> They used a vehicle called an Employe Stock Ownership Plan, or ESOP, an employe benefit device similar to a pension or profit-sharing plan. Enjoying many of the same tax benefits of pension funds, the South Bend Lathe ESOP was able to borrow the full purchase price to buy the unit. The $10 million borrowing will be paid back over a number of years out of the enterprise's profits. Thus, the workers eventually will end up with 100% ownership of South Bend Lathe, though they didn't put up any capital in the acquisition.
>
> The company, which makes and markets machine tools, was acquired by Amsted in 1959. In recent years Amsted has been trying to divest itself of the unit, raising the possibility that the South Bend operation might be closed.
>
> The purchase package put together by the South Bend ESOP includes a $5 million grant from the Federal Economic Development Administration to the city of South Bend to be lent to the ESOP. The loan is for 25 years and carries an annual interest charge of 3%. In addition, the ESOP is borrowing $5 million from two Indiana banks and Heller International Inc., a diversified Chicago finance concern, at an average cost of four percentage points above the prime, or minimum lending, rate.
>
> Under ESOP, principal and interest payments on the debt are tax-deductible, a distinct tax advantage.
>
> The South Bend transaction is one of the largest such purchases using the ESOP method and also is unusual in its use of federal funds.
>
> Management of the South Bend company will remain intact and business operations will be unaffected, a company spokesman said.

DEBT REFINANCE DEVICE

The same general principles set forth in Chapter 4 involving the use of an ESOP to conserve and raise capital may enable an employer to refinance its debt through the vehicle of an ESOP. If a transaction is properly structured, it should permit the employer to repay outstanding indebtedness, both principal and interest, with tax deductible dollars.

Example. For example, assume that an employer has $1,000,000 of debt outstanding. The employer's ESOP may borrow $1,000,000 from a lender, and buy $1,000,000 of stock from the employer. The employer may then utilize the $1,000,000 cash it receives from the ESOP to retire its $1,000,000 of indebtedness. As security for repayment of the loan, the ESOP may pledge the stock of the employer, and the employer may guarantee the indebtedness of the ESOP or contract to make sufficient future cash contributions to the ESOP to amortize the debt and interest. An employer may also offer additional security in the way of liens on its assets to assure repayment of the indebtedness.

Same Creditor. Where the lender to the ESOP is the same creditor to whom the employer is indebted, the refinancing of the loan through the ESOP should offer no difficulties. Where the creditor remains the same but the debt is shifted from the employer to the ESOP, the refinanced indebtedness may normally be secured in the same manner as the indebtedness was secured prior to the refinancing. In addition, the increased cash flow available to the employer through tax-deductibility of both principal and interest should provide the lending institution with greater assurance of the employer's capability to meet the payments on the loan.

Assuming the same amortization and interest payment schedule for the loan as is contained in the illustration in Chapter 4, at page 73, the net effect on the employer of the refinancing of the indebtedness through an ESOP is an increase in after-tax working capital of $500,000 over the term of the loan. Amortization of principal at the rate of $100,000 per year and payment of interest at the rate of 10% per annum on the unpaid balances, the total after-tax cost to the employer of repayment of the borrowing and interest, if the employer does not refinance through an ESOP, equals $1,275,000, whereas by refinancing through an ESOP, the total after-tax cost amounts to $775,000.

Accounting Treatment. The effect of the transaction on the employer's balance sheet should be an improvement. By the transaction, the employer eliminates $1,000,000 of direct debt from its balance sheet, and its net worth reflected in its capital stock account should be increased by $1,000,000. However, employers should seek the opinion of their accountants as to the accounting treatment of each transaction, depending upon whether (1) the employer guarantees the indebtedness of the ESOP, or (2) contracts to make annual contributions to the ESOP sufficient in amount to amortize both the principal and interest on the outstanding indebtedness, and (3) whether an employer's guarantee or promise to pay ESOP indebtedness should be reflected in the asset and liability sides of a balance sheet or in a footnote.

ESOP—SPECIAL SITUATIONS

Banks. In certain types of business, more than in others, working capital and stockholder equity are the foundation of earning capacity. A bank is a good example of such a business. The lending capacity of a bank, and, therefore, its earning capacity, is a direct multiple of the equity invested in the bank. For every increased dollar of capital, a bank increases its lending capacity many times, i.e., it increases its earning capacity many times. Consider this basic nature of banking in conjunction with an ESOP's primary purpose to invest in employer securities and an employer's ability to increase working capital by stock contributions to an ESOP, and possible special advantages of an ESOP to a bank become evident. Insurance companies are also heavily dependent upon working capital or equity to increase the amount of insurance the companies may write. Such companies may also utilize stock contributions to an ESOP to increase cash reserves and earning capacity. Finally, as a general observation, corporations in capital intensive industries may find the use of ESOPs to increase and conserve working capital of greater value than corporations which depend less on capital and more on employee skills and know-how to support earnings.

Takeover Bids. During the bear market of the early 70's, stock market prices for many listed companies declined sharply, causing stock prices to drop below net book value in many instances. When stock prices are depressed, companies become possible targets of takeover bids by raiders. Since employer's stock held in an ESOP Trust is voted by a trustee, and the trustee normally votes the stock under instructions from a committee appointed by the employer's Board of Directors, it is evident that, to the extent the ESOP Trust acquires ownership of employer stock, the ESOP provides a degree of safety for management and employees against a takeover. The vote represented by the stock in the trust, if it remains under the control of the employer's Board of Directors may make a takeover bid unsuccessful. Whether an ESOP may be used to support management in a takeover situation, depends on whether the plan fiduciary fulfills his fiduciary obligations under the circumstances and the extent to which the fiduciary has the capacity to vote the stock.

Avoiding S.E.C. Registration. A situation often exists in which an officer or director owns substantial blocks of stock, or other stockholders own such substantial blocks that they are deemed to be controlling stockholders under S.E.C. rules. Such stockholders who wish to sell their stock may not be able to do so legally without filing a registration statement with the S.E.C. The details of the S.E.C. problems are discussed in Chapter 9; however, where a substantial stockholder wishes to sell stock, he may arrange a sale of his stock to an ESOP rather than the public, and may thereby, subject to the rules set forth in Chapter 9 succeed in avoiding the expense of registration of the sale of the stock. Registration may not only be expensive, but may require a great deal of an employer's executives' time, and may limit severely the activities of an employer during the period of registration before the registration statement becomes effective.

Summary. Where an employer must borrow the funds to make an acquisition, an indirect borrowing of the purchase price by an ESOP may provide substantial savings in working capital. An employer may save $500,000 in working capital on an acquisition costing $1,000,000, by indirect repayment of the borrowing by contributions to an ESOP. Where an employer wishes to sell a subsidiary or a division, establishing an ESOP may provide funds to employees of the subsidiary or division to enable them to make the purchase. Moreover, an employer may refinance existing indebtedness through the use of an ESOP, and convert nondeductible repayment of principal to tax-deductible repayment of the same principal indebtedness. In special situations, such as capital intensive businesses, takeover attempts, and S.E.C. registration areas an ESOP may offer employers fringe support.

PART III

Special Applications
of an ESOP to
Closely-Held Corporations

6

ESOP AS A MARKET
FOR STOCK OF
CLOSELY-HELD CORPORATIONS

This part of the book discusses special advantages and problems of an ESOP formed by a closely-held corporation. This Chapter considers ESOP's possible solutions to problems of a controlling shareholder of a closely-held corporation, and the next Chapter, Chapter 7, discusses ESOP as an adjunct to estate planning. The problems and solutions developed in these two Chapters are based upon a hypothetical, but typical, situation of a controlling stockholder of a successful closely-held corporation who is locked into the ownership of his stock due to its lack of marketability.

Opposing Fundamental Principles. Often a closely-held corporation which has been consistently profitable for years remains under the control of the corporation's founder or the founder's family. The controlling stockholders may find that they own a valuable asset, but that the asset lacks liquidity, because no market exists for their stock. Two basic opposing forces are inextricably enmeshed which hinder efforts of controlling stockholders to sell some of their stock, to make current use of a portion of their economic wealth represented by stock ownership. On the one hand, the Internal Revenue Code may impose a prohibitive tax at ordinary income tax rates on a sale of stock by a controlling stockholder to the most likely buyer, the closely-held corporation, unless the controlling stockholder is willing to part with control or terminate his interest in the corporation. On the other hand, the controlling stockholder, whether the founder of the business or a member of the founder's family, does not want to part with control, or terminate his interest in the corporation to realize current cash from the sale of a portion of his stock.

Closely-held Corporation Fact Pattern. This chapter explains a method for a controlling stockholder of a closely-held corporation to realize cash by sale of a portion of his stock ownership in his corporation to make the sale at capital gains rates, and at the same time not sever his interest or lose control of the business to which he may have devoted a substantial part of his business life. To illustrate the methods for accomplishing these goals of a controlling stockholder, assume a hypothetical but typical fact pattern involving a profitable closely-held corporation. The closely-held corporation ("Closely-held Corp.") was founded twenty years ago. The founder ("Founder") owns 90% of the outstanding stock, and the vice-president, the treasurer, and the secretary of the company own the remaining 10% of the stock between them. From its inception, Closely-held Corp. has been profitable and has accumulated a substantial amount of earnings and profits. At this time, the balance sheet of the company is as follows:

Closely-held Corporation
Balance Sheet

Assets

Current assets:		
Cash and marketable securities	$ 225,000	
Accounts receivable:		
Trade, less allowance for doubt-		
ful accounts 0f $20,250	340,000	
Inventories:		
Finished parts and assemblies	190,000	
Work in process	360,000	
Raw materials, parts and subassemblies	500,000	
	$1,615,000	
Prepaid expenses	20,000	
Total current assets	$1,635,000	
Property, plant and equipment—at cost		
Land	25,000	
Building and improvements	365,000	
Machinery and equipment	680,000	
Furniture and fixtures	60,000	
Leasehold improvements	100,000	
	$1,230,000	
Less accumulated depreciation and amortization	800,000	
	$ 430,000	
Other assets	10,000	
Total Assets		$2,075,000

Liabilities and Shareholders' Equity

Current liabilities:		
Current portion of long-term debt	$ 40,000	

Accounts payable	130,000
Accrued Federal income taxes	75,000
Accrued expenses	130,000
Total current liabilities	$ 375,000
Long-term debt, less current portion	400,000

Shareholders' equity:

Common stock—par value $1; authorized 10,000 shares, issued 1,000 shares	1,000
Additional paid-in capital	99,000
Retained earnings	1,200,000
Total shareholders' equity	1,300,000
Total Liabilities and Shareholders' Equity	$2,075,000

In its last fiscal year Closely-held Corp. realized net income of $600,000 before taxes and net income of $300,000 after taxes, and its payroll totaled $2,000,000. Based upon its history of earnings and its industry, a recent appraisal of the fair market value of Closely-held Corp. indicates it should be valued at approximately six times after-tax earnings, or a total fair market value of $1,800,000 for Closely-held Corp. Since the founder owns 90% of the stock of the Company, the value of his stock amounts to $1,620,000.

The Founder has devoted the last 20 years of his business life to the building of his company. He is now in his late fifties and wishes to begin enjoying a portion of the wealth he has built during his working career. He is a rich man, but the bulk of his wealth consists of stock in Closely-held Corp. for which no market exists. He would be willing to sell a portion of his stock if the sale would not cause him to lose control of the company. He feels he is still young, and would like to continue active in the business, in a control position, until he is 65. Assume he is willing to sell a portion of his stock, no more than 25% of his holdings, to leave himself with 67½% of the stock. Based on the value of Closely-held Corp., and assuming it were possible to sell a minority interest in such a closely-held corporation to a third party, he should realize $405,000 (25% of $1,620,000 total value of Founder's stock) for 25% of his interest in Closely-held Corp.

Key Employees or Closely-Held Corp. as Purchasers. The logical third-party purchasers of Founder's stock, of course, are the three officers who already own 10% of the company. However, they are unable to raise sufficient capital to make the purchase, and find that no lender will lend $405,000 secured by stock representing a minority interest in Closely-held Corp., since no market exists for the stock. The next alternative which suggests itself to the founder is a sale of his stock to Closely-held Corp. The company has sufficient assets and sufficient available funds to buy out 25% of his interest for the projected purchase price of $405,000. However, under our tax laws, the purchase of the stock by Closely-held Corp. would amount to a redemption, and the $405,000 received by Founder from the sale of 25% of his interest would be taxed to him as ordinary income, a dividend, at an income tax rate possibly as high as 70%.

Redemption Equivalent to Dividend. Section 302 of the Internal Revenue Code of 1954, and the regulations under that Section set forth two basic rules under which a redemption of stock by a corporation is considered to be "not essentially equivalent to a dividend," and is to be treated as payment in exchange for stock, a capital gain transaction. If either of these rules applies to our Founder, the purchase from him of 25% of Closely-held Corp. would result in capital gain. The first rule requires that the purchase of his stock by Closely-held Corp. be a "substantially disproportionate redemption of stock" within the meaning of the Section, or under the second alternative rule the Founder must "terminate" his interest as a shareholder. Our Founder is unwilling to terminate his interest as a shareholder in Closely-held Corp., and, further, under the Code a sale of 25% of his Closely-held Corp. stock to the company would not qualify as a "substantially disproportionate distribution." Under Section 302(b)(2)(B), no distribution may be substantially disproportionate, unless a shareholder owns less than 50% of the voting stock after a portion of his stock is redeemed. Since our Founder would still own 67½% of the stock of Closely-held Corp., disproportionate distribution under Section 302 would be denied him. The regulations to avoid dividend taxation under the law state that "the question whether a distribution in redemption of stock of a shareholder is not essentially equivalent to a dividend under Section 302(b)(1) depends upon the facts and circumstances of each case." Under the facts and circumstances of our case, unfortunately, the proposed redemption of 25% of Founder's interest in Closely-held Corp. stock would be equivalent to a dividend and taxed as such.

Use of an Esop. Assume that Closely-held Corp. has an ESOP and that Founder agrees to sell to the ESOP 25% of his interest in the corporation for a price of $405,000. The ESOP may borrow the $405,000 from a lender, and Founder may personally guarantee repayment of the loan, and as further security the ESOP may pledge the stock of Closely-held Corp. In addition, Closely-held Corp. contracts to make sufficient annual contributions to the ESOP to amortize both the principal and interest on the loan as they fall due annually. The terms of the loan provide for annual amortization payments of $100,000 each on the first three anniversaries and a final amortization payment of $105,000 on the fourth anniversary of the borrowing date, together with interest at the rate of 10% per annum on unpaid balances. With the $405,000 of borrowed cash the ESOP purchases 225 shares of Closely-held stock from Founder (25% of the 900 shares owned by Founder). What is the effect of the use of the ESOP to provide a market for a portion of Founder's stock?

Sale from ESOP's Viewpoint. From the viewpoint of the ESOP and its employee beneficiaries, the ESOP has become the owner of 225 shares of common stock of Closely-held Corp., or 22½% of the total outstanding stock of the company. It has become indebted to the lender for $405,000, the value of the stock, but the indebtedness is guaranteed by the Founder, and Closely-held Corp. has contracted to make annual contributions to the ESOP to amortize both the principal and the interest of the indebtedness. As an employee incentive program, the employees of the corporation have had 22½% of the outstanding stock of their employer irrevocably set aside on their behalf. As the indebtedness of the ESOP is reduced through contributions by the employer, and as they receive their allocated portions of the stock upon retirement or other separation from service, they will become the owners of this 22½% of their employer's business.

Sale from Founder's Viewpoint. From the viewpoint of Founder, the transaction results in his receipt of $405,000 upon the sale of 225 shares of Closely-held Corp.'s capital stock. The $405,000 from the sale of the stock is subject to capital gains and preference item tax rates (amounting to approximately 30%) and the net after-tax proceeds of $283,500 may be used by Founder to diversify his investments. In addition, Founder retains control of Closely-held Corp., because the trustee of the ESOP must vote the stock in accordance with instructions given by the committee appointed by the Board of Directors. On the other hand, if the redemption proceeds of $405,000 were taxed as a dividend, i.e. ordinary income, the tax resulting from the redemption by Closely-held Corp. could be as high as 70%, or $280,000, leaving only $125,000 in after-tax proceeds available to Founder for his benefit. By utilization of an ESOP to make the purchase, no corporate redemption of stock is involved, the dividend problem should be avoided, and the sale should be subject to capital gains tax treatment.

Sale from Closely-held Corp.'s Viewpoint. From the viewpoint of the corporation, where the corporation redeems the Founder's stock directly the effect on the corporation's balance sheet is immediate. By the payment of $405,000 in cash to the Founder in exchange for the Founder's stock, the corporation immediately reduces its equity by $405,000. After the redemption, the balance sheet of Closely-held Corp. at page 92, above, would indicate total shareholders' equity in the amount of $895,000, rather than the amount of $1,300,000 shown at present, and current assets would be reduced by the same amount. The effect on the corporation's balance sheet is detrimental and could weaken the corporation's ability to borrow funds in the future. Payment for the stock by Closely-held Corp. is not deductible for income tax purposes; it is made out of after-tax accumulated earnings, and has no effect on the profit and loss statement of Closely-held Corp. Where Founder sells his stock to the ESOP, no reduction in current assets or equity of Closely-held Corp. occurs. If, however, Closely-held Corp. contracts to make annual contributions to the ESOP, or guarantees repayment of the loan to a lender, the transaction should be reflected in the financial statements of Closely-held Corp., although accountants may not agree unanimously how the transaction should be treated for accounting purposes.

Installment Sale by Founder. If the ESOP cannot borrow the $405,000 purchase price from a third-party lender, Founder may still sell his stock to the ESOP by permitting the ESOP to buy his stock on an installment basis, under the same terms as if the funds had been advanced by a third-party lender. Assume that the ESOP buys the stock from the founder for $100,000 in cash and the balance in notes aggregating $305,000 bearing interest at 10% per annum.

The installment sale contemplates that Closely-held Corp. will make sufficient cash contributions to the ESOP to make the downpayment and amortize the $405,000 loan, plus the interest. The table below indicates the after-tax cost to the employer of contributions to the ESOP to pay for Founder's stock:

	Contributions	*After-Tax Cost*
Down payment	$100,000	$ 50,000
1st Anniversary	100,000	50,000
2nd Anniversary	100,000	50,000
3rd Anniversary	105,000	52,500
TOTALS	$405,000	$202,500

Since the contributions to the ESOP are tax-deductible, the total after-tax cost to Closely-held Corp. of the purchase of Founder's stock amounts to $202,500. The net after-tax income of Closely-held Corp. is reduced by $50,000 in the year of the transaction by $50,000 in each of the next two years, and is reduced $52,500 in the fourth year following the close of the transaction. The indirect effect of the $405,000 purchase of stock by the ESOP on the working capital of the employer is a reduction of working capital of $50,000 in the first year, and an additional reduction of $50,000 in each of the next two succeeding years, and $52,500 in the fourth year for a total reduction of $202,500 in net working capital over the four-year period of payments for the stock.

From the viewpoint of Founder of Closely-held Corp., since the installment sale does not involve a redemption by Closely-held Corp., the founder receives payment for his 225 shares of Closely-held Corp. at capital gains' rates. If the ESOP borrows the $405,000 for the payment of the stock from a third-party lender and pays the full consideration at closing, the Founder receives the entire payment of $405,000 in one taxable year, and pays his capital gains tax and preference tax in the amount of approximately $121,500. The balance of the cash funds are available to him to diversify his investments or for other personal uses. On the other hand, if the Founder sells his stock to the ESOP on an installment basis, and accepts $100,000 in cash from the ESOP during the year the transaction is closed with the balance paid in three subsequent annual installments, the transaction may be treated as an installment sale by the Founder under section 453(b) of the Internal Revenue Code. Under these circumstances, the Founder will be required to pay the applicable capital gains taxes as each annual cash installment is received. Through his continued ownership of 67½% of the stock of Closely-held Corp. the Founder also continues to control his company.

EMPLOYER STOCK VALUATION

Appraisal. To qualify for exemption from the prohibited transaction rules, purchases and sales of employer stock by the ESOP must be made for "adequate consideration" as that term is defined in ERISA, whether the sales to the ESOP are made by a stockholder or the employer corporation itself. Appraisals or valuations of stock should therefore always be made at the time of such sale, if any question exists that the sale is for "adequate consideration."

Possible Penalties. If a sale is made to an ESOP for more than fair market value, the trustee of the ESOP faces the possibility of being required to make good any loss to the ESOP under ERISA Section 409, or even criminal penalties under ERISA Section 501, if the overpayment is willful. In addition, if a controlling stockholder or an employer corporation receives more than "adequate consideration" upon the sale of employer stock to the ESOP, under Section 4975 of the Code the stockholder or the corporation may be liable for a tax on prohibited transactions ranging from 5% to 100% of the amount involved in the transaction. The matter of penalties is discussed in greater detail in Chapter 10.

Adequate Consideration—Definitions. The problem of evaluating stock sold to an ESOP is present throughout the ERISA legislation. The prohibited transactions set forth in Sections 406 and 407 of ERISA, which are described in greater detail in Chapter 3, do not apply to the purchase by an ESOP of qualifying employer securities if such purchase is for "adequate consideration" as defined in ERISA Section 3(18):

(18) The term "adequate consideration" when used in part 4 of subtitle B of this subchapter means (A) in the case of a security for which there is a generally recognized market, either (i) the price of the security prevailing on a national securities exchange which is registered under section 78f of Title 15, or (ii) if the security is not traded on such a national securities exchange, a price not less favorable to the plan than the offering price for the security as established by the current bid and asked prices quoted by persons independent of the issuer and of any party in interest; and (B) in the case of an asset other than a security for which there is a generally recognized market, the fair market value of the asset as determined in good faith by the trustee or named fiduciary pursuant to the terms of the plan and in accordance with regulations promulgated by the Secretary.

Valuation Problems–OTC Stocks. In the case of a Closely-held Corp. the above definition may cause valuation problems of two basically different types. Under Portion (A) of the definition of "adequate consideration," in a situation where there is a "generally recognized market" for a security, adequate consideration means the "prevailing" price on a national securities exchange for securities listed on such exchanges. Where a security is traded in the over-the-counter market and is not listed on a national exchange, however, adequate consideration means "a price not less favorable to the plan than the 'offering price' for the security as established by the current bid and asked prices quoted by persons independent of the issuer and of any party in interest." Many corporations which went public during the public-offering boom of the 1960's have remained over-the-counter stocks, but the bid and asked prices for these stocks and the trading in such stock is for all practical purposes non-existent. Although stock ownership is widely dispersed in some of these corporations, basic stock ownership and control is often lodged in comparitively few hands. Furthermore, the bid prices for these stocks often have no relationship to the intrinsic value of the stocks, and bids are often substantially below book and at prices which do not reflect price-earnings ratios within any accepted meaning of the term. If such corporations are required to apply the definition of "adequate consideration" set forth in ERISA to sales of stock to ESOPs, the requirement could severely limit any incidental benefits in the form of increased working capital by stock contributions to ESOPs by such corporations. Under many circumstances, except perhaps heavily traded securities listed on a national securities exchange, market price should be one of the elements taken into consideration in determining fair market value of a stock, but should not be determinative of fair market value. Certainly market price should not be determinative where a stock has a small float and is rarely traded.

Apparently, the ERISA definition of "adequate consideration" assumes that a "generally recognized market" exists where a security is listed on a national securities exchange, or where the security, although not listed on an exchange, is traded in the over-the-counter market. Presumably, the "prevailing" price of a stock listed on a national exchange means the traded price of the stock on the date the stock is purchased by the ESOP or contributed to the ESOP. As a solution, presumably a transaction may be safely consummated by valuing a contribution to the ESOP at the low price for the stock on the day of the contribution, and at the same low price upon any sale to the ESOP by a controlling shareholder.

In the case of a closely-held corporation not listed on NASDAQ but which is traded in the over-the-counter market the valuation problem may be even more difficult. The over-the-counter market is a "generally recognized market," and under the ERISA definition adequate consideration would be the "offering price" as established by bid and asked prices. The float in such stocks may be thin, with infrequent trades made at prices which may vary greatly from one sale to the next. Where the float in a stock traded in the over-the-counter market is especially thin, the "offering price" for the stock as established by the current bid and asked prices should not be the sole criterion in determining fair market value. As the sole criterion for valuing a sparsely traded over-the-counter stock a substantial distortion could result in the value used for ESOP purposes.

Perhaps one solution to the problem of valuation where closely-held stock suffers from a small float and infrequent trades in the over-the-counter market is to treat such stock as not having "a generally recognized market."

No Generally Recognized Market. Where a closely-held stock is not listed on a national securities exchange and is not traded in the over-the-counter market, ERISA provides that "the fair market value of the asset" shall be the fair market value "as determined in good faith by the trustee or named fiduciary pursuant to the terms of the plan and in accordance with regulations promulgated by the Secretary [of Labor]." It is generally assumed that these regulations will incorporate Internal Revenue Service guidelines of long standing which were issued to value securities in closely-held corporations for estate tax purposes. In the meantime, the National Office of the Internal Revenue Service Pension Trust Section has expressed its opinion that reliance on such guidelines by a trustee or plan fiduciary is proper. The existing Internal Revenue Service guidelines for valuing stock of closely-held corporations, set forth in Rev. Rule 59-60, are discussed below.

Tax Reduction Act of 1975–Valuation. The Tax Reduction Act of 1975, referred to at page 30 in Chapter 1, apparently recognized that some stocks not listed on national securities exchanges but traded over-the-counter have a thin float, and that bid and asked prices may not be representative of the fair market value of such stocks. In describing the requirements for an employee stock ownership plan as defined under that act, the Tax Reduction Act of 1975 defines the "value" of a stock contributed to a Tax Reduction Act ESOP as follows:

> Act Sec. 301(d)(9)(B). "[V]alue" means the average of closing prices of the employer's securities, as reported by a national exchange on which securities are listed, for the 20 consecutive trading days immediately preceding the date of transfer or allocation of such securities or, in the case of securities not listed on a national exchange, the fair market value as determined in good faith and in accordance with regulations issued by the Secretary of the Treasury or his delegate.

Note that the above definition of "value" of stock contributed to or sold to a Tax Reduction Act ESOP differs in important respects from the definition of "adequate consideration" under ERISA, and note further that a good faith determination of fair market value is to be made under regulations of the Secretary of the Treasury, not the Secretary of Labor as under ERISA. The definition of value contained in the Tax Reduction Act of 1975, is simpler and should cause fewer valuation problems. Under the definition in the Tax Reduction Act of 1975, the value of a stock means "the average of closing prices of the employer's securities, as reported by a national exchange on which securities are listed, for the 20 consecutive trading days immediately preceding the date of transfer. . . ." For all other stocks not listed on a national exchange, and this includes stock traded in the over-the-counter market, the fair market value shall be "the value as determined in good faith and in accordance with regulations issued by the Secretary of the Treasury or his delegate." It is generally presumed that these regulations will be substantially similar to Internal Revenue Service guidelines for valuing closely-held stock for estate tax purposes. A detailed discussion of existing valuation guidelines for valuing stock of closely-held corporations follows in the balance of this Chapter.

IRS VALUATION GUIDELINES

Rev. Rule 59-60–Value a Question of Fact. Rev. Rule 59-60, promulgated by the Internal Revenue Service in 1959, summarized the IRS's approach to the valuation of closely-held stock for estate and gift tax purposes. The Rev. Rule acknowledges that the determination of fair market value, is a question of fact, the answer to which depends upon the circumstances of each case. It recognizes that no formula may be devised that will be generally applicable to the multitude of different valuation issues which may arise in valuing closely-held stock. Where market quotations are not available, the Rev. Rule provides that all other financial data, as well as all relevant factors affecting the fair market value of the stock must be considered. Although no general formula is applicable to the many different valuation situations which may arise in the valuation of a stock of a closely-held corporation, the Rev. Rule sets forth the IRS's opinion of acceptable guidelines, and the general approach, methods, and factors which should be considered in valuing the stock of a closely-held corporation.

Scarcity of Market Quotations. Of the two definitions of value quoted above, that in ERISA and that in the Tax Reduction Act of 1975, the Rev. Rule more closely follows the philosophy of valuing a closely-held corporation contained in the Tax Reduction Act of 1975, than contained in ERISA. The Rev. Rule treats as a closely-held corporation any corporation where market quotations for its stock are unavailable or scarce. In this connection, the first section of the Rev. Rule provides as follows:

> . . . The methods discussed herein will apply likewise to the valuation of corporate stocks on which market quotations are either unavailable or are of such scarcity that they do not reflect the fair market value.

In further defining a closely-held corporation the Rev. Rule states that "little, if any, trading in the shares of such a corporation takes place," and emphasizes that irregular sales seldom reflect the elements contained in a definition of "fair market value." In this connection, the following comment is made in the Rev. Rule:

> Closely held corporations are those corporations the shares of which are owned by a relatively limited number of stockholders. Often the entire stock issue is held by one family. The result of this situation is that little, if any, trading in the shares takes place. There is, therefore, no established market for the stock and such sales as occur

at irregular intervals seldom reflect all of the elements of a representative transaction as defined by the term "fair market value."

Willing Buyer and Seller. The fair market value of a stock is defined, speaking generally, as the price at which a willing buyer and a willing seller both of whom are not acting under compulsion, would buy and sell. In this connection the Rev. Rule states as follows:

> . . . [F]air market value . . . is the price at which the property would change hands between a willing buyer and a willing seller when the former is not under any compulsion to buy and the latter is not under any compulsion to sell, both parties having reasonable knowledge of relevant facts.

Prophecy of Future. The Rev. Rule acknowledges that valuation of securities is a prophecy of the future, and that prices of stock traded in volume best reflect fair market value, but that stock which is infrequently traded requires a different measure of value.

> Valuation of securities is, in essence, a prophecy as to the future and must be based on facts available at the required date of appraisal. As a generalization, the prices of stocks which are traded in volume in a free and active market by informed persons best reflect the consensus of the investing public as to what the future holds for the corporation and industries represented.

Eight Fundamental Factors. In establishing the elements for valuing the stock of a closely-held corporation, the Rev. Rule sets forth eight fundamental factors which require thorough analysis in each valuation situation. The Rev. Rule states as follows:

> It is advisable to emphasize that in the valuation of the stock of closely held corporations or the stock of corporations where market quotations are either lacking or too scarce to be recognized, all available financial data, as well as all relevant factors affecting the fair market value, should be considered. The following factors, although not all-inclusive are fundamental and require careful analysis in each case:
>
> (a)   The nature of the business and the history of the enterprise from its inception.
> (b)   The economic outlook in general and the condition and outlook of the specific industry in particular.
> (c)   The book value of the stock and the financial condition of the business.
> (d)   The earning capacity of the company.
> (e)   The dividend-paying capacity.
> (f)   Whether or not the enterprise has goodwill or other intangible value.
> (g)   Sales of the stock and the size of the block of stock to be valued.
> (h)   The market price of stocks of corporations engaged in the same or a similar line of business having their stocks actively traded in a free and open market, either on an exchange or over-the-counter.

Weighting the Factors. After describing or discussing each of the above fundamental factors in some detail, the Rev. Rule goes on to explain that, under the circumstances of a particular case, certain of the above factors may carry more weight than others because of the nature of the company's business. For example, in the case of a company which sells products or services to the public, generally primary consideration should be given to earnings in making the valuation, whereas in a real estate investment company the greatest weight of the above factors may also be given to the value of the underlying assets. The Rev. Rule recognizes that capitalization rates of earnings may vary substantially depending upon (1) the nature of the business, (2) the risk involved, and (3) the stability or irregularity of the earnings. The Rev. Rule also points out that valuations cannot be made on the basis of a prescribed formula, and therefore no useful purpose is served by taking an average of the several factors and basing the valuation on the results. Nor, the Rev. Rule continues, should the valuation be made by assigning mathematical weights to each of the factors in deriving the fair market value.

Stock Subject to Restriction. Finally, the Rev. Rule recognizes that at least for the purpose of determining values for estate tax purposes, where the shares of stock are subject to an option reserved by the issuing corporation to repurchase at a certain price, the option price is usually accepted as the fair market value. In this connection, the Rev. Rule states as follows:

> Frequently, in the valuation of closely held stock for estate and gift tax purposes, it will be found that the stock is subject to an agreement restricting its sale or transfer. Where shares of stock were acquired by a decedent subject to an option reserved by the issuing corporation to repurchase at a certain price, the option price is usually accepted as the fair market value for estate tax purposes. See Rev. Rul. 54-76, C.B. 1954-1, 194. However, in such case the option price is not determinative of fair market value for gift tax purposes. Where the option, or buy and sell agreement, is the result of voluntary action by the stockholders and is binding during the life as well as at the death of the stockholders, such agreement may or may not, depending upon the circumstances of each case, fix the value for estate tax purposes. However, such agreement is a factor to be considered, with other relevant factors, in determining fair market value. Where the stockholder is free to dispose of his shares during life and the option is to become effective only upon his death, the fair market value is not limited to the option price.

Summary. A closely-held corporation may itself be the only logical buyer for a controlling shareholder's stock. Where a controlling shareholder wishes to sell only a portion of his stock, not all of his stock, a sale of some stock to the corporation may for tax purposes be treated as a redemption "essentially equivalent to a dividend," and may result in imposition of ordinary income tax at prohibitive rates upon the controlling shareholder's proceeds of sale. Use of an ESOP may avoid such dividend taxation for a controlling stockholder. In addition, indirect repayment by a closely-held corporation of funds borrowed by an ESOP to purchase controlling shareholder stock may conserve substantial working capital for the corporation. The most difficult problem in a purchase of stock of a closely-held corporation by an ESOP involves the valuation of the stock to comply with ERISA. The definition of "adequate consideration" under ERISA, and fair market value under the Internal Revenue Code are indefinite and may lead to the imposition of penalties. Guidelines for IRS valuations are set forth in detail in Rev. Rule 59-60.

ESOP AS AN ADJUNCT
TO ESTATE PLANNING

From an estate planning point of view, Founder of Closely-held Corp. described in Chapter 6 should be aware that his estate may face the initial problem of finding a purchaser for his stock in Closely-held Corp. after his death. The purchaser should be willing and able to purchase the stock for its fair market value. Three logical purchasers may exist for the Founder's stock: (1) Closely-held Corp., (2) an ESOP, and (3) the key employees who already own 10% of the stock. In choosing the possible purchaser, each must be considered in the light of tax and financial problems which may arise and must be solved to make the estate plan workable within the structure of our income and estate tax laws—and palatable to our Founder. The problems which may arise involve (1) income tax aspects of the purchase of Founder's stock from his estate, (2) valuation problems from the viewpoint of ERISA and for estate tax purposes, and (3) the funding of the purchase.

Purchase by Closely-held Corp. As set forth in Chapter 6, where Closely-held Corp. redeems stock of Founder, a serious income tax problem arises. Is the redemption of the stock by Closely-held Corp. essentially equivalent to a dividend and therefore taxable to Founder as ordinary income? The same income tax problem may arise where an estate attempts to sell stock in Closely-held Corp. to the corporation itself. However, the difference in tax treatment as ordinary income or as capital gain, becomes of significantly greater importance where the sale of Closely-held Corp. stock is to the corporation by the estate after the death of Founder. If the sale of stock by the estate is treated as a sale or exchange from an income tax point of view, i.e., as a capital gain transaction, the net result may be that the estate pays no income tax upon the sale of the stock. The estate may achieve this income tax result where the stock in Closely-held Corp. is sold by the estate at a price equal to the stepped-up tax basis of the stock, normally the value at which the stock is included in the gross estate of the decedent. On the other hand, if the redemption of stock from Founder's estate by Closely-held Corp. is treated as a dividend, an income tax of as much as 70% of the total distribution received from Closely-held Corp. may be assessed against the estate. In each instance, whether Closely-held Corp. stock is transferred in a sale or exchange transaction, or in a transaction treated as a dividend subject to a possible income tax of 70%, the estate tax valuation of Closely-held Corp. stock is the same, and the amount of estate tax attributable to the stock is identical. As set forth in Chapter 6, if Closely-held Corp. redeems the stock, under Section 302 of the Internal Revenue Code the redemption may be treated as a sale or exchange, and not as a distribution equivalent to a dividend, if the redemption is substantially disproportionate or results in a termination of the estate's interest in Closely-held Corp..

Section 318 of the Code. In determining whether or not a redemption by a corporation is "substantially disproportionate" or results in a "termination" of a shareholder's interest in a corporation under Section 302, the constructive ownership provisions of Section 318 of the Code must be considered. Under Section 318 an individual is considered as owning stock owned by his spouse, his children, grandchildren, and parents. He is also considered as owning stock owned by an estate in proportion to his interest in the estate as a beneficiary, and by a trust in proportion to his actuarial interest as a beneficiary in the trust. Moreover, if a shareholder owns 50% or more in value of stock of a corporation, the shareholder is considered as owning stock owned by such corporation in the proportion the value of the shareholder's interest bears to the value of all the stock of such corporation. Finally, these attribution rules also work in reverse in that estates or trusts or corporations are deemed to own the stock owned by the beneficiaries or stockholders.

As an example of the effect of the constructive ownership rules of Section 318, assume that Founder bequeaths 450 shares of his stock in Closely-held Corp. to his estate and 450 shares as a specific legacy to his son. If the executor should sell the estate's 450 shares to Closely-held Corp., although this is all of the stock owned by the estate, the sale of the stock by the executor may not constitute a "termination" of the estate's interest in Closely-held Corp., because the estate is deemed still to own the stock of Closely-held Corp. owned by the decedent's son, under the attribution rules of Section 318.

Redemption to Pay Death Taxes—Section 303. Section 303 of the Internal Revenue Code of 1954 sets forth special rules under which distributions by Closely-held Corp. to the estate of Founder in the redemption of the stock to pay death taxes, may be treated as payments in exchange for the stock and not as dividends, although payments which qualify for such treatment are strictly limited in amount.

Under Section 303 of the Internal Revenue Code the maximum amount of the distribution from Closely-held Corp. entitled to treatment as payment in exchange for the stock may not exceed the sum of (1) estate, inheritance, legacy, and succession taxes imposed because of the decedent's death, and (2) the amount of funeral and administration expenses allowable as deductions to the estate. In addition, the distribution in redemption of stock from Closely-held Corp. to the estate must be made, under the general rule, within three years and 90-days after the filing of the estate tax return, unless a petition for redetermination of a deficiency in estate tax has been filed with the Tax Court, in which event the period for distribution is extended until 60 days after the decision of the Tax Court becomes final. Moreover, for Section 303 of the Code to apply to a distribution by Closely-held Corp., the value of Closely-held Corp.'s stock in the decedent's gross estate must equal prescribed percentages of the value of the estate. The tests require that the value of the stock held in the decedent's estate must be more than 35% of the gross estate or more than 50% of the taxable estate. In this connection, Section 303(b)(2)(A) states as follows:

> (A) IN GENERAL.—Subsection (a) shall apply to a distribution by a corporation only if the value (for Federal estate tax purposes) of all of the stock of such corporation which is included in determining the value of the decedent's gross estate is either—
> (i) more than 35 percent of the value of the gross estate of such decedent, or
> (ii) more than 50 percent of the taxable estate of such decedent.

Problems in Section 303 Redemptions. Section 303 provides protection against treatment of a corporate redemption of stock from an estate as a dividend where the requirements of the Section are met. The Section may cause difficulties in estate planning prior to the death of the Founder, because of the uncertainty of meeting the percentage relationship of the value of the Closely-held Corp. stock to the other assets in Founder's estate. The relationship of the value of the Closely-held Corp. stock to the value of the other assets in the Founder's estate is beyond the control of the Founder. An unexpected increase in value of the other assets forming a part of the estate may reduce the value of the Closely-held Corp. stock below 35% of the gross value of the estate or below 50% of the value of the taxable estate. Occurrence of such an increase in value of other assets could cause the redemption of stock by Closely-held Corp. to be treated as the payment of a dividend with the drastic income tax results mentioned above.

General Effect of ESOP Purchase. If Closely-held Corp. has an ESOP at the time of the Founder's death, the problem of finding a buyer may be solved. Since the ESOP is formed to invest "primarily" in employer stock, the ESOP may be the prospective purchaser and may offer a market for the stock which the estate will seek to sell. As the potential purchaser for the Founder's stock, the ESOP may help solve the income tax problems incidental to the sale of the stock by the estate. The basic estate planning technique for use of an ESOP contemplates the sale of the Founder's Closely-held Corp. stock to the ESOP Trust. The parties may arrange for a sale by an inter-vivos agreement between the Founder and the ESOP, or may contemplate that the executors of the Founder's estate will negotiate the sale with the ESOP. Under either approach, problems of valuation of the Closely-held Corp. stock may arise, and problems of funding the purchase of the stock may exist, but the serious income tax problems involved in a redemption of stock by Closely-held Corp. may be solved where the sale is made to the ESOP.

Valuation Conflicts. As in the case of any sale of employer stock to an ESOP, an estate's sale to the ESOP must be at "adequate consideration" under ERISA. Valuation problems involved in sales of employer's stock to ESOP were discussed in Chapter 6. Complications in the valuation problem caused by the requirement that sales be at fair market value, when related to the estate tax problem of fixing value in a buy-out agreement, are discussed in greater detail later in this chapter. However, that a conflict may exist is evident since the estate must sell to the ESOP at fair market value, whereas the executors may attempt to value the Closely-held Corp. stock for estate tax purposes as low as possible.

SALE TO ESOP vs. CORPORATE REDEMPTION

Income Tax Dividend Problem. Where the sale of Closely-held Corp. stock by the estate is to the ESOP, the sale is, of course, not a sale to Closely-held Corp., and the problem of a redemption taxed as a dividend may be avoided. Since the corporation makes no distribution with respect to the stock, the provisions of Section 302 of the Code generally do not come into play, and when the estate sells the stock to the ESOP a sale or exchange of a capital asset should result. The income tax treatment would be identical to the treatment of a sale of stock of Closely-held Corp. by the Founder to the ESOP during the Founder's lifetime as set forth in Chapter 6.

Corporate Income Tax Saving. In addition to offering a possible solution to the dividend problem, purchase of the stock by the ESOP, rather than by the corporation, provides other incidental benefits to Closely-held Corp. As developed in Chapter 6 in the discussion of purchases of Closely-held Corp. stock from a controlling stockholder, such as the Founder, the direct purchase of the stock by contributions to the ESOP by Closely-held Corp., results in stock purchases with pre-tax dollars, or in payments which are deductible for income tax purposes. The income tax saving enables the equivalent retention of working capital by Closely-held Corp., and, to the extent of the income tax saving, strengthens the financial position and balance sheet of Closely-held Corp. by the additional retained working capital. On the other hand, if Closely-held Corp. redeems the stock, the redemption is non-deductible for income tax purposes and reduces available after-tax funds. Each non-deductible payment reduces the working capital and shareholder equity in the full amount of the payment.

Accumulated Earnings Tax–Section 531. As is set forth in Chapter 6, an ESOP formed by Closely-held Corp. may be used to purchase stock from the Founder from time to time. Such purchases of stock will not only provide cash to the Founder at capital gain rates, but may also help to avoid the accumulated earnings tax problem of Section 531 of the Code. Note from the Closely-held Corp.'s Balance Sheet in Chapter 6 at page 92 that Closely-held Corp. has retained earnings of $1,200,000. To the extent that the retained earnings are not "retained for the reasonable needs of the business" they may be subject to an accumulated earnings tax equal to 27½% of the accumulated taxable income up to $100,000, plus 38½% of the accumulated taxable income in excess of $100,000.

Section 537 Relief vs. ESOP Contributions. Section 537 of the Code may provide assistance to Closely-held Corp. in avoiding the accumulated earnings tax. The Section provides that funds required to redeem stock of Closely-held Corp. owned by

Founder's estate to the maximum amount of death taxes defined under Section 303(a), are funds held for a reasonable need of the business. The Section 537 exemption, however, only comes into play for a taxable year of a corporation "in which a shareholder of the corporation died or any taxable year thereafter." Under this Section, then, accumulations may only be considered as required for reasonable needs of the business to the extent such accumulations are needed for Section 303 redemptions after the death of Founder. The Section does not offer any tax comfort for the $1,200,000 of retained earnings of Closely-held Corp. already accumulated on its books during the decedent's lifetime. As a general principle, contributions to an ESOP, whether in cash or stock are tax deductible within the limits provided in the Code, and reduce accumulated earnings. In this manner, cash contributions to the ESOP used to purchase Founder's stock reduce the possibility that Closely-held Corp. may be subject to the accumulated earnings tax.

Buy-sell Agreements. The buy-sell agreement is an estate planning device often used to provide for transfers of stock ownership in a closely-held corporation. Such an agreement normally provides for the buy-out of a deceased shockholder's stock interest by the corporation, or by the remaining major shareholders, all of whom are normally parties to the agreement. Customarily, practitioners provide a purchase price for the stock in the agreement, often setting forth a formula which defines the price. Such a formula may be based upon book value, or a multiple of earnings, or any other reasonable price-fixing method acceptable to the parties. The prices contained in such buy-out agreements are normally accepted by the Internal Revenue Service as fixing the value of the stock for estate tax purposes, provided the price is arrived at by arms-length dealings between the parties and is reasonable.

Buy-sell Agreement–ESOP Valuation Problem. Where Closely-held Corp. has an ESOP, a contract by the Founder with the ESOP to buy the Founder's stock from his estate may act as a substitute for a buy-sell agreement for estate planning purposes. The difficulty in reaching such agreement with an ESOP lies in the problems of valuing stock of closely-held corporations for ESOP purposes discussed in Chapter 6. The estate tax advantage of fixing a price for a decedent's stock in a buy-sell agreement, may cause a sale of Founder's stock to the ESOP at the fixed price to violate the fair market value requirements of ERISA.

Parties to a buy-sell agreement are generally the major or controlling stockholders and the corporation. Such agreements normally provide that any party to the agreement wishing to sell his stock must first offer the stock to the corporation and if the corporation does not buy, to the other stockholders on a pro-rata basis. Such agreements may also bind the estate of a participant. A basic provision in any buy-sell agreement fixes the price at which the stock must be offered for sale and may be bought. Such price is often provided as a formula, based upon book value of the stock of the corporation, or some multiple or average of prior years earnings of the corporation.

Consider our example of the Founder and Closely-held Corp. in Chapter 6. An ESOP Trust may, of course, be a party to a buy-sell agreement with the Founder, Closely-held Corp., and the remaining stockholders. By becoming a party to the agreement the ESOP may have the first opportunity to purchase the stock of Closely-held Corp. from the estate of the Founder, or of any of the other stockholders. Chapter

6 indicates that the purchase of Founder's stock from his estate by the ESOP must be for "adequate consideration." Under ERISA, in the case of Closely-held Corp., adequate consideration means the "fair market value of [Closely-held Corp. stock] as determined in good faith by the Trustee or named fiduciary pursuant to the terms of the plan and in accordance with regulations promulgated by the Secretary of Labor." The buy-sell agreement with the ESOP Trust as a party, if it contains a fixed formula price for Closely-held Corp.'s stock, may not comply with ERISA, because the fixed formula price may not meet ERISA's definition of "adequate consideration" at the time of sale. If the formula price should require the ESOP Trust to pay more than adequate consideration for Closely-held Corp. stock, the penalties discussed in Chapter 10 for failure to comply with the fiduciary duties may come into play.

Use of ERISA Definition of Adequate Consideration. Where the ESOP Trust is a party to a buy-sell agreement, a possible solution to the valuation problem may be the use of a definition of sale price in the agreement based upon the ERISA definition of adequate consideration. Such a definition of price would result in a flexible price and would probably incorporate, by reference or otherwise, many of the elements contained in Rev. Rule 59-60 discussed in Chapter 6. The Trustee's determination of fair market value pursuant to such a definition of price may meet the requirements of ERISA that a sale of the stock to the ESOP Trust be for "adequate consideration." However, the flexible pricing formula may result in disadvantages in establishing valuations since the Internal Revenue Service may apply its own construction of the valuation elements in arriving at a price for estate tax purposes. The basic advantage of a fixed price contained in a buy-sell agreement and used to determine the estate tax valuation of the stock would be lost.

Integration of ESOP Purchase with Section 303 Redemption. As set forth above, under Section 303 of the Code, if at the time of the Founder's death, the stock of Closely-held Corp. in the Founder's estate meets the percentage requirements set forth in that Section, stock of Closely-held Corp. may be redeemed by the Corporation without imposition of a dividend tax upon the estate. Where an ESOP is in existence, a buy-sell agreement among Closely-held Corp., the ESOP, and the Founder and other stockholders of Closely-held Corp. may contemplate the redemption of a portion of Closely-held Corp. stock in the Founder's estate by the corporation under Section 303 and the purchase of the balance of the stock by the ESOP. Again, the basic valuation problem of the stock upon redemption by Closely-held Corp. on the one hand and upon sale to the ESOP on the other remains. Two separate agreements, one with the ESOP for a sale of of a portion of the Founder's stock, and the other with Closely-held Corp. for a redemption of stock under Section 303 or a sale to the remaining shareholders may be utilized. The definitions of price contained in the two separate agreements should be identical, to avoid a situation involving one valuation for estate tax purposes, and a different valuation for determining whether the sale to the ESOP Trust meets the requirements of ERISA.

Negotiation of Price After Death. Where Closely-held Corp. has an ESOP, an estate planner could consider the sale of the Founder's stock by his estate to the ESOP at a negotiated price equal to the "adequate consideration" or fair market value required under ERISA. Such an approach to the use of an ESOP in estate planning permits the flexibility to meet the requirements of ERISA and at the same time provides an opportunity for estate planning by the Founder's executor. The sale to the ESOP could be in addition to a redemption of stock under Section 303 to the extent, if any, that the requirements of that Section are met.

FUNDING ESOP PURCHASE

Funding the purchase of employer stock by an ESOP presents an additional problem for consideration in utilizing an ESOP as an adjunct to an estate plan. Many estate plans involving closely-held corporations include the use of life insurance to fund the purchase of stock from an estate of a deceased shareholder. Where no ESOP is involved, a closely-held corporation often insures the life of a key-employee who is also a stockholder, or the life of a substantial stockholder where the corporation and the stockholder have entered into a buy-sell agreement. In either instance, where the corporation owns the insurance and pays the premiums, the corporation does not receive an income tax deduction for the premiums. The premium payments by the corporation are made in after-tax dollars.

ESOP Ownership of Life Insurance. Consider the use of an ESOP to purchase the insurance and pay the premiums. Insurance on the life of a key-employee who is not a stockholder should meet the "exclusive benefit" test, since the key-man insurance could theoretically offset loss in the value of employer stock owned by the ESOP due to the death of the employee. The insurance funds may offset any loss in value of stock, and the insurance would not benefit the key-employee's estate since he may not be a stockholder. If circumstances indicate that the "exclusive benefit" test is met, and that insurance on the life of a key-employee is a proper investment for the ESOP, the premiums may be paid by the employer corporation with tax-deductible contributions to the ESOP. Therefore, the premiums on the life insurance are indirectly paid with pre-tax dollars.

Purchase of Founder's Stock. In addition to insurance on the life of key-employees, an estate planner should consider whether an ESOP may fund obligations under a buy-sell agreement to buy a Founder's stock with life insurance proceeds. Under a buy-sell agreement, the Founder would commit himself and his estate to sell his stock to the ESOP. Subject to the valuation problems discussed above, the ESOP may agree to purchase the stock from the Founder's estate, and the ESOP, subject to ERISA restrictions, could purchase life insurance on the life of the Founder to fund the purchase obligation. The parties would contemplate that the premiums on the life insurance would be paid by tax-deductible contributions by Closely-held Corp. to the ESOP.

Deduction of Premiums. Under Section 264(a) of the Code the general income tax rule disallows any deduction to a corporation for the payment of premiums on life insurance on the life of an employee or a stockholder like our Founder, where the corporation is directly or indirectly a beneficiary of the insurance. Therefore, premiums paid by a corporation on the life of a stockholder to provide funds to redeem his stock are not deductible. On the other hand, if the ESOP is the beneficiary under the policy, provided the investment in life insurance to buy out Founder's estate is a proper investment for an ESOP, funding a buy-sell agreement through insurance owned by the ESOP converts non-deductible premiums to premiums which are indirectly deductible by the corporation through contributions to the ESOP. If the parties determine that under the circumstances of a particular case investment in life insurance by an ESOP would violate either the "exclusive benefit" rule or the fiduciary duties of the Trustee, they may consider the possible advantage of ownership of the insurance and payment of non-deductible premiums by Closely-held Corp. Contributions of stock to the ESOP equal in value to each premium paid may provide tax deductions equal to each premium payment. If the ESOP is the beneficiary of the insurance, this fact alone should not violate the "exclusive benefit" rule or any fiduciary duty.

Exclusive Benefit Rule. Authorities disagree whether insurance to fund the purchase of employer stock by an ESOP from a stockholder's estate under a buy-sell agreement is an acceptable investment for an ESOP. As developed in preceding chapters of this book, the ESOP must be maintained for the "exclusive benefit" of employees or their beneficiaries, to qualify under Section 401(a) of the Code. In determining whether an ESOP meets the requirements of Section 401, the regulations promulgated under that Section of the Code provide that all of the circumstances in a particular situation must be considered:

> All of the surrounding and attendant circumstances and the details of the plan will be indicative of whether it is a bona fide stock bonus plan for the exclusive benefit of employees in general.

At first glance, since the purpose of the life insurance upon Founder's life is to purchase employer stock, investment by the ESOP in the insurance would appear to meet the exclusive benefit test. However, an incidental benefit would accrue to the Founder's estate since the insurance proceeds would provide the cash to buy the Founder's stock. Under these circumstances some District Offices of the Internal Revenue Service take the position that statutory and case law provide no authority for the investment of ESOP funds in life insurance on the life of a stockholder to buy stock from his estate under a buy-sell agreement. Since District Directors may have differing opinions on this issue, until it is settled by definitive ruling or regulation, before proceeding with the purchase of insurance to fund a stockholder buy-sell agreement for an ESOP, the status of the law at the time of the proposed transaction should be carefully reviewed.

Fiduciary Investment Restrictions. In addition to the basic problem whether insurance on the life of a stockholder meets the "exclusive benefit" requirement under Section 401 of the Code, an investment in life insurance by an ESOP must meet the prudent man investment test of Section 404 of ERISA. As explained in Chapter 3, where the ESOP invests in qualified employer securities, the normal requirement of a fair return on an investment need not be met. However, no similar exemption applies to an investment by a trustee in life insurance to fund a buy-sell agreement. The investments of the ESOP should also be made to provide sufficient liquidity to permit distributions to participants in the ESOP in accordance with the terms of the plan. Whether the investment of funds in life insurance affects this requirement for ESOP investments should be given thought by a plan fiduciary in light of the circumstances of the particular ESOP.

Borrowing Cash Surrender Values. Once an ESOP fiduciary determines that life insurance is a proper investment for the particular ESOP, astonishing results may be obtained by utilizing the borrowing power generated by the cash surrender value of life insurance. Fiduciaries may develop plans for an ESOP to purchase whole life insurance, and annually borrow the cash surrender value of the policy from the insurance company to purchase qualified employer stock, in our case, from Closely-held Corp. Closely-held Corp., in turn, contributes this cash to the ESOP to pay the premiums and interest to the insurance company. Since the contributions to the ESOP to pay the premiums and interest are deductible for tax purposes by Closely-held Corp., the after-tax cost to Closely-held Corp. is only 50% of the amount contributed to the ESOP. Frequently, it is possible for the ESOP to borrow sufficient funds periodically in the form of the cash surrender value of the insurance to purchase stock from an employer in an amount in excess of the annual after-tax cost of the contributions made by the employer to the ESOP for payment of premiums and interest. Such a plan may bring about the purchase of insurance at no net after-tax cost to Closely-held Corp. for the premiums and interest paid.

Summary. As an estate planning instrument, an ESOP is a prospective purchaser of a controlling shareholder's stock from his estate, and may provide protection against possible dividend treatment of a redemption of stock by a closely-held corporation and imposition of income taxes at rates as high as 70%. Where an ESOP is utilized, not only may the dividend tax be avoided, but a purchase of the stock by the ESOP at the estate tax valuation may avoid all income taxes, both dividend tax and capital gains tax. Section 303 of the Code contains special rules for redemptions of stock by a corporation which may avoid dividend treatment. To qualify, the stock in a decedent's estate must constitute more than 35% of the value of the gross estate and more than 50% of the taxable estate. Because of possible changes in value of estate assets prior to death, the exemption provided under Section 303 may not be available. Sale of stock by an estate to an ESOP, and indirect payment for the stock by corporate contributions to the ESOP may permit purchase of the stock with tax-deductible dollars. In addition, cash contributions to an ESOP by a closely-held corporation to purchase stock may help avoid the imposition of the accumulated earnings tax under Section 531 of the Code. The valuation of closely-held stock presents similar problems to those discussed in Chapter 6, where the estate planning device of a buy-sell agreement is utilized. Finally, if in a particular case an investment in life insurance by an ESOP meets fiduciary investment obligations, payment of premiums with deductible contributions by an employer and borrowing on cash surrender values may make possible a purchase of insurance at no after-tax cost to a corporation.

PART IV

Tax Treatment of
Beneficiaries, Securities
Laws, and General Commentary

8

INCOME TAX TREATMENT
OF EMPLOYEE BENEFICIARIES

An ESOP is a stock bonus plan qualified under Section 401(a) of the Code, and exempt from income taxes under Section 501(a). Employee beneficiaries of trusts forming a part of such plans are not subject to income tax when contributions are made to the trusts by employers. Furthermore, the employee is not subject to income tax on the income realized by the trusts from trust assets, although the income is exclusively for employees or their beneficiaries. The beneficiaries of an ESOP are subject to income tax only when the funds in the employees' accounts are actually distributed or made available to them. At the time of distribution, employees or their beneficiaries may be taxed in different ways, depending upon the circumstances of the distribution. Emloyees may (1) receive a portion of the distribution tax-free, (2) pay capital gains tax on other portions of the distribution, (3) pay a separate income tax under a special ten-year averaging method on a different portion of the distribution, or (4) pay a tax under rules for the taxation of annuity payments. This chapter explains the income tax treatment of employee beneficiaries of ESOPs.

Section 402 of the Code. Section 402 of the Internal Revenue Code governs the income tax treatment of a beneficiary of an ESOP Trust. This section of the Code sets forth the rules governing the taxability of beneficiaries of qualified employee trusts under pension, profit sharing, and stock bonus plans. Section 402 establishes the general rule that "the amount actually distributed or made available to any distributee by any employee trust described in Section 401(a) which is exempt from tax under Section 501(a)" is taxable to such distributee in the year in which the distribution occurs or the funds are made available to the distributee under Code Section 72. Section 72 provides for the taxation of annuities. The general rule is subject to many qualifications and refinements, and under specific circumstances permits postponement of taxation of portions of the distributions, permits some portions to be taxed at capital gains rates, and permits other portions to be taxed under a separate tax computed on a 10-year forward averaging of income.

Annuity Taxation Under Section 72. In the case of all qualified employee trusts exempt from taxation under Section 501(a) of the Code, contributions by an employer to the trust are not taxed to the employee at the time of the contribution, but are taxed upon "distribution" or when the funds are "made available" to the beneficiary. Such contributions are exempt from income tax to the participant whether or not the contributions for the participant are forfeitable or nonforfeitable, and distributions from the trust, other than lump sum distributions discussed below, are taxable to a beneficiary as if the distributions were annuity payments in accordance with the rules for the taxation of such payments under Section 72 of the Code. Under Section 72, payments received under an annuity form part of a recipient's gross income, subject to the material exception that gross income does not include "that part of any amount received as an annuity . . . which bears the same ratio to such amount as the investment in the contract bears to the expected return" from the annuity. In effect, a portion of each payment (referred to as the "exclusion ratio") representing cost of the annuity to the annuitant is received tax-free. In determining the exclusion ratio to ascertain non-taxable portions of annuity payments from employee trusts, contributions by an employee to the trust are treated as part of the cost of the annuity to the employee. Furthermore, where the aggregate amount receivable by an employee during the first three years of annuity payments is equal to or greater than the consideration for the contract contributed by the employee, all amounts received are excluded from gross income until the payments equal the total contributed by the employee.

Lump Sum Distributions–History. From 1942 to 1969 lump sum distributions by employee tax exempt trusts, upon retirement or severance from employment, were subject to special income tax treatment as long-term capital gains. To the extent such distributions exceeded the amount contributed by an employee the lump sum distribution was treated as a long-term capital gain for income tax purposes. However, the Tax Reform Act of 1969 amended this income tax treatment of lump sum distributions, and under the amendments contained in this act, any portion of a lump sum distribution after 1969, attributable to employer contributions made after 1969, was no longer entitled to capital gain treatment.

ERISA Amendments. Effective for distributions made in taxable years beginning after December 31, 1973, ERISA again amended the income tax rules applicable to lump sum distributions by employee trusts by adding Section 402(e) to the Code. By its amendments, ERISA changed substantially the concept for taxation of lump sum distributions from qualified employee trusts. The amended scheme of taxation incorporated in Section 402(e) preserves capital gain treatment for that portion of a lump sum distribution to an employee which is attributable to the employee's participation in the plan prior to 1974. In addition, as discussed in greater detail below, income taxation is postponed on the net unrealized appreciation of employer securities forming a part of the lump sum distribution. Finally, ERISA provides a new "separate tax" at ordinary income tax rates on that portion of the taxable lump sum distribution which is attributable to the employee's participation in the plan after 1973 under Section 402(e)(1) of the Code. The tax on the portion of a lump sum distribution subject to ordinary income tax, is computed under a special income tax averaging system based on the premise that the life expectancy of an employee who retires at age 65 is approximately 10 years. The separate tax under Section 402(e)(1) is determined as an amount equal to ten times the tax which would be imposed upon a single individual whose taxable income equalled one-tenth of the total taxable portion of the lump sum distribution in excess of a "minimum distribution allowance." These concepts are discussed in greater detail below, but the general effect of ERISA's tax treatment of the ordinary income tax portion of a lump sum distribution results in a 10-year forward averaging of the taxable portion of the distribution.

ESOP Distributions. To qualify an ESOP under Section 401(a) of the Code, as set forth in Chapter 2, the plan must provide that distributions from the trust to its beneficiaries be made in stock of the employer. Normally, such distributions of stock will be made in a lump sum, although the law contains no prohibitions against installment distributions of stock from an ESOP. Any such installment distributions of stock would be subject to the annuity tax rules contained in Section 72 of the Code, as set forth above. However, since lump sum distributions in stock constitute the most frequent type of distribution from an ESOP, income tax rules applicable to lump sum distributions by ESOPs to employee beneficiaries are discussed in detail below.

Definition of Lump Sum Distribution. To qualify for the special tax treatment under Code Section 402(e), a distribution must first meet the requirements of a "lump sum distribution." Under the Code, a lump sum distribution means a distribution or payment within one taxable year of a recipient of the balance to his credit under a qualified trust. The distribution must become payable to the recipient (1) on account of the employee's death, (2) after the employee attains the age of 59½ years, (3) on account of the employee's separation from service, or (4) after the employee becomes disabled. As a condition to treatment of the amount received as a lump sum distribution, the recipient must elect for the taxable year to have all similar amounts received during such year treated as lump sum distributions. Finally, to qualify for lump sum treatment, the employee must have been a participant in the plan for five or more taxable years before the taxable year in which the lump sum is distributed to him.

Net Unrealized Appreciation in Employer Stock. Where the requirements for a lump sum distribution are met, an employee may realize a substantial tax benefit from the lump sum distribution of qualified employer stock: the net unrealized appreciation of qualified employer securities is excluded from gross income, and is not taxable at the time of distribution. In this connection, Code Section 402(e)(4)(J) provides as follows:

> In the case of any distribution including securities of the employer corporation . . . there shall be excluded from gross income the net unrealized appreciation attributable to that part of the distribution which consists of securities of the employer corporation so distributed.

Deduction of Employee Contributions. Code Section 402(e)(4)(D)(i) eliminates amounts considered contributed by the employee from the total taxable amount of a lump sum distribution. This elimination of employee contributions is generally unimportant with respect to distributions from an ESOP, since ESOPs are generally noncontributory plans.

Taxation of Net Unrealized Appreciation Upon Sale. Upon sale of the employer securities with respect to which net unrealized appreciation was eliminated from the taxable amount of a lump sum distribution, realization of the previously unrealized appreciation results in long-term capital gain to the employee, regardless of the length of time the employee has held the stock after distribution and before sale, whether more than 6 months or less. If the gain from the sale of such employer securities exceeds the unrealized appreciation which went untaxed at the time of distribution, the excess gain is treated as either short-term or long-term capital gain, depending on whether the employee held the stock or securities for more than six months after distribution. As a result of this rule any appreciation in employer securities realized after the date of distribution to the date of sale will be taxed to the employee as short-term or long-term capital gain, depending on the length of time the employee holds the securities. If the employee dies after the lump sum distribution but before selling the employer's stock, the general tax basis rules come into play and the employer stock receives a new income tax basis equal to its fair market value in the estate valuation. Under these circumstances the unrealized appreciation in an employer's stock which forms part of a lump sum distribution may escape income taxation in its entirety.

Initial Separate Tax. To the extent that a lump sum distribution exceeds amounts considered contributed by the employee and the net unrealized appreciation attributable to the employer's securities, the full amount of the lump sum distribution forms part of the "total taxable amount" of the distribution used in computing an "initial separate tax." In determining the amount of separate tax to be imposed upon the lump sum distribution, the Code first provides for the computation of an initial separate tax. Under Code Section 402(e)(1)(C) the "initial separate tax" is an amount equal to 10 times the tax which would be imposed if the recipient were a single individual, and his taxable income were an amount equal to 1/10th of the excess of (1) the total taxable amount of the lump sum distribution over (2) the "minimum distribution allowable."

Minimum Distribution Allowance. The Code defines the minimum distribution allowance as an amount equal to (1) the lesser of $10,000 or one-half of the total taxable amount of the lump sum distribution for the taxable year, reduced by (2) 20% of the amount by which such total taxable amount exceeds $20,000. The net effect of the definition of minimum distribution allowance is to reduce the minimum distribution allowance to zero where the total taxable amount of a lump sum distribution is equal to or exceeds $70,000. If an employee trust makes a lum sum distribution including a total taxable amount of $70,000, the minimum distribution allowance of $10,000 is reduced to zero by one-fifth of the excess of the total taxable amount over $20,000, i.e., by $10,000 (excess of the total taxable amount, $70,000, over $20,000 equals $50,000, and 1/5 of $50,000 results in a reduction in the minimum distribution allowance of $10,000).

Ordinary Income Portion. The balance of the lump sum distribution is taxable. Of this balance, the "ordinary income portion" subject to the imposition of the separate tax of Section 402(e) is that portion of the distribution attributable to participation by the employee in the ESOP after December 31, 1973. In this connection, Code Section 402(e)(4)(E) provides that:

> [T]he term "ordinary income portion" means . . . so much of the total taxable amount of such distribution as is equal to the product of such total taxable amount multiplied by a fraction—
> (i) the numerator of which is the number of calendar years of active participation by the employee in such plan after December 31, 1973, and
> (ii) the denominator of which is the number of calendar years of active participation by the employee in such plan.

Summary of Separate Tax Computation. The computation of the separate tax on the ordinary income portion of a lump sum distribution, to summarize the above discussion of the law, involves the following five basic steps:

1. *Compute the lump sum distribution.* Under Section 402(e)(4)(A) a lump sum distribution means the total amount of the distribution received in one taxable year of the balance to the credit of an employee in an employee trust. Where the taxpayer elects lump sum treatment, all qualified trusts with an employer are treated as a single pension, profit-sharing, or stock bonus plan, as the case may be, to determine whether the balance to the credit of an employee is paid out.

2. *Compute the total taxable amount.* Code Section 402(e)(4)(D) defines the total taxable amount as the lump sum distribution, less (1) employee contributions and (2) net unrealized appreciation attributable to securities of the employer corporation.

3. *Compute the ordinary income portion of the total taxable amount.* Section 402(e)(4)(E) provides that the ordinary income portion of the total taxable amount is that portion of the total taxable amount represented by a fraction, the numerator of which is made up of the years of participation of the employee in the plan after December 31, 1973, and the denominator of which is equal to the total number of years of participation of the employee in the plan.

4. *Compute the initial separate tax.* Section 402(e)(1)(C) provides for an initial separate tax computed as if the taxable income were an amount equal to one-tenth of the excess of (1) the total taxable amount (computed under paragraph 2 above) over (2) the minimum distribution allowance. A tax is then determined equal to the tax on the taxable income imposed under Section 1(c) of the Code (the tax rates applied to unmarried individuals). This tax is then multiplied by ten to arrive at the initial separate tax. As set forth above, the minimum distribution allowance is the lesser of $10,000 or one-half of the total taxable amount, subject to reduction because of excess taxable distributions in the year.

5. *Compute the amount of separate tax.* Section 402(e)(1)(B) provides that the amount of separate tax is equal to the amount of the initial separate tax multiplied by a fraction, the numerator of which is the ordinary income portion of the lump sum distribution (Step 3 preceding) and the denominator of which is the total taxable amount of the distribution (Step 2, preceding).

Capital Gains Treatment. The Code also provides capital gains treatment for a portion of a taxable lump sum distribution by an ESOP or other qualified employee trust to the extent the distribution is from participation of an employee in the plan prior to January 1, 1974. In this connection, Code Section 402(a)(2) provides that the capital gain portion of the total taxable amount of a lump sum distribution is "equal to the product of such total taxable amount multiplied by a fraction (A) the numerator of which is the number of calendar years of active participation by the employee in such plan before January 1, 1974 and (B) the denominator of which is the number of calendar years of active participation by the employee in such plan." The Secretary of the Treasury may prescribe regulations under which plan years may be used in lieu of calendar years to determine the capital gain portion of a distribution under this Section of the Code, as well as the ordinary income portion of the total taxable amount set forth in Section 402(e)(4)(E).

EXAMPLES OF TAX COMPUTATIONS

Profit-Sharing Plan Distribution. Examples may help clarify the application of income tax rules set forth in Section 402(e) of the Code to lump sum distributions from employees' trusts. Assume that John Jones, a participant in Employer Corp.'s qualified profit-sharing plan, retired on December 31, 1975. Upon retirement he received a lump sum distribution of $60,000 from the profit-sharing plan, made up of cash of $20,000 and employer stock valued at $40,000. Assume further that Jones contributed $5,000 to the plan during his period of participation, which began on January 1, 1966, and that the tax basis of the stock contributed to the plan by Employer Corp. totalled $15,000. Applying the five steps outlined above to the lump sum distribution to Jones, the income tax treatment of the distribution, including both the imposition of the separate tax under Section 402(e) of the Code and the capital gains treatment of a portion of the distribution under Section 402(a)(2), is as follows:

Profit-Sharing Plan
Lump Sum Distribution

1. *Lump Sum Distribution* ($20,000 cash, plus $40,000 Employer Stock)...........$60,000

2. *Total Taxable Amount* ($60,000, less sum of $5,000 employee contribution
   and $25,000 net unrealized appreciation of Employer stock) $30,000

3. *Ordinary Income Portion:*
   (a)   Fraction (by Code definition):
         Calendar years of participation after 12/31/73 ÷ the full
         number of Calendar years of participation × total taxable amount
   (b)   Fraction (by figures):
         $\frac{2}{10} \times \$30,000$ ....$ 6,000

4. *Initial Separate Tax* (10 × tax on 1/10 of excess of Total Taxable Amount
   over Minimum Distribution Allowance):
   (a)   Total Taxable Amount..$30,000
   (b)   Total Taxable Amount less Minimum Distribution Allowance,

$10,000, reduced by $2,000 [20% of excess of Total Taxable Amount over $20,000]...$22,000

(c) Tax on $\frac{1}{10}$ of Total Taxable Amount ($2,200) at unmarried individual tax rates..$ 348

(d) Initial Separate Tax, 10 × $348...$ 3,480

5. *Separate Tax Under §402(e)*

(a) Initial Separate Tax × Fraction:

$$\frac{\text{Ordinary Portion (Step 3)}}{\text{Total Taxable Amount (Step 2)}}$$

(b) $3,480 × $\frac{\$\ 6,000}{\$30,000}$ = ...$ 696

Separate Tax. The foregoing computation of the income tax on a lump sum distribution of $60,000 to John Jones indicates that the income tax payable by Jones, as a separate tax under Section 402(e) of the Code, on the ordinary income portion of the distribution totals $696.00. This separate tax on the ordinary income portion is based upon a theory of forward averaging of the ordinary income portion of the distribution for 10 years. Under the general concept, the separate tax is computed by determining the tax on 1/10th of the taxable ordinary income portion of the lump sum distribution and then multiplying this tax by ten. In addition to the separate tax, the lump sum distribution is subject to a capital gains tax to the extent Jones was a participant in the plan prior to 1974.

Capital Gains Tax. Section 402(a)(2) contains the rules for determining the portion of a lump sum distribution taxable at capital gains rate. It provides that so much of the total taxable amount as is equal to the product of the total taxable amount multiplied by a fraction, the numerator of which is the number of calendar years of active participation of Jones in the plan before January 1, 1974, and the denominator of which is the total number of calendar years of participation by Jones in the plan. Under this Section of the Code the portion of the total taxable amount so determined, is treated as a gain from the sale or exchange of a capital asset held for more than six months. Application of these rules to the lump sum distribution received by Jones results in the inclusion of a total long-term capital gain of $24,000 in the gross income of Jones during 1975, computed as follows: The total taxable amount of $30,000 (item 2 in the above example) multiplied by 8/10—years of participation before 1974 (January 1, 1966 to and including December 31, 1973), 8, divided by total years of participation (January 1, 1966 to and including December 31, 1975), 10.

Assume that Jones is married and files a joint return with his wife. Their combined taxable income, other than the lump sum distribution received by Jones from the profit-sharing plan, and after having taken all deductions and exemptions to which they were entitled for the year 1975 amounted to $16,000. It should be noted that the $16,000 of net taxable income of Jones and his wife was arrived at after deducting the ordinary income portion of the lump sum distribution received by Jones, in accordance with Section 402(e)(3) of the Code. The tax on $16,000 on a joint basis amounted to

$3,260, and the total income tax payable by Jones and his wife by including an additional $12,000 in income, as a result of the long-term capital gain of $24,000, increased the total income tax payable to $7,100. The long-term capital gain portion of the lump sum distribution from the profit-sharing plan to Jones increased his joint tax by $3,840 (total tax of $7,100, less tax payable without capital gain $3,260).

Combined Taxes from Profit-Sharing Distribution. When Jones combined all income taxes payable with respect to the $60,000 lump sum distribution from the profit-sharing plan, he found that his total income tax bill for the lump sum distribution of $60,000 amounted to $4,536 ($696 separate tax plus $3,840 long-term capital gains tax).

Future Taxation of Net Unrealized Appreciation. In addition to the tax payable for the year 1975 during which the lump sum distribution was received, Jones may be subject to income taxes in the future as a result of the net unrealized appreciation in employer stock received as part of the lump sum distribution. Jones received employer stock valued at $40,000 which had a basis in the hands of the profit-sharing trust of $15,000. The stock Jones received carried with it $25,000 in net unrealized appreciation. This net unrealized appreciation was carried over to Jones upon his receipt of the lump sum distribution, because the tax basis of the employer stock in Jones' hands is the same as the tax basis of the stock in the hands of the profit sharing trust. Whether or not Jones ever pays an income tax with respect to the net unrealized appreciation in employer stock depends upon whether Jones sells the stock during his lifetime, or retains the stock which ultimately becomes part of his estate.

Upon the sale of the stock, to the extent the price exceeds $15,000, the amount of the net unrealized appreciation realized at that time is taxed at long-term capital gains rates regardless of the holding period for the stock at the time of sale. If the gain upon the sale exceeds the net unrealized appreciation, the excess gain is treated as short-term or long-term capital gain, depending on whether Jones held the stock for more than six months after distribution. Finally, as indicated above, if Jones dies before selling the stock, the stock receives a stepped-up basis of its fair market value at the applicable valuation date, and the unrealized appreciation in the employer stock distributed to Jones escapes income taxation in its entirety.

ESOP Distribution. Assume that the qualified employee benefit plan which made the lump sum distribution to Jones during 1975 was an ESOP, rather than a profit-sharing plan. If an ESOP had been involved as the employee incentive plan, certain assumptions in respect to the lump sum distribution to Jones would have changed. Since the distribution from the ESOP could only have been made in stock, item 1, the Lump Sum Distribution in the example, at page 120, would have consisted of $60,000 in employer stock, without the distribution of any cash.

Item 2, the total taxable amount, would presumably not have been reduced by any amount of employee contributions, since ESOPs normally are non-contributory on the part of the employees. As a result of such changes in the assumptions in the example the total taxable amount of the lump sum distribution would increase to $35,000. (The deduction of $5,000 for employee contributions would not exist.) With these changes, what would have been the income tax effect upon Jones of a lump sum distribution of $60,000 from an ESOP during the calendar year 1975?

The distribution to Jones as a lump sum distribution in stock from an ESOP would result in the following changes in the example of a lump sum distribution from the profit-sharing plan, and the tax computations would be as follows:

ESOP—Lump Sum Distribution

1. *Lump Sum Distribution* ($60,000 all in employer stock) $60,000.00

2. *Total Taxable Amount* ($60,000, less $45,000 net unrealized appreciation of employer stock, stock value $60,000 less stock basis $15,000).......... $15,000.00

3. *Ordinary Income Portion* (2/10th times $15,000) .... $ 3,000.00

4. *Initial Separate Tax* (10 times tax on 1/10th of excess of total taxable amount over minimum distribution allowance):

   (a)   Total·taxable amount, $15,000, less minimum distribution allowance (one-half of total taxable amount, $7,500) results in an excess of total taxable amount equal to............................$ 7,500.00

   (b)   Tax on 1/10th of excess total taxable amount ($750.00) at single individual income tax rates...$ 107.50

   (c)   Initial separate tax (10 × $107.50) ....$ 1,075.00

5. *Separate Tax Under Section* 402(c):

   (a) $1,075.00 × $\dfrac{\$\ 3,000}{\$15,000}$ = ...$ 215.00

Capital Gains Tax. The computation of the capital gain portion of the tax paid by Jones as a result of the lump sum distribution involves the following computation where the distribution is made by an ESOP in stock of the employer:

Item 2 of the foregoing example indicates that the total taxable amount of the distribution is $15,000. Multiplying $15,000 by a fraction, the numerator of which is years of service before 1974 and the denominator is total years of service, i.e. 8/10ths, the capital gains portion of the total taxable amount is computed as $12,000.

Continuing the assumption that the net taxable income of Jones is $16,000 before the lump sum distribution, with a total federal tax of $3,260, the addition of a long-term capital gain of $12,000 (of which 50% or $6,000 is added to taxable income) results in total taxable income of $22,000, and a total joint federal income tax of $5,020. The long-term capital gain portion of the distribution is, therefore, subject to a net long-term capital gains tax of $1,760 (total tax including capital gain of $5,020, less total tax, excluding the capital gain, of $3,260).

Combined Taxes from ESOP Distribution. The total combined taxes from the $60,000 lump sum ESOP distribution therefore amount to $1,975 ($215 of Separate Tax, plus $1,760 of capital gains tax). The taxes payable on the lump sum distribution of $60,000 from the ESOP are therefore $2,561 less than the taxes payable on the same distribution from the profit-sharing plan ($4,536 less $1,975). However, with the distribution from the ESOP Jones receives net unrealized appreciation in employer stock equal to $45,000 which may be taxed on a future sale of the stock, as opposed to a net unrealized appreciation in employer stock of $25,000 from the profit-sharing plan which may also be taxed on a future sale.

Summary. Under Section 402 of the Code distributions to beneficiaries of an ESOP receive advantageous income tax treatment. When a beneficiary receives an employer's stock upon retirement as a lump sum distribution, a portion of the distribution (1) is tax-free to the beneficiary, (2) may be taxed at capital gains rates, and (3) the balance is taxable on the basis of a ten year forward-averaging method. Where a lump sum distribution from an ESOP is made solely in employer stock, rather than in the form of stock and cash from a profit-sharing plan, the tax treatment of a beneficiary of an ESOP may be substantially more favorable than the tax treatment of a beneficiary of a profit-sharing plan.

9

SECURITIES LAWS AND ESOP

An ESOP is formed to invest primarily in employer securities, and distributions from an ESOP must be made in the employer's stock. After such distribution, employees or participants who receive stock from the ESOP, may sell the stock. Therefore ESOPs and their participants, due to the very nature of ESOPs, regularly engage in transactions involving the transfer, purchase, distribution, and sale of securities. As in the case of all persons involved in security transactions, an ESOP trust, an employer corporation, and an employee or participant must comply with the requirements of securities laws where they engage in transactions involving transfers of stock or securities.

Securities Act of 1933 and Securities Exchange Act of 1934. The two federal securities laws most directly involved in the maintenance and operation of an ESOP are the Securities Act of 1933 ('33 Act) and the Securities Exchange Act of 1934 ('34 Act). In general, the '33 Act sets forth the circumstances under which a registration statement must be filed with the Securities and Exchange Commission upon the sale of a security. The '34 Act makes it unlawful to use any deceptive device in the purchase or sale of securities, and also sets forth the circumstances under which a corporate insider is liable to a corporation for short-swing profits in the purchase and sale of the corporation's stock. Both the '33 Act and the '34 Act concern themselves with individual transactions. In this sense, each transaction, involving a security, engaged in by an ESOP Trust, the employer corporation, and a participant or beneficiary, should be scrutinized to determine whether the registration provisions of the '33 Act, or the anti-fraud or short-swing profit provisions of the '34 Act may be applicable or violated. Securities transactions involving ESOPs which require analysis include:

(1) *Receipt of Securities by Trust.* The contribution by the employer and the receipt of securities by the ESOP Trust may occur in any one of the following four ways:

   (a) The employer may make contributions of stock or other qualified securities to the trust, without payment of any consideration by the trust for the stock;

   (b) The trust may purchase the stock or securities from the employer;

   (c) The trust may purchase the stock or securities directly from a stockholder of the employer, without making the purchase in the open market; and

   (d) The trust may purchase securities in the open market, where such market exists for the securities.

(2) *Distributions of Securities by Trust.* When a trust distributes securities to a participant, the participant's beneficiary, or his estate, as the case may be, the trustee must consider whether the distribution meets the requirements of the '33 Act, and does not violate any of the provisions of the '34 Act.

(3) *Sale of Securities by Employee, Beneficiary, or Estate.* Finally, a participant, or a beneficiary, or the estate of a participant may sell the employer's stock. At the time of any such sale, the seller must consider whether the requirements of the '33 Act are met and whether any violations of the '34 Act may occur as a result of the sale.

Each proposed transaction falling within the categories of transactions set forth under paragraphs (1), (2), and (3) above, should be analysed under the applicable federal securities laws, both the '33 Act and the '34 Act, to confirm that the proposed transaction does not violate any of the provisions of either of these securities acts. This chapter sets forth the status of the rules promulgated by the Securities and Exchange Commission under the acts, and where appropriate, attempts to point out where future problems may arise.

THE SECURITIES ACT OF 1933

Registration Requirements–Section 5. The '33 Act provides that it is "unlawful" for any person to sell a security through use of any means of interstate commerce unless a registration statement under the Act is in effect at the time of the sale or offer to sell. The basic operative provision in the '33 Act, Section 5, is as follows:

> Sec. 5. (a) Unless a registration statement is in effect as to a security, it shall be unlawful for any person, directly or indirectly—
> (1) to make use of any means or instruments of transportation or communication in interstate commerce or of the mails to sell such security through the use or medium of any prospectus or otherwise. . . .

Under Section 5 of the '33 Act, any offer to sell a security or any sale of a security involving interstate commerce would require filing a registration statement with the Securities and Exchange Commission if the Act did not provide certain exemptions from the filing requirement, and if the Securities and Exchange Commission did not also exempt, by interpretive ruling, certain types of transactions from the registration requirements.

Statutory Exemptions from Registration–Section 4. Paragraphs (1) and (2) of Section 4 of the '33 Act contain basic statutory exemptions from registration requirements as follows:

> Sec. 4. The provisions of section 5 shall not apply to—
> (1) transactions by any person other than an issuer, underwriter, or dealer.
> (2) transactions by an issuer not involving any public offering.

Under the exemptions provided in Section 4 of the '33 Act, (1) if the person offering to sell the security is not an issuer, underwriter, or dealer the restrictions of Section 5 do not apply, or (2) if the proposed transaction does not involve a public offering, the Section 5 prohibition is also inapplicable.

Contributions by Employer. When an employer contributes its securities to a trust, the Securities and Exchange Commission has ruled that registration under the '33 Act is not required, because no payment is made by the trust for the securities. This is the so-called "no-sale" theory. However, when a plan contains conditions which benefit the employer, the "no-sale" theory may not exempt the transaction. For example, where the plan requires an employee undertaking to continue working for the duration of the plan or until earlier retirement, disability, or death, the employer may be deemed to receive value from the inducement of participants to continue their employment. Additionally, provisions in a plan granting an employee discretion regarding the form of investment, time of distribution, or option to contribute to the plan, may make the interest of the employee in the plan, as well as the securities of the employer, a "security" under the '33 Act, and may require registration before the plan may be implemented. Since under such a plan, an employee is offered an opportunity to make an investment decision, it is reasoned that the employee should be offered the information necessary to make such investment decision.

Purchase from Employer. Where a trust pays an employer cash or other consideration for employer securities, since value is received, a sale occurs and registration under the '33 Act is required unless an exemption applies. One such exemption is provided for the interest of an employee in the plan under Section 3(a)(2) of the '33 Act. This section exempts from the definition of "security" to which the Act applies, any ". . . interest or participation in a single or collective trust fund maintained by a bank or in a separate account maintained by an insurance company, which interest or participation is issued in connection with (A) a stock bonus, pension, or profit-sharing plan which meets the requirements for qualification under section 401 of the Internal Revenue Code of 1954. . . ." The exemption provided by Section 3(a)(2) applies only to the interest of the employee in the plan, and does not include in its terms the securities of the employer acquired by the trust. Furthermore, the exemption is only available where a bank is a trustee, and where no employee contributions are used to acquire stock of the employer.

Section 4(1) Exemption. The trust is not the issuer or a dealer in the securities of the employer in the normal sense of security law definitions. However, to be exempt under Section 4(1) of the '33 Act, quoted above, the trust may not be an "underwriter" as that term is used in the Act. Where a person receives securities from an issuer (in our case the employer corporation) with a view to the distribution of such securities to others, such a person may be an underwriter within the meaning of the Act. An ESOP Trust would purchase the stock of an employer with a view to distributing the stock to participants in the future and, in this sense, may be an underwriter not exempt under Section 4(1) of the Act, and may be required to look for a different exemption to avoid registration.

Non-Public Offering Exemption–Section 4(2). If the trust itself, and not the participants, is deemed the purchaser, the exemption, quoted above, under Section 4(2) (transactions by an issuer not involving any public offering) may be available. Since the trust is a single purchaser, on the surface it appears that this exemption should be available, but its availability may be affected by security law theories making the trust part of a single distribution to participants. Possible application of these theories depends upon the number of participants (whether or not the trust is deemed the purchaser), since the trust contemplates distribution of the securities to the participants in due course. Under one theory the trust, at the time of purchase, may have a present intention to distribute the employer securities in the future, all as part of a single distribution, to such a number of participants that the transaction would involve a public offering.

Non-public Offering–Rule 146. Where there are fewer than 35 participants when the trust purchases stock, Rule 146 may be followed to provide exemption from the registration requirements of the '33 Act for the transaction as non-public offerings. The Rule is not an exclusive definition of a non-public offering, and transactions may comply as non-offerings even though all the requirements of Rule 146 are not met. However, Rule 146 provides exemption as a non-public offering upon a purchase of stock from an employer, if the following conditions are satisfied:

(a) The employer has made no other sales (or offers of sale) within a period of six months before or after the sale to the trust.

(b) The employer has made no general solicitation or general advertising.

(c) Prior to the sale (or offer) the employer shall have reasonable grounds to believe, and shall believe that the trust has sufficient knowledge and experience in financial and business matters to evaluate the merits of the purchase *or* that the trust is able to bear the economic risk of the purchase.

(d) At the time of the sale, the employer must reasonably believe that the trust has the knowledge and experience referred to above *or* where the trust is represented by an advisor, that the trust and its advisor have the knowledge and experience referred to above, *and* that the trust is able to bear the economic risk of the purchase.

(e) The trust must either have access (prior to purchase) to the type of information that would be in a prospectus forming part of a registration statement filed under the '33 Act, or be furnished such information.

(f) The trust should not have more than thirty-five participants at the time of the purchase.

(g) Reasonable care must be exercised to assure that future transfers of the securities are not part of a distribution. Such care requires that resales by participants be limited to compliance with Rule 144 and placing a restrictive legend on the stock.

Sales to Residents of a Single State–Rule 147. Another exemption from registration that may apply is Section 3(a)(11) of the '33 Act. Section 3(a)(11) provide a general exemption for sales (and offers) limited to residents within a single state or territory, which must be the same state in which the employer does business. As in the case of Rule 146, Rule 147 sets forth specific requirements which, when met, provide assurance to an issuer that Section 3(a)(11) had been complied with, although the Rule is not an exclusive definition of an intra-state sale. General conditions of Rule 147 are as follows:

(a) The employer must have made no other non-conforming sales during a period of six months prior to or after sale.

(b) The employer must be incorporated, and have its principal office located in the state in which the participants reside.

(c) The employer must derive at least 80% of its gross revenues and those of its subsidiaries on a consolidated basis from the resident state.

(d) At least 80% of the assets of the employer and those of its subsidiaries on a consolidated basis must be located in the state.

(e) At least 80% of the proceeds from the purchase by the trust must be used by the employer in the resident state.

(f) Since an ESOP is formed for the specific purpose of acquiring securities of the employer, each of the participants must be a resident (principal residence) of the state.

(g) Any resales by participants during the nine-month period following the purchase by the trust, must be made (if otherwise permissible) only to residents of the state.

(h) The employer must take appropriate steps to police subsequent resales by placing legends on certificates, issuing stop transfer instructions to the transfer agent, and obtaining written representations from each purchaser or participant as to his residence.

Beneficial Ownership by Less Than 100 Persons–Rule 240. For employers whose stock is owned by less than 100 stockholders, Rule 240 may provide another exemption from registration under the '33 Act. The conditions for bringing a transaction within the protection of Rule 240 are as follows:

(a) The employer may make no general advertising or general solicitation for the stock.

(b) No commission may be charged for soliciting buyers.

(c) The aggregate sales price may not exceed $100,000 for securities sold within any twelve-month period.

(d) Both before and after the sale, the employer must reasonably believe that the securities of the employer are beneficially owned by not more than 100 persons, and for this computation, since the ESOP Trust is formed to acquire securities of the employer, all participants in the trust must be counted together with other stockholders of the employer.

(e) Subsequent dispositions of securities by the trust must be based on an exemption that would be available if shares had been acquired in a transaction exempt as a non-public offering by virtue of section 4(2).

(f) The employer is required to police transactions under Rule 240 in the same manner required under Rules 146 and 147.

(g) The employer must file three copies of Form 240 with the Regional Office of the Securities and Exchange Commission within ten days after the end of the month in which a sale in reliance on Rule 240 is made.

Instructions for Form 240. The following are the instructions for Form 240:

FORM 240

Securities and Exchange Commission

Washington, D.C. 20549

Notice of Sales of Securities Pursuant to Rule 240

(to be filed with the Regional Office of the Securites and Exchange Commission
for the region in which the issuer's principal business operations are conducted
not more than 10 days after the close of the first month during the calendar year
in which a sale is made in reliance on the rule)

1. Name, address and telephone number (including area code) of the issuer of the securities to be sold.

2. Names (in full) of the executive officers, directors and promoters of the issuer (or of persons serving in similar capacities for noncorporate issuers) and of any persons beneficially owning 10 percent or more of the equity securities of, or equity interest in, the issuer;

3. Title of class of securities sold;

4. Aggregate sales price of unregistered securities sold within the preceding twelve months, computed in accordance with paragraph (e) of the rule;

   Note: Sales prior to March 15, 1975 need not be reported.

5. Number of persons who are beneficial owners of securities of the insurer as of the date of filing this Notice, computed in accordance with paragraph (f) of the rule.

Pursuant to the requirements of Rule 240 under the Securities Act of 1933, the issuer has duly caused this notice to be signed on its behalf by the undersigned duly authorized officer or person acting in a similar capacity.

Date of Notice

                                                                                    Issuer

                                                                            (Officer)

Instruction. Print the name and title of the signing representative under his signature. At least one copy of the notice shall be manually signed. Any copies not manually signed shall bear typed or printed signatures.

Attention: Intentional misstatements or omission of facts constitute Federal criminal violations (See 18 U.S.C. 1001).

COMPLETED FORM 240

The following is an example of Form 240 completely filled out for a sale by XYZ Corporation to its trust of 300 shares of Common Stock for $60,000.

Securities and Exchange Commission

Washington, D.C. 20549

FORM 240

Notice of Sales of Securities Pursuant to
Rule 240

1. *Issuer.*

   XYZ Corporation, 1234 Main Street, New York, New York 10017. Telephone No. (212) 123-4567.

2. *Names of Officers, Directors, Promoters and 10% Holders.*

   John Doe, Richard Roe, John Smith and Robert Jones.

3. *Securities Sold.*

   Common Stock, par value $.10 per share.

4. *Sales Price.*

   $60,000.00

5. *Number of Beneficial Owners.*

   75.

Pursuant to the requirements of Rule 240 under the Securities Act of 1933, the issuer has duly caused this Notice to be signed on its behalf by the undersigned duly authorized officer or person acting in a similar capacity.

XYZ CORPORATION

By   John Doe

JOHN DOE, PRESIDENT

Date of Notice
January 3, 19

Purchase from Controlling Shareholder. Where a trust purchases securities of an employer from a shareholder, and such shareholder, directly or indirectly, controls the employer, the trust is deemed to have purchased the securities from the employer and one of the foregoing exemptions must be available to avoid the registration requirements of the '33 Act.

Distributions by the Trust. Theoretically, distributions of employer stock by a trust to participants should not require registration under the '33 Act, since participants do not pay for the stock. Therefore, the "no-sale" theory described above should exempt distribution transactions from the operation of Section 5 of the '33 Act. Where, however, an investment decision is offered to participants by offering them a choice of receiving cash or securities, the "no-sale" theory may not apply. Where a trust relied upon a specific exemption to acquire securities without registration, such exemption may affect the time within which the trust may make a distribution. For example, if a trust acquires securities in a transaction in reliance on Rule 146 or Rule 240, both described earlier, the trust may not distribute the securities until 2 years after the date of acquisition. Similarly, where a trust pays for stock with a note, special provisions of Rule 144 (which is discussed below) relating to payment and collateral may apply.

Resale by Participants. Where an ESOP Trust distributes stock to a participant without registration at the time of distribution, the participant, generally speaking, receives stock which is "restricted" stock under the federal securities laws. Upon distribution of such stock to a participant, the ESOP Trust should legend the certificates to indicate that the stock is "restricted" as to resale by the participant. A participant who receives restricted stock may sell the shares only (1) by causing a registration statement to be filed and become effective, or (2) by complying with an exemption or SEC rule which would permit the sale without registration. The rule most frequently used by sellers to permit sale of restricted stock is Rule 144, promulgated under authority of the '33 Act.

The foregoing paragraph states the general rule respecting the sale of restricted employer stock by a participant, although, at least one anomalous no-action letter by the SEC permitted resale by a participant of stock received from a qualified plan without registration where (1) the participant could make no investment choice, (2) no conditions were imposed under the plan or by the employer with respect to the investment or distribution of the employer stock, and (3) a minimum number of shares were involved in light of the trading volume of the stock. This no-action letter, however, should not be relied upon as superseding the general rule or permitting sale without registration in any other case.

Rule 144. Rule 144 sets forth the requirements to enable a participant to resell restricted employer shares without registering the shares. In order to comply with Rule 144, the following conditions must be met:

(1) The securities of the employer must have been registered under Section 12 of the '34 Act or the employer must file the information reports specified under Section 15 of the '34 Act.

(2) The securities of the employer must be held by the participant (the period during which such securities are held by the trust, even when the interest the participant has vested, does not count) for a period of at least 2 years.

(3) The number of shares that may be sold by the participant may not exceed, in any six month period, specified differing amounts of securities, depending upon whether the securities are traded on a national exchange. With respect to securities traded on a national securities exchange, the amount of securities which may be sold is the *lesser* of (a) one percent of the total number of employer securities outstanding or (b) the average weekly reported volume of trading in such securities on all exchanges during the four calendar weeks preceding the filing of a Form 144 or the receipt by the broker of the order to execute the transaction. With respect to securities not traded on an exchange the amount of securities sold may not exceed one percent of the total number of employer shares outstanding.

(4) The sales must be in "brokers' transactions," and the seller may not solicit or arrange for the solicitation of orders to buy in anticipation of or in connection with the sale, and may not make any payment in connection with the offer or sale except normal commissions to the broker who executes the sell order.

(5) Concurrently with placing the sell order with the broker, the seller must file with the Securities and Exchange Commission 3 copies of Form 144, when the number of shares to be sold exceeds 500 or the aggregate sale price exceeds $10,000. A copy of Form 144 must also be filed with any national exchange on which such securities are admitted to trading.

Aggregation Rules. Questions may arise whether sales made by the trust and participants must be aggregated under SEC rules to determine if the volume limitations under Rule 144 have been exceeded. In ruling on one situation where members of a committee administering a qualified plan and the trustee were selected by and were also members of the board of directors of an employer, the SEC held that aggregation of sales would be required in the following situations:

(1) Sales by the trustee with sales by the trust.

(2) Sales by the trust with sales by the trustee.

(3) Sales by the individual members of the committee with sales by the trust.

(4) Sales by the trust with sales by individual members of the committee.

However, the SEC ruled that aggregation was not required with respect to distributions by the trust to retiring participants with sales by the trust.

Rule 237. Where the securities of the employer distributed by the trust to the participant are not registered securities within the meaning of Sections 12 or 15 of the '34 Act, Rule 144 may not be used by a participant to resell the securities of an employer. In such an event, if the requirements of Rule 237 are met, this Rule may permit a sale without registration under the '33 Act. The requirements of Rule 237 are:

(1) The employer must be incorporated in the United States and have its principal business operations in the United States;

(2) The employer must have been actively engaged in business as a going concern for at least five years;

(3) The participant must own the employer securities for at least five years;

(4) The participant must sell the securities in a negotiated transaction, otherwise then through a broker or dealer;

(5) The gross proceeds from all sales of shares which may be sold under this Rule by any person during any period of one year

(a) may not exceed the *lesser* of

(i) the gross proceeds from the sale of one percent of the securities outstanding or,

(ii) $50,000, and

(b) shall be reduced by the amount of gross proceeds from any shares sold during such year pursuant to (i) the additional exemption under Section 3(b) of the '33 Act, and (ii) the exemption afforded by Rule 144.

(6) At least 10 business days prior to the sale, three copies of Form 237 must be filed with the Regional Office of the Commission for the region in which the employer's principal business operations are conducted, and at the same time, one copy of Form 237 must be sent to the employer.

The following are the instructions for completing Form 237:

Form 237

**NOTICE OF PROPOSED SALE OF SECURITIES
PURSUANT TO RULE 237**

SECURITIES AND EXCHANGE COMMISSION
Washington, D. C. 20549

FORM 237

NOTICE OF PROPOSED SALE OF SECURITIES PURSUANT TO RULE 237

1. Name, address and telephone number (including area code) of the issuer of the securites to be sold:

2. Name and address of the person who is selling the securities to which this notice relates:

3. Title of the class of securities to be sold:

4. Number of shares or other units to be sold (if debt securities, give the aggregate face amount):

5. Aggregate price at which the securities are proposed to be sold:

6. Date on which the securities to be sold were acquired by the person by whom they are to be sold, and if they were purchased, the date on which the full purchase price was paid:

7. State the manner in which the person selling the securities will seek to obtain buyers for the securities and indicate the class of persons to which sales of the securities will be made:

8. Furnish the following information as to all securities of the issuer sold during the past 12 months by the person who is selling the securities to which this notice relates, pursuant to Rule 144, Rule 237 or any other exemption under Section 3(b) of the Act:

Name and address of seller	Title of securities sold	Date of sale	Amount sold	Gross proceeds

Instruction. See the definition of "person" in Rule 237(d). Information is to be given not only as to sales by the person who is selling the securities to which this notice relates but also as to sales under the rules and exemptions referred to by all other persons included in that definition.

9. State the approximate total number of shares or other units (or if debt securities, the aggregate face amount) of the class, of which the securities to be sold are a part, outstanding as shown by a recent published report or statement of the issuer or by a letter from the issuer setting forth the number outstanding as of a recent date.

THE PERSON FILING THIS NOTICE HEREBY REPRESENTS BY SIGNING THIS NOTICE THAT HE DOES NOT KNOW OF ANY MATERIAL INFORMATION IN REGARD TO THE CURRENT AND PROSPECTIVE OPERATIONS OF THE ISSUER OF THE SE-

CURITIES TO BE SOLD WHICH HAS NOT BEEN DISCLOSED TO THE BUYERS OF THE SECURITIES TO BE SOLD.

Date of Notice

(Signature)

Instruction. The notice shall be signed by the selling security holder. At least one copy of the notice shall be manually signed. Any copies not manually signed shall bear typed or printed signatures.

Attention: Intentional misstatements or omission of facts
constitute Federal Criminal Violations (See 18 U.S.C. 1001).

Registration Forms. Where no exemption is available, either for distributions from the trust or for sales by the employer or by a participant, registration under the '33 Act may be required. Such registration may be accomplished by filing one of a number of applicable registration forms, including:

Form S-1. A general form of registration statement which may be used to register any type of transaction;

Form S-8. A form of registration statement generally used to register interests in, and the underlying securities of an ESOP. The registration statement on Form S-8 may also be used to register resales by participants where such resales occur on a national exchange; and

Form S-16. A simplified form of registration statement which may be used to register any type of transaction, but is limited in its use to certain issuers which meet its requirements.

THE SECURITIES EXCHANGE ACT OF 1934

Open Market Purchases–Rule 10b-5. Where the securities of an employer are not registered pursuant to Section 12 of the '34 Act, the Federal Securities law problems involved in purchases made by an ESOP Trust in the open market generally are limited to Section 10(b) of the '34 Act and Rule 10b-5 promulgated by the Securities and Exchange Commission under that Section of the '34 Act. In essence, Rule 10b-5 provides that if the trust purchases (or sells) securities of the employer when the trust knows or should know material information about the employer which would affect the investment decision of the seller, and such information is not available to the seller, the trust would violate the Rule. Upon such violation, the trust could be forced to return the shares to the seller, or pay damages to the seller. The disclosure requirements of Rule 10b-5 are applicable to both publicly traded and privately held securities.

Prohibitions Against Trading by Trust–Rule 10b-6. Where the securities of an employer are registered pursuant to Section 12 of the '34 Act, additional Securities and Exchange Commission rules come into play. Rule 10b-6 prohibits trading by an issuer while engaged in a distribution. Where an employer has outstanding convertible securities or option plans which are registered under the '33 Act, the employer is generally in registration and continuously engaged in a distribution. Since an ESOP Trust is generally a creature of the employer, the rules prohibiting the issuer or employer from engaging in certain conduct are equally applicable to the trust. Various SEC rules and proposals specify the conditions under which issuers (and trusts created by the issuers) may purchase their own securities in open-market or negotiated transactions in a manner to avoid a manipulative or misleading impact on the trading market for an issuer's securities. Among the SEC proposals is Rule 13e-2 set forth in SEC Release No. 10539. Under the SEC rules, and proposals, purchases by an issuer of its own securities may be limited to a single broker or dealer on any one day and may be restricted to certain price and volume limitations to insure that an issuer neither leads nor dominates the trading market in its securities. Where the investment power of an ESOP Trust is vested in or exercised by a trustee completely independently of the employer, however, there would appear to be no requirement for the trustee to follow the detailed guidelines of the Securities and Exchange Commission respecting trading by an issuer.

Trust Ownership of Stock–Section 16(a). Once an ESOP Trust owns 10% or more of the outstanding securities of an employer whose securities are registered pursuant to Section 12 of the '34 Act, it must file a Form 3—Statement of Beneficial Ownership, disclosing the securities registered in its name or beneficially owned by the trust. Thereafter, the trust must file a Form 4—Statement of Changes in Beneficial Ownership, within 10 days after the end of any month in which the number of shares owned by the trust increases or decreases.

Participants–Rule 16(a). Although generally under the '34 Act beneficial ownership of a security through the medium of a trust is equivalent to direct ownership for the purposes of Section 16(a), Rule 16a-8(g)(3) provides that no report is required under Section 16(a) by any person with respect to his indirect interest in securities held by a retirement plan which holds securities of an issuer whose employees are generally beneficiaries of the plan. However, the SEC requests that individuals, otherwise required to file reports under Section 16(a), include, by footnote, in such reports, a statement of the number of shares vested in such individual under the plan as shown by the trustee's latest annual report, and a statement indicating whether any shares accrued under the plan for such individual since the trustee's last annual report.

Short Swing Profits Under Section 16(b)–Trust. Section 16(b) of the '34 Act provides that upon any purchase and sale, or sale and purchase, of any security registered pursuant to Section 12 of the '34 Act, within six months, by any officer, director, or holder of 10% or more of such securities, such officer, director, or holder shall be liable to the issuer of such securities for any profit realized on such transaction. Therefore, after the trust acquires 10% or more of the outstanding securities of the employer, the trust may be liable for any "short-swing" profits. Rule 16b-3, however, exempts from Section 16(b) the acquisition of shares of stock from a trust pursuant to the terms of an ESOP by a director or officer of the issuer, if the ESOP meets the following conditions:

(1) The ESOP must be approved by the holders of a majority of the outstanding securities of the issuer present, or represented and entitled to vote at a shareholders' meeting, and the shareholders must have received the information required to be furnished under the proxy solicitation rules.

(2) The terms of the ESOP must limit either the aggregate dollar amount or aggregate number of shares which may be allocated to each participant or to all participants as a whole. Generally, the limitations of 15% of payroll and $25,000 per year or

25% of compensation established under the Internal Revenue Code result in compliance with this requirement.

Rule 13d. When a trust acquires 5% of the outstanding securities of an employer, the trust may be required to file a Schedule 13D with the SEC and with the employer. Schedule 13D must be filed within 10 days after the acquisition of securities by the trust which brings trust ownership to more than five percent of such outstanding securities. When the trust becomes liable to file Schedule 13D, it must send one copy of the Schedule to the employer at its principal executive office, eight copies to the SEC with a filing fee of $100, and one copy to any exchange on which the security is traded.

Contents of Schedule 13D. The following are the items of information to be included in Schedule 13D, as contained in the instructions to the Schedule:

Item 1. Security and Issuer.

State the title of the class of equity securities to which this statement relates and the name and address of the issuer of such securities.

Item 2. Identity and Background.

State the following with respect to the person filing this statement:

(a) Name and business address;

(b) Residence address;

(c) Present principal occupation or employment and the name, principal business and address of any corporation or other organization in which such employment is carried on;

(d) Material occupations, positions, offices or employments during the last 10 years, giving the starting and ending dates of each and the name, principal business and address of any business corporation or other organization in which each such occupation, position, office or employment was carried on; and

(e) Whether or not, during the last 10 years, such person has been convicted in a criminal proceeding (excluding traffic violations or similar misdemeanors) and, if so, give the dates, nature of conviction, name and location of court, and penalty imposed, or other disposition of the case. A negative answer to this sub-item need not be furnished to security holders.

Item 3. Source and Amount of Funds or Other Consideration.

State the source and amount of funds or other consideration used or to be used in making the purchases, and if any part of the purchase price or proposed purchase price is represented or is to be represented by funds or other consideration borrowed or otherwise obtained for the purpose of acquiring, holding, or trading the securities, a description of the transaction and the names of the parties thereto.

Item 4. Purpose of Transaction.

State the purpose or purposes of the purchase or proposed purchase of securities of the issuer. If the purpose or one of the purposes of the purchase or proposed purchase is to acquire control of the business of the issuer, describe any plans or proposals which the purchasers may have to liquidate the issuer, to sell its assets or to merge it with any other persons, or to make any other major change in its business or corporate structure, including, if the issuer is a registered closed-end investment company, any plans or proposals to make any changes in its investment policy for which a vote would be required by Section 13 of the Investment Company Act of 1940 (15 U.S.C. 80a-13).

Item 5. Interest in Securities of the Issuer.

State the number of shares of the security which are beneficially owned, and the number of shares concerning which there is a right to acquire, directly or indirectly, by (i) such persons, and (ii) each associate of such person, giving the name and address of each such associate. Furnish information as to all transactions in the class of securities to which this statement relates which were effected during the past 60 days by the person filing this statement and by its subsidiaries and their officers, directors and affiliated persons.

Item 6. Contracts, Arrangements, or Understandings with Respect to Securities of the Issuer.

Furnish information as to any contracts, arrangements, or understandings with any person with respect to any securities of the issuer, including but not limited to transfer of any of the securities, joint ventures, loan or option arrangements, puts or calls, guaranties of loans, guaranties against loss or guaranties of profits, division of losses or profits, or the giving or withholding of proxies, naming the persons with whom such contracts, arrangements, or understandings have been entered into, and giving the details thereof.

Item 7. Persons Retained, Employed or to Be Compensated.

Where the Schedule 13D relates to a tender offer, or request or invitation for tenders, identify all persons and classes of persons employed, retained or to be compensated by the person filing this Schedule 13D, or by any person on his behalf, to make solicitations or recommendations to security holders and describe briefly the terms of such employment, retainer or arrangement for compensation.

Item 8. Material to be Filed as Exhibits.

Copies of all requests or invitations for tenders or advertisements making a tender offer or requesting or inviting tenders, additional material soliciting or requesting such tender offers, solicitations or recommendations to the holders of the security to accept or reject a tender offer or request or invitation for tenders shall be filed as an exhibit.

Summary. Since ESOPs deal primarily in employer securities, transactions involving ESOPs should be carefully tailored to comply with securities laws. The federal securities laws most directly concerned with ESOP transactions are the Securities Act of 1933 and the Securities Exchange Act of 1934. ESOP transactions which should be scrutinized are (1) receipt of securities by ESOP Trust, (2) distribution of securities by the trust, and (3) sale of securities by the employees or beneficiaries. Under the '33 Act, contributions of stock by an employer to the trust, without payment of consideration by the trust, are normally exempt from registration requirements. Purchases of stock by the ESOP may be exempt under Sections 3(a)(2) or 4(1) of the '33 Act. Additional registration exemptions may apply under 4(2) of the Act, the non-public offering exemption, and the exceptions for sales to residents of a single state under Rule 147 or sales by employers with less than 100 stockholders under Rule 240. Distributions by a trust to a beneficiary may normally be exempt from registration, unless the beneficiary is offered an investment choice. A beneficiary receiving stock, non-registered stock, receives restricted stock and may only sell in accordance with the provisions of Rule 144 if the securities of the employer are registered within the meaning of Sections 12 or 15 of the '34 Act. The short-swing profit rules of Section 16(b) of the '34 Act may apply to an ESOP, although distributions from an ESOP to a director or officer are exempt, if the ESOP has been approved by vote of the shareholders.

10

COMMENTARY: THE LOGICAL ESOP CANDIDATE, AND SPECIAL ESOP PROBLEMS

The preceding chapters of this book have discussed ESOP's two basic goals, i.e., (1) provide the average American wage earner with an interest in American corporate capital, and (2) assist American corporations to obtain additional needed capital. These chapters have also set forth legal requirements to establish and maintain an ESOP, and have indicated some pitfalls for the unknowing ESOP fiduciary or ESOP employer. ESOP is not for every employer. And each interested employer should consider ESOP from its own particular viewpoint, considering not only ESOP's advantages, but also possible ESOP disadvantages. This Chapter contains criteria to determine the logical ESOP candidate. It also discusses favorable and unfavorable aspects of ESOP, with emphasis on those aspects of ESOP most often subjected to public criticism.

LOGICAL ESOP CANDIDATES

Exclusive Benefit Rule. An ESOP must be established and maintained exclusively for the benefit of employees or their beneficiaries. This condition precedent for all employee-benefit plans to qualify under Section 401(a) of the Code suggests a special consideration for an ESOP candidate. An ESOP must be formed to invest primarily in employer securities and may distribute only employer stock to its employees. Under these circumstances, if employees are to derive any benefit from the ESOP, the benefit must arise from the value of employer stock distributed to employees under the terms of the plan. If stock distributed to the employees or their beneficiaries is valueless, the employees will derive no benefit from the ESOP. Therefore, a first basic criterion for the logical ESOP candidate requires that the candidate have reasonable prospects for a successful financial future. A corporation in financial difficulty, with uncertain prospects for future earnings, is not a good ESOP candidate. If an employer obtains tax advantages from contributions of stock to an ESOP, and then the employer's stock loses value, distributions of stock of diminished value to employees may result not only in reduced employee morale, but may lead to lawsuits against both plan fiduciaries and employer corporations. A corporation would be foolhardy to guarantee the value of its stock for all time, but future prospects should be an important consideration in deciding whether to adopt an ESOP.

Fiduciary Obligations. An employer should also consider the effect on an ESOP fiduciary of a decline in price of an employer's stock. As the fair market value of an employer's stock declines, a plan fiduciary may find it more and more difficult to fulfill his fiduciary duties, particularly where the plan assets consist of a 100% investment in employer stock. As indicated in Chapter 3, an ESOP fiduciary need not comply with all fiduciary obligations imposed by ERISA upon fiduciaries of other employee-benefit plans. An ESOP fiduciary is exempt from the requirement of diversification in the investment of trust assets and may invest 100% of trust assets in employer securities. Actually, an ESOP fiduciary is obligated to invest primarily in employer securities, and to operate the ESOP Trust to enable the fiduciary to distribute employer stock to employees entitled to distributions from the ESOP Trust. Consider these characteristics of an ESOP Trust, unique in comparison to trusts of other employee-benefit plans, in the light of a fiduciary's obligations. How should a fiduciary react to a decline in the price of an employer's stock or in an employer's business prospects? Must the ESOP fiduciary sell the stock when earnings decline? Due to the nature of ESOP, formed to acquire and distribute securities and stock of an employer, an ESOP fiduciary is theoretically under less of an obligation to sell employer securities or stock under adverse conditions than other fiduciaries of employee-benefit plans who are under an obligation to maintain a diversified income-producing portfolio. In spite of a decline in value of an employer's stock, an ESOP fiduciary who retains the stock as a trust asset is at least technically fulfilling a fundamental purpose of the ESOP Trust. An employer who appreciates possible future fiduciary problems will require that the ESOP clearly obligate the plan fiduciary to invest in and hold the employer's securities as the trust assets, providing the fiduciary the protection of the contractual obligations.

ESOP Employer Benefits. The ESOP candidate should be able to project realistic benefits it may anticipate from an ESOP. If the candidate has no employee-benefit program, it should consider the value of improved employee morale and loyalty by the adoption of an ESOP. If the employer already has an employee-benefit program, it should consider possibilities of supplementing such a program with an ESOP, or substituting an ESOP. From the viewpoint of the employer's future need for capital, the ESOP candidate should determine the employer's capital needs for a reasonable period into the future, and should attempt to determine how an ESOP may assist in providing the needed capital. A projection of future capital needs may be developed from a five-year forecast of the business, which takes into account such items as product lines, prices, costs and industry trends, required capital improvements, expense and personnel requirements, past and estimated future income, and estimated future cash requirements. A form of such a five-year forecast is contained in *Acquisitions, Mergers, Sales, and Takeovers* by Charles A. Scharf, published by Prentice-Hall Inc., Englewood Cliffs, New Jersey.

The ESOP candidate may determine from the projection of capital needs the extent to which an ESOP may assist in providing this capital. In addition, where a candidate is closely-held as Closely-held Corp., discussed in Chapters 6 and 7, the candidate should determine whether a market for its stock may provide continuity of ownership or assist in formulating an estate plan for major stockholders. If an ESOP may not only afford employees an opportunity to become part owners of the business, but may also create a market for stock to avoid possible liquidation or transfer of stock to unfriendly hands, these possibilities should be considered to decide whether to establish an ESOP.

Tax Benefit and Maximum Contributions. An ESOP's benefits to an employer are largely derived from tax deductible contributions. Where an employer has no taxable income such benefits are not available to the employer. As a consequence, to be a logical candidate for an ESOP, an employer should be profitable. In addition, the amount of tax benefit an employer may derive from an ESOP is limited by the amount of compensation paid to covered employees.

An ESOP is expensive to establish and to maintain. It requires skilled legal services to draft the plan and to operate within the legal restrictions of ERISA, and the tax and securities laws. If employer stock is closely held, the ESOP may also incur the expense of annual stock valuations. In view of expenses involved in establishing and maintaining an ESOP, the logical ESOP candidate should have a large enough payroll to permit deductible contributions of meaningful financial benefit to the candidate. As set forth in Chapter 4, the maximum tax deduction for contributions to an ESOP is 15% of compensation of employees covered by the plan, or 25% of such compensation in the case of certain carryovers. In view of the expenses involved in an ESOP, for an ESOP to be an economically sound business project, an employer should be of sufficient minimum size to contribute approximately $50,000 annually to an ESOP should it so choose. A general yardstick employed to determine whether an employer is sizeable enough to establish an ESOP, is that the employer's payroll for covered employees should amount to approximately $300,000 per year.

DILUTION OF EARNINGS PER SHARE

In the normal course of events, an employer which establishes an ESOP contemplates the sale or contribution of newly issued stock to the ESOP. Issuance of additional shares of stock will reduce earnings per share until an employer's earnings increase sufficiently to absorb the additional outstanding shares. This dilution in earnings per share is one of the most frequent criticisms raised against the establishment of an ESOP.

Public vs. Private Corporation. Where newly issued stock is contributed or sold to an ESOP, the capital and cash flow of an employer increases. Funds available to conduct the employer's business increase. Upon such issuance, however, book value per share may decrease, and as indicated above, earnings per share will decrease.

Generally, the importance of a decrease in book value or earnings per share is greater for a public corporation than for a closely-held corporation. In the case of a corporation whose stock is publicly traded, financial statements become public knowledge, and stockholders and security analysts rely on the financial statements to value the stock of the corporation, often with particular emphasis on reported earnings per share. Management of a publicly-held company is, therefore, often reluctant to make any decision which may decrease earnings per share, although the decision may increase the working capital of the corporation.

On the other hand, in a privately-owned corporation, or even in a publicly-held corporation where management places less stress on reported earnings per share and more stress on cash flow, reported earnings per share may be looked upon more as an accounting concept rather than a yardstick to measure sound business decisions. Contributions or sales of stock to an ESOP by such a corporation may strengthen its financial position and provide needed capital in the judgment of management; and management may make contributions or sales of stock to an ESOP in spite of possible adverse effects upon reported earnings per share for accounting purposes.

Example of Dilution Computation. Where reported earnings per share are important to management, computations should be made to establish the earnings which must be realized on the funds provided to an employer by the ESOP from a stock contribution or sale to avoid dilution in such earnings. As an example of such a computation, assume that an ESOP borrows $5,000,000, at 10% annual interest on a ten year level repayment basis, and utilizes the $5,000,000 to purchase employer stock. Assume further that the market price of the employer's stock is $12 per share, permitting the ESOP to purchase 416,667 shares, and that the ESOP will receive $100,000 annually in dividends on the 416,667 shares. Based on the assumptions, the additional funds needed for debt service by the ESOP, in addition to the dividends, will amount to $714,000 annually for the ten year period.

If the stock of the employer earns $1.50 per share after taxes, and 2,375,000 shares are outstanding before the sale to the ESOP, the employer has $3,562,500 of after-tax earnings prior to the ESOP's purchase of stock (2,375,000 shares × $1.50 per share). For the 416,667 newly issued shares sold to the ESOP not to dilute future earnings, the after-tax earnings of the employer must increase by $625,000 (416,667 shares × $1.50 per share). Therefore, the total after-tax earnings of the employer after the purchase of the stock by the ESOP must equal at least $4,187,500 to avoid dilution. Stated differently, the $5,000,000 received by the employer for its newly issued stock must earn a 12.5% return after taxes, or based upon a 50% combined federal and local tax bracket, it must earn 25% before taxes not to dilute earnings per share.

The foregoing assumptions, refined to reflect discounted cash flow based upon a return of 12-1/2% per annum over the ten year period, are set forth in the following example, in which it is assumed the cost of establishing and maintaining the ESOP is $50,000:

	Present Val. 12.5	Contribution to ESOP	After Tax Cost	Neg. Cash Flow Inc. Div.	Present Val. (Rt. at 12-1/2)	Net Disc. Cash Flow Aft Tax
						(25,000)
Start-up Date	1.000000	50,000	25,000	25,000	25,000	5,000,000
1st Anniversary	.888888	714,000	357,000	457,000	406,222	4,568,778
2nd Anniversary	.790123	714,000	357,000	457,000	361,086	4,207,692
3rd Anniversary	.702332	714,000	357,000	457,000	320,966	3,886,726
4th Anniversary	.624295	714,000	357,000	457,000	285,303	3,601,423
5th Anniversary	.554929	714,000	357,000	457,000	253,603	3,347,820
6th Anniversary	.493270	714,000	357,000	457,000	225,164	3,122,656
7th Anniversary	.438462	714,000	357,000	457,000	200,377	2,922,279
8th Anniversary	.389744	714,000	357,000	457,000	178,113	2,744,166
9th Anniversary	.346439	714,000	357,000	457,000	158,322	2,585,844
10th Anniversary	.307946	714,000	357,000	457,000	140,731	2,445,113
		7,190,000	3,595,000	4,595,000	2,554,887	

Plus discounted Cash Flow 2,445,113

5,000,000

The above example demonstrates that the employer realized increased discounted cash flow after taxes totaling $2,445,113, as a result of a $5,000,000 purchase of stock by the ESOP, and the repayment of the ESOP borrowing by contributions to the ESOP. However, as stated, unless this employer finds a use for the $5,000,000 from the sale of stock which earns a 25% pre-tax return, the ESOP loan and purchase transaction will dilute earnings per share.

VOTING ESOP STOCK

Normally, the stock held in an ESOP Trust is voted by the turstee, or other named fiduciary of the trust, and the ESOP also provides that the trustee vote the stock as directed by a committee appointed by the Board of Directors. Under these circumstances, while the stock remains in the trust, whether allocated to the accounts of individual employees or not, voting of the stock remains under the control of the Board of Directors. Management need have no apprehension concerning dilution of control of the employer. Future voting of stock received by employees under the terms of the plan in most situations may, as a practical matter, be provided for. Some authorities feel, however, that participants in an ESOP should be given the right to vote stock allocated to their accounts as their interests vest. This proposition does not reflect the congressional intent expressed concerning the ERISA legislation, but raises questions of the relationship between management, on the one hand, and labor, on the other. These questions appear destined to continue as part of the debate involving the ESOP concept.

Experience of Western Europe. The industrialized countries of Western Europe have divided over the proposition that workers should participate in a corporation's decision making. In this connection, eight European countries, led by West Germany, provide for some form of worker representation or participation on management boards, or in the company decision making process. In addition to West Germany, Sweden, The Netherlands, Luxemburgh, Norway, Switzerland, Austria, and Denmark approve of worker participation in management decisions.

Other countries, forming part of the European Common Market are of the opposite opinion: there should be no worker representation on management boards. Apparently, labor leaders in these countries, Belgium, France, Italy, Britain, and Ireland, believe that representation of workers on management boards may hurt the labor movement. Such leaders feel that participation in management may hamper a union's freedom to confront management with necessary demands for the improvement of the worker's position in our industrial societies. On the other hand, from management's point of view, a board on which workers are represented, may not be as free to make the difficult decisions necessary to reduce labor costs from time to time to maintain profits. The issue is not free from doubt in Western Europe, and the industrialized countries which have not yet adopted procedures for the participation of workers in management decisions, particularly France and Britain, believe that a long time will pass before a cooperative approach between management and labor to making business decisions will become a reality.

United States Legislation. Chapter 1 discussed miscellaneous federal legislation incorporating the ESOP concept. Among the federal acts discussed were the Trade Act of 1974, and the Tax Reduction Act of 1975. Both these Acts provide that in order to qualify under their provisions, an ESOP must entitle a participant to vote stock allocated to his account in which he has a vested interest.

In addition to federal legislation which contemplates a vote of the stock by participants, legislation in at least one state also contemplates employee participation in the management of an ESOP employer through an advisory committee to the trustee. The state of Minnesota has enacted tax legislation which affords special treatment to employee stock ownership trusts. This legislation grants special income tax treatment for contributions made by an employer to such a trust, and also provides special exemptions from estate taxes and gift taxes for devises, bequests or transfers of property to ESOP Trusts. The income tax provisions permit an employer to contribute up to 30% of compensation of covered employees to an ESOP Trust in the form of tax deductible contributions. Under Minnesota's estate and gift tax laws, bequests and gifts to ESOPs are exempt from estate and gift taxation. Generally, under Minnesota law, the type of ESOP which entitles donors or employers to the special tax treatment is similar to ESOP as defined in ERISA, with the additional provision that "the employees eligible as beneficiaries of the trust shall have the right to elect by majority vote thereof an advisory committee to the trustee or trustees."

The provisions of the Trade Act of 1974, the Tax Reduction Act of 1975, and the Minnesota ESOP legislation indicate that a sufficient number of legislative representatives in the United States hold the opinion that employees should have a voice in the vote of stock held in ESOP trusts on their behalf to enact legislation to this effect.

Neither the ERISA legislation nor the Congressional Committee Reports which explain the underlying intent of Congress in the enactment of ERISA contain a requirement that employees be entitled to vote the stock allocated to them in an ESOP Trust. On the contrary, under ERISA non-voting preferred stock is a qualified security, which could, of course, not be voted by employees under any circumstances. The ERISA legislation, and the intent of Congress in enacting that legislation, clearly establish a basic purpose for the legislation: that employees become part owners of the capital which enables them to be productive in their work. Nowhere does the legislation contemplate or require that employees become managers of that capital. No more justification exists to require that employees vote stock held for their benefit in an ESOP Trust, than to require that employees have the right to determine the form of investment of assets held by trustees in pension and profit-sharing plans generally. In all instances, employees are beneficiaries of a trust, and, by the nature of trust arrangements, the trustees, not the beneficiaries, are obligated to determine the disposition of trust assets. Historically, the opportunity to choose a trustee considered more capable of administering trust assets than a beneficiary, underlies the trust concept.

Whether employees should vote the stock held in their accounts by an ESOP will ultimately be determined by the attitude and intent of legislators. In making their determinations, the legislators should be mindful that a clear distinction exists between owning capital, and managing that capital. One of the fundamental purposes of ESOP as set forth in ERISA is to give the average American worker an ownership interest in capital. Nowhere is the purpose stated to give the average working man control of the management of the capital. Participation by the average worker in the management of his employer places the worker in a conflict of interest situation. Where hard business decisions must be made, such as lay-offs, reduction in overtime, increased automation, or other decisions by management which may adversely affect workers, it is difficult to imagine a more direct conflict of interest than to request the average worker to vote objectively on such issues.

Voting by Trustee—NYSE Rule 452. Rule 452, adopted by The New York Stock Exchange provides that without specific authorization from the beneficial owner, the registered owner (subject to the rules of the NYSE) may not vote stock in connection with a merger, consolidation or any other matter which may affect substantially the rights or privileges of such stock.

The New York Stock Exchange has also adopted a policy with respect to stock plans which requires the trustee, where the incidents of ownership of the shares are exercisable by the participants, to poll the participants by forwarding to them the proxy material and to vote shares registered in the name of the trustee at a shareholders' meeting as directed by the participants. Where the incidents of ownership are not exercisable by the participants, the trustee is required by the NYSE to vote shares in proportion to votes cast by other shareholders, at the meeting. Where the incidents of ownership are exercisable by participants, the SEC has requested that the trustee abstain from voting such shares when the participant has failed to indicate a voting preference, unless shares so treated are not valid for quorum purposes under State law.

PENALTIES FOR ERISA VIOLATIONS

Chapter 3 describes obligations of a plan fiduciary in administering ESOPs. In addition, Chapter 6 sets forth the difficult valuation problems which may arise in purchases and sales of employer stock involving an ESOP Trustee and a closely-held employer. The premise that dealings between an ESOP Trust and a party in interest (as that term is used in ERISA) and a disqualified person (as that term is used in the Internal Revenue Code of 1954) must be for "adequate consideration" lies at the root of the valuation problems. The difficulty of meeting the adequate consideration or fair market value requirement in the case of a closely-held stock with a thin float is discussed in some detail in Chapter 6. In spite of the difficulty, under the terms of ERISA and Code if an ESOP fiduciary pays more for the stock of an employer than "adequate consideration," the fiduciary, and other parties in interest or disqualified persons may be subject to substantial penalties.

Restitution. Section 409 of ERISA provides that a plan fiduciary who violates the terms of ERISA is personally liable to the plan for any losses incurred by the plan from the breach. In this connection, Section 409 of ERISA provides as follows:

> Act Sec. 409. (a) Any person who is a fiduciary with respect to a plan who breaches any of the responsibilities, obligations, or duties imposed upon fiduciaries by this title shall be personally liable to make good to such plan any losses to the plan resulting from each such breach, and to restore to such plan any profits of such fiduciary which have been made through use of assets of the plan by the fiduciary, and shall be subject to such other equitable or remedial relief as the court may deem appropriate, including removal of such fiduciary. A fiduciary may also be removed for a violation of section 411 of this Act.
>
> (b) No fiduciary shall be liable with respect to a breach of fiduciary duty under this title if such breach was committed before he became a fiduciary or after he ceased to be a fiduciary.

Tax Penalties. In addition to penalties imposed by ERISA for breaches of fiduciary duties, the Internal Revenue Code imposes taxes upon any disqualified person who participates in a prohibited transaction. The definition of a disqualified person is contained in Section 4975(e)(2) of the Code, which defines a "disqualified person" in the same terms as ERISA's definition of a party in interest. Section 4975(e)(2) provides as follows:

> (2) DISQUALIFIED PERSON.—For purposes of this section, the term "disqualified person" means a person who is—
> (A) a fiduciary;
> (B) a person providing services to the plan;
> (C) an employer any of whose employees are covered by the plan;
> (D) an employee organization any of whose members are covered by the plan;
> (E) an owner, direct or indirect, of 50 percent or more of—
>   (i) the combined voting power of all classes of stock entitled to vote or the total value of shares of all classes of stock of a corporation,
>   (ii) the capital interest or the profits interest of a partnership, or
>   (iii) the beneficial interest of a trust or unincorporated enterprise, which is an employer or an employee organization described in subparagraph (C) or (D):
> (F) a member of the family (as defined in paragraph (6)) of any individual described in subparagraph (A), (B), (C), or (E);
> (G) a corporation, partnership, or trust or estate of which (or in which) 50 percent or more of—

      (i) the combined voting power of all classes of stock entitled to vote or the total value of shares of all classes of stock of such corporation,

      (ii) the capital interest or profits interest of such partnership, or

      (iii) the beneficial interest of such trust or estate, is owned directly or indirectly, or held by persons described in subparagraph (A), (B), (C), (D), or (E);

  (H) an officer, director (or an individual having powers or responsibilities similar to those of officers or directors), a 10 percent or more shareholder, or a highly compensated employee (earning 10 percent or more of the yearly wages of an employer) of a person described in subparagraph (C), (D), (E), or (G); or

  (I) a 10 percent or more (in capital or profits) partner or joint venturer of a person described in subparagraph (C), (D), (E), or (G).

The Secretary, after consultation and coordination with the Secretary of Labor or his delegate, may by regulation prescribe a percentage lower than 50 percent for subparagraphs (E) and (G) and lower than 10 percent for subparagraphs (H) and (I).

The above quotation includes within the definition of a disqualified person (1) a fiduciary, (2) an employer and (3) an owner of 50% or more of the combined voting power of all classes of stock of an employer. Therefore the definition of disqualified person includes a plan fiduciary, and the Founder and Closely-held Corp. discussed in Chapters 5 and 6.

Section 4975(a) imposes an initial tax on a disqualified person equal to 5% of the amount involved in a prohibited transaction for each year in the taxable period. The tax imposed is to be paid by any disqualified person who participates in the prohibited transaction (other than a fiduciary acting only as such). In this connection, Section 4975(a) provides as follows:

    (a) INITIAL TAXES ON DISQUALIFIED PERSON.—There is hereby imposed a tax on each prohibited transaction. The rate of tax shall be equal to 5 percent of the amount involved with respect to the prohibited transaction for each year (or part thereof) in the taxable period. The tax imposed by this subsection shall be paid by any disqualified person who participates in the prohibited transaction (other than a fiduciary acting only as such).

In addition to the initial tax, in any case in which an initial tax is imposed and the prohibited transaction is not corrected within ninety days after the date of the mailing of a notice of deficiency, an additional tax equal to 100% of the amount involved in the prohibited transaction is imposed and must be paid by any disqualified person who participated in the prohibited transaction (other than a fiduciary acting only as such). In this connection, Section 4975(b) provides as follows:

    (b) ADDITIONAL TAXES ON DISQUALIFIED PERSON.—In any case in which an initial tax is imposed by subjection (a) on a prohibited transaction and the transaction is not corrected within the correction period, there is hereby imposed a tax equal to 100 percent of the amount involved. The tax imposed by this subsection shall be paid by any disqualified person who participated in the prohibited transaction (other than a fiduciary acting only as such).

The definition of a prohibited transaction is contained in Section 4975(c) of the

Code. This definition is indentical with the definition of a prohibited transaction contained in Section 406(a) of ERISA, except that ERISA speaks in terms of transactions with a "party in interest," rather than in terms of transactions with a "disqualified person." Section 4975(c) provides as follows:

(C) PROHIBITED TRANSACTION.—

(1) GENERAL RULE.—For purposes of this section, the term "prohibited transaction" means any direct or indirect—

(A) sale or exchange, or leasing, of any property between a plan and a disqualified person;

(B) lending of money or other extension of credit between a plan and a disqualified person;

(C) furnishing of goods, services, or facilities between a plan and a disqualified person;

(D) transfer to, or use by or for the benefit of, a disqualified person of the income or assets of a plan;

(E) act by a disqualified person who is a fiduciary whereby he deals with the income or assets of a plan in his own interest or for his own account; or

(F) receipt of any consideration for his own personal account by any disqualified person who is a fiduciary from any party dealing with the plan in connection with a transaction involving the income or assets of the plan.

In view of the serious consequences of a fiduciary violation of the prohibited transaction sections, and in view of the difficulty of ascertaining with certainty that the ERISA requirements of "adequate consideration" or fair market value have been met where valuations of an employer's stock are necessary, procedures should be established for a plan fiduciary to obtain an advance ruling from the Internal Revenue Service concerning a particular proposed transaction, similar to requests for no action letters addressed to the Securities and Exchange Commission. The Accelerated Capital Formation Act of 1975 contains such a proposal. This act proposes to add a new section, Section 416(d)(2), to the Code which would provide as follows:

(2) Upon application by an employee stock ownership plan, the Secretary of the Treasury or his delegate shall issue an advance opinion as to whether a proposed transaction involving that employee stock ownership plan will satisfy all the requirements described in paragraph (1) of this subsection, and any such opinion shall be binding upon the Secretary.

ESOP· vs. PUBLIC OFFERING

Comparisons are often made between an ESOP as a financing vehicle and a public offering of an employer's stock, although little or no valid basis exists for such comparison. An ESOP, in the first instance, is an employee benefit plan. Its primary purpose is to give employees an interest in the capital of their employer. An ESOP is only incidentally an instrument of corporate finance. On the other hand, a public sale of an employer's stock is purely a financing transaction.

Consider these differences between the nature of ESOP and a public offering of stock. The ESOP (1) provides employees with incentive from stock ownership, (2) offers continuing control of the vote of the stock by the employer, (3) provides a continuing market for employer stock and (4) permits the indirect repayment of borrowed funds by the employer with tax-deductible dollars. On the other hand, an initial public offering of an employer's stock involves a single transaction, which is solely a financing, and which carries with it no other incidental benefits to the employer.

Where the comparison between formation of an ESOP or a public offering of stock assumes that the ESOP must borrow funds from a third party to buy an employer's stock, the net available cash to an employer from an ESOP transaction must obviously be substantially less than the net available cash to the employer after an initial public offering of stock. Where an ESOP borrows money to purchase an employer's stock, the employer must, through contributions to the ESOP, repay the loan, and, as a consequence, assuming a 50% effective combined Federal and state income tax bracket, the employer must repay approximately one-half of the proceeds of the sale of stock to the lender in after-tax dollars. A fairer comparison between an ESOP purchase of stock and a public offering of stock results if it is assumed that the ESOP has the cash available to purchase the employer's stock, from prior contributions or otherwise.

An ESOP transaction involving no outside borrowing, provides at least as much working capital to an employer as a public offering of stock (an initial public offering of stock will entail substantial expense for such items as printing, accounting, and legal fees). Because of the incidental valuable benefits which may flow from an ESOP, an ESOP may be a preferable vehicle of finance, although comparing an ESOP to a public offering of stock is like comparing apples and oranges.

MISCELLANEOUS

Treatment of Existing Plans. Where an employer has a pension plan, conversion of the plan to an ESOP normally will not be permitted by the Internal Revenue Service. If an employer with such a pension plan wishes to adopt an ESOP in its stead, the employer is required to terminate the pension plan, unless the employer obtains the written consent of all the employees with respect to the conversion to an ESOP. Termination of such a pension plan normally requires the vesting of the interests of all employees in the plan.

An alternative may be to add the ESOP as a supplemental or additional benefit plan to the pension plan. From a business point of view, additional employee benefits represented by the ESOP may be prohibitively expensive for the employer.

Since profit-sharing plans are individual account plans, they lend themselves more readily to conversion to ESOPs. However, plan fiduciaries would assume substantial risks of violation of fiduciary obligations if as part of a conversion to ESOP, a diversified portfolio of assets is sold and invested solely in employer stock. One solution to this problem may be that upon conversion, two separate accounts may be maintained for each employee. One account could contain the original diversified portfolio, and the second account could be utilized to purchase employer securities.

Bank Regulations. Where an employer's stock is stock registered on a national securities exchange or is an over-the-counter margin stock, the amount of money which a bank may lend with respect to such stock is limited under the Code of Federal Regulations. An attorney for such an employer should, in each instance, review a proposed transaction to determine that no federal regulations are violated. In this connection, Regulation 221.1(a) of Title 12, Code of Federal Regulations provides as follows:

> . . . No Bank shall extend any credit secured directly or indirectly by any stock for the purpose of purchasing or carrying any margin stock in an amount exceeding the maximum loan value of the collateral . . .

General Cautions. ESOP may provide all of the possible advantages described in this book, but future legislation will determine whether or not ESOP will remain a viable tool to enhance employee benefits as well as supply needed capital for corporate employers. From an employer's point of view, the basic financial advantages of ESOP consist of tax advantages it offers employers. Past history has demonstrated that where a basic valuable tax advantage is available, taxpayers have a tendency to abuse such a tax advantage by misuse. Hopefully, ESOPs will not be so abused by employers that legislators feel impelled to curb their use, and in so doing minimize the advantages of the ESOP, both as an employee benefit plan and as a vehicle of corporate finance.

Summary. A logical candidate for an ESOP should be (1) profitable, (2) with reasonable prospects of continued financial success, and (3) of a minimum size, with a covered employee payroll of no less than $300,000. Where an employer sells or contributes newly issued stock to an ESOP, upon such issuance an employer's earnings per share are reduced. The dilution in earnings per share frequently raises objections against the formation of an ESOP. In public corporations, management is often jealous of the earnings per share reported to the public, its stockholders, and security analysts. However, reported earnings per share may be of less importance in closely-held corporations. In situations where reported earnings per share are important to management, proposed ESOP transactions should be analyzed by making computations of possible dilution of earnings per share. In the chapter an example of such a computation, limited to its assumed facts, concluded that upon a sale of newly issued stock by the employer to an ESOP for $5,000,000 the ESOP may increase discounted cash flow over the ten year period of the loan to purchase the stock, by an amount of $2,445,113. However, in order to avoid dilution of earnings per share, the employer in the example should be able to earn a return of after-tax income of 12-1/2% on the $5,000,000 received for its stock. ERISA does not require that beneficiaries of an ESOP have the right to vote the stock held for their benefit in the ESOP Trust, although miscellaneous legislation indicates some belief that the right to vote should be vested in employee participants. Where violations of fiduciary obligations occur, parties in interest such as the fiduciary, the employer, or a controlling stockholder may be subject to a tax ranging from 5% to 100% of the value of a prohibited transaction. Comparisons between ESOP transactions and public stock offerings should not be made since the comparisons are between fundamentally different concepts, like comparing apples and oranges. Converting pension plans to ESOPs may not be possible and conversions of profit-sharing plans should be approached cautiously. Finally, leveraged ESOP transactions should be reviewed to determine whether margin requirements are violated by the borrowing of funds by an ESOP to purchase stock.

Appendix Of Model
ESOP and Forms

CONTENTS OF APPENDIX

This Appendix includes forms of basic documents which may be utilized by a draftsman as a starting point in preparing an ESOP. The documents are the following:

1. A form of Employees' stock ownership trust.
2. A form of outline of an explanation of an ESOP to employees.
3. A form of accounting procedures which may be adapted for the administration of an ESOP trust.
4. A form of Application for Determination to the Internal Revenue Service for an advance determination of qualification of an ESOP under Section 401(a) of the Code, Form 5301.
5. Instruction for completing Form 5301.
6. Form 5302, an employee census to be attached to application for determination and the general instructions to complete the census.
7. A form of notice to interested parties of an Application for Determination.

The above form of Employees' stock ownership trust and form of accounting procedures incorporate provisions generally required by ERISA and the Code to establish and maintain an ESOP. The form of trust reproduced is adapted from a trust submitted to the Internal Revenue Service and contains changes by the Internal Revenue Service to adapt the trust to ESOP requirements. The form of trust should not be used without careful review of an employer's situation by counsel and the adaptation of the form to the circumstances of the particular employer, after a careful review of the Internal Revenue Service requirements for qualification of ESOPs at the time of its preparation.

EMPLOYEES' STOCK OWNERSHIP TRUST

Employer Corporation
Employees' Stock Ownership Trust

1. *Name.*

The Trust hereby established shall be known as "THE EMPLOYER CORPORATION EMPLOYEES' STOCK OWNERSHIP TRUST," (the "Trust").

2. *Definitions.*

When used in this Trust Agreement, unless otherwise specified when used:

(a) The term "Company" means Employer Corporation, a New York corporation.

(b) The term "Subsidiary" means any domestic corporation, at least eighty percent (80%) of the stock of which is owned by the Company or another corporation, at least eighty percent (80%) of the stock of which other corporation is owned by the Company.

(c) The term "Employer" means the Company or any Subsidiary which adopts this Trust for its employees.

(d) The term "Employee" means every full-time employee (as herein defined) of an Employer who is not covered by a collective bargaining agreement.

(e) The term "Compensation" means monies paid to an Employee by an Employer for services in regularly stated hourly, weekly, bi-weekly, semi-monthly or monthly amounts, including payments for commissions, bonuses and overtime.

(f) The term "Fiscal Year" means the period beginning with April 1st of one calendar year and expiring on March 31st of the following year.

(g) The terms "he," "him," or "his" shall include "she" and "her;" and the singular number shall include the plural and the plural the singular.

(h) The term "Participant" shall mean any Employee participating in the benefits provided by this Trust.

(i) The term "Disability" shall include the term "sickness" and shall mean a permanent physical or mental condition of a Participant resulting from a bodily injury or disease or mental disorder which renders him incapable of continuing in the employment of an Employer and is permanent and continuous in nature.

(j) The term "Full-Time Employee" means an employee continuously employed by the Company or its Subsidiaries for One Thousand (1000) hours or more during any Fiscal Year.

(k) The term "Trustee" means Bank, or such Trustee as from time to time may be acting as such hereunder.

(l) The term "Advisory Committee" means the committee appointed by the Company's Board of Directors to administer this Trust as hereinafter provided.

(m) The term "Trust Fund" means the assets of the Trust established pursuant to this Trust Agreement.

3. *Purposes of the Trust.*

This Trust is created for the sole purpose of enabling Employees of the Company and its Subsidiaries to share in the ownership of the Company. In no event shall any part of the principal or income of the Trust Fund be paid to or revert to the Company or any of its Subsidiaries or be used for any purpose whatsoever other than the exclusive benefit of their Employees and their beneficiaries.

4. *Contributions under the Trust.*

The Employer shall contribute to the Trustee as of March 31st of each year, commencing March 31, 19 , such amount as the Board of Directors of such Employer shall determine by resolution properly presented and duly passed prior to March 31st of such year and communicated to the Participants. Each Employer's contribution shall be paid either in cash or in common shares of the Company valued at the fair market value thereof at the time of the contribution and shall be made within the period permitted for the filing of the Employer's Federal Income Tax return for such period.

5. *Participating Employees.*

All Employees of the Company on March 31, 19 , who are at least eighteen (18) years of age and have completed one (1) or more years of continuous service to the Company or any of its Subsidiaries are eligible to participate in the Plan. All new Employees whose continuous service to the Company or any of its Subsidiaries shall have amounted to one (1) year, to and including March 31st of any subsequent year, shall become eligible to participate in the Plan on March 31st of such year.

No Employee shall be excluded from participation in this Trust by being classed as a temporary employee if his customary employment is for One Thousand (1000) hours or more in any Fiscal Year.

Any Employee whose employment is less than Five Hundred (500) hours during any Fiscal Year shall be determined a new Employee after the first Fiscal Year in which he works at least One Thousand (1000) hours.

Employment shall not be deemed to have been severed nor shall its permanency be affected by the fact that an Employee has been on a leave of absence for service in the armed forces, sickness or disability with the consent of the Board of Directors of an Employer, provided such leave of absence is uniformly granted to all Participants.

Officers and directors of the Company who are Employees shall participate in this Trust on the same basis as the other Employees.

All doubtful cases of eligibility to participate in this Trust shall be resolved by the Advisory Committee, whose determination shall be final in such cases.

6. *Allocation of Benefits.*

(a) *Participants' Accounts.*

A separate bookkeeping account (the "Account") shall be opened by the Advisory Committee in the name of each Participant. Annually, as of March 31 of each year, the Committee shall adjust the Account of each Participant in order to reflect increases or decreases by reason of the following: (i) the contribution of the Company to the Trust Fund for the Fiscal Year; (ii) the earnings or losses of the Trust Fund for the Fiscal Year; (iii) any increase or decrease in value of the investments of the Trust Fund; and (iv) forfeitures, if any.

(b) *Employer Contributions.*

An Employer's contribution for each Fiscal Year will be allocated by the Advisory

Committee among the Participants employed by said Employer who are Employees on March 31 of each year and will be credited to them as of that date on the following basis: Each Participant shall be credited with two (2) units for each year of service as a Full-Time Employee and one (1) unit for each $100.00 of his Compensation or major fraction thereof for the Fiscal Year for which the contribution is to be made. The amount to be credited to the Participant shall be determined by dividing the amount of the Employer's contribution for the year for which the contribution is made by the total number of such units of all Participants employed by said Employer calculated on the same basis and multiplying the quotient by the number of such units of the individual Participant. The contribution made by each Employer will be allocated only to the Participants employed by that Employer.

(c) *Income of Trust Fund.*

Within ninety (90) days after the close of each Fiscal Year that the Trust Fund shall have have been in existence, the Advisory Committee shall apportion among all Participants (as of the last day of the prior Fiscal Year) the net income earned by said Fund that has not theretofore been apportioned. The calculation of this proration of net income and the apportionment of the same shall be made on the basis of the Participants' Accounts as they stood on the last day of such Fiscal Year and without regard to new Employees who may have become eligible to participate during that prior Fiscal Year.

(d) *Revaluation of Investments.*

The Advisory Committee shall determine the fair market of the Trust Fund as of: March 31 of each Fiscal Year that this Trust shall have been in existence; the date of the occurrence of any of the events described in Paragraph 7; and such other time or times that the Advisory Committee shall deem proper. Any increase or decrease in fair market value of the investments of the Trust Fund since the preceding March 31 shall be reflected in the Participants' Accounts annually as provided in Paragraph 6(a), except for those Participants' Accounts that are subject to distribution as provided in Paragraph 7, as to which said increase or decrease shall be reflected in said accounts as of the date of the occurrence of the events described in Paragraph 7. The apportionment of the increase or decrease in the fair market value of the investments of the Trust Fund shall be made on the basis of the Participants' Accounts as they stood as of March 31 of the preceding Fiscal Year, without regard to Employees who may have become eligible to participate during the current Fiscal Year.

(e) *Forfeitures.*

All credits and interests of Participants in the Trust Fund which are forfeited as hereinafter provided will be reallocated by the Advisory Committee among the Participants who are in the employ of an Employer on April 1st of the year following the year in which such forfeiture occurs. Such reallocation shall be made upon the basis of the units described in paragraph 6(b). No Participant who is not in the employ of an Employer at the time of reallocation of forfeited interests and credits shall be entitled to share in the reallocation thereof.

(f) *Limit on Allocations.*

In no event shall the amount allocated to the Account of any Participant for any Fiscal Year, including such Participant's share of forfeitures, exceed Twenty-Five Thousand and 00/100 dollars ($25,000.00) or Twenty-Five Percent (25%) of such Participant's Compensation, whichever is less. Any amounts not allocated to Participants because of this limitation shall be reallocated to the other Participants on the basis of their units described in Paragraph 6(b).

7. *Distribution of Benefits.*

Distributions under this Trust shall be made to the Participants, their beneficiaries, executors or administrators, as the case may be, upon instruction from the Advisory Committee to the Trustee, only upon the following events and in the manner provided hereunder:

(a) On the death of a Participant prior to complete distribution to him of his Account, his death benefits shall be One Hundred percent (100%) of the value of his Account at the time of his death, as of the most recent valuation date. Such benefit shall be paid to his designated beneficiary or beneficiaries.

At any time and from time to time each Participant shall have the unrestricted right to designate the beneficiary or beneficiaries to receive his death benefit, if any, (the "Beneficiary"), and to revoke any such designation. Each such designation (or revocation) shall be evidenced by a written instrument filed with the Advisory Committee, signed by the Participant and, if the primary Beneficiary is other than his spouse, then his spouse, if any. If no such designation is on file with the Advisory Committee at the time of the death of the Participant, or if such designation is not effective for any reason as determined by the Advisory Committee, then to such Participant's spouse, if any, or if no spouse is then surviving, to the executor of the will or administrator of the estate of such Participant.

(b) On retirement of a Participant from the employ of an Employer, his retirement benefit shall be One Hundred percent (100%) of the value of his Account at the date of his retirement. Any Participant who attains the normal retirement age of sixty-five (65) years shall retire from the employment of an Employer unless permitted by such Employer's Board of Directors to remain in the Employer's employ beyond such date.

(c) If a Participant shall become totally and permanently disabled in the judgment of the Advisory Committee, his disability benefit shall be One Hundred percent (100%) of the value of his Account as of the date the Advisory Committee recognizes such Disability. The Advisory Committee may require such evidence as it deems necessary in judging the permanency of such Disability. If a Participant is discharged without cause, then he shall be entitled to One Hundred percent (100%) of the value of his Account as of the date of his discharge.

(d) A Participant who is discharged by an Employer for cause or who voluntarily resigns from the employ of the Employer shall be entitled to a severance benefit equal to the value of the vested portion of his Account at the date of the severance of employment. The balance of his Account shall thereupon be forfeited.

For the purpose of this subsection (d) and subsection (e) below, a Participant's vested portion of his Account shall be an amount equal to the percentage of the value of his Account in the Trust Fund determined on the basis of the number of years that such Participant has been a Full-Time Employee, according to the following schedule.

	Percent
Less than one year	0
One year but less than two years	10
Two years but less than three years	20
Three years but less than four years	30
Four years but less than five years	40
Five years but less than six years	50
Six years but less than seven years	60
Seven years but less than eight years	70
Eight years but less than nine years	80
Nine years but less than ten years	90
Ten years or more	100

Within ninety (90) days after the close of a Fiscal Year in which any Participant voluntarily resigns or is discharged for cause, the Advisory Committee shall apportion among the separate Accounts of all other Participants, as of the last day of such Fiscal Year in which such

Participant voluntarily resigns or is discharged, the forfeitable interest, if any, of such Participant in the Trust Fund as provided in Section 6 hereof.

The nonforfeitable interest of such a resigned or discharged Participant shall be distributed to him as provided in the following paragraph.

(e) The distribution provided in subsections (a), (b), (c) and (d) above shall be made solely in Company stock, except for cash paid to compensate for a fraction of a share, in one or more of the following methods as the Advisory Committee, in its sole discretion, may determine:

(i) One lump sum payment
(ii) Payments in semi-annual or annual installments commencing ninety (90) days from the date of such Employee's death, disability, retirement, discharge or resignation over any period not exceeding fifteen (15) years from such Participant's 65th birthday, which installments shall be in approximately equal numbers of shares of Company stock, any income earned on the undistributed portion of the Participant's account being used to continue such installments until the entire account of the Participant is exhausted.

8. *Inalienability of Benefits.*

(a) *Spendthrift Clause.*

No Participant shall have any right to pledge, hypothecate, anticipate, or in any way create a lien upon any part of the Trust Fund. Except as respecting any indebtedness owing to an Employer (which will be deducted), distributions to Participants, their beneficiaries, heirs or legal representatives, excepting minors and persons under legal Disability, shall be made only to them and upon their personal receipt or endorsements, and no interest in the Trust Fund, or any part thereof, shall be assignable in anticipation of payment, either by voluntary or involuntary act, or by operation of law, or be liable in any way for the debts or defaults of such Participants, their beneficiaries, or heirs. If by reason of any judgment, bankruptcy, or other cause, any Participant, or his beneficiary, cannot receive and enjoy his share in the Trust Fund, the distributions or payments accruing during the existence of such judgment or the pendency of such proceeding may, in the discretion and at the election of the Advisory Committee, (1) be held by the Trustee temporarily, (2) be used by the Trustee in purchasing necessaries for the Participant or his beneficiary, or in such other manner as the Advisory Committee shall deem best for the Participant, or (3) be distributed or paid by the Trustee to the Participant's beneficiary or to the person or persons who at the time of distribution or payment would receive the same were the Participant to die intestate. Any payment made in accordance with the provisions of this subsection shall be final and conclusive upon all persons.

(b) *Distributions to Persons Under Disability.*

Distributions to minors or persons under legal Disability may be made by the Trustee either, (1) directly to said persons, (2) to the legal guardians or conservators of said persons, or (3) by itself expending the same for the education and maintenance of said persons. Except as to (3) immediately above, the Trustee shall not be required to see to the application of such distributions so made to any of said persons, but his or their receipt therefor shall be a full discharge for the Trustee.

9. *Appointment and Membership of Advisory Committee.*

The Board of Directors of the Company shall appoint not less than two (2) nor more than eight (8) Employees to a committee to be known as the Advisory Committee. Each member shall continue to serve until his successor is appointed. Upon a vacancy occurring by reason of death or resignation of a member of the Committee, a successor shall be appointed by the Board. At least one member of the Advisory Committee shall be a director and/or officer of the Company and at least one member shall be a Participant other than a director or officer of the Company.

10. *Organization of Advisory Committee.*

The Advisory Committee shall select a Chairman and a Secretary from among its members. The Advisory Committee may appoint such other agents, who need not be members of such Committee, as it may deem necessary for the effective performance of its duties, whether ministerial or discretionary, as the said Committee may deem expedient or appropriate. The compensation of such agents shall be fixed by the said Committee within limitations set by the Board of Directors of the Employers. The Advisory Committee shall act by majority vote. Its members shall serve as such without compensation. The proper expenses of the Committee, including the compensation of its agents, if any, shall be paid equally by the Employers.

11. *Powers of the Advisory Committee.*

The Advisory Committee shall have complete control of the administration of the Trust herein embodied, with all powers necessary to enable it properly to carry out its duties in that respect. Without limiting the generality of the foregoing, the Committee shall have the power to construe this instrument and to determine all questions that shall arise hereunder, and shall also have all the powers elsewhere in this instrument conferred upon it. It shall decide all questions relating to the eligibility of Employees to participate in the benefits of this Trust, and all questions relative to the length of continuous service of an Employee. The Advisory Committee shall establish investment policy and may retain investment advisors. All investment transactions and disbursements by the Trustee, except for the ordinary expenses of the administration of this Trust, shall be made upon the written direction of the Advisory Committee. The decisions of the Advisory Committee upon all matters within the scope of its authority shall be final.

12. *Records of Advisory Committee.*

All acts and determinations of the Advisory Committee shall be duly recorded by the Secretary thereof, or under his supervision, and all such records, together with such other documents as may be necessary for the administration of the Trust herein embodied shall be preserved in the custody of said Secretary or his successor.

13. *Trust Fund.*

The Trust Fund shall consist of all payments made by the Employers to the Trustee, as provided for hereinabove, together with the net income which shall be produced by the investments of the Trust Fund, which shall be added to the principal annually by the Trustee. The said Trust Fund shall be held, administered and invested in the manner hereinafter provided, as a single fund.

14. *Investment of the Trust Fund.*

(a) The Trust Fund shall be invested and reinvested in common and/or preferred stock of the Company to the extent necessary to enable the Trustee to make the distributions required under the provisions of this Agreement, up to the whole thereof, and to the extent not so invested, may be invested and reinvested in bonds, notes, debentures and stocks, common and preferred, of other Companies; co-mingled trust funds managed by the Trustee; life insurance policies for investment purposes and not for the Account of any individual Participant; mortgages; vendor's interest in contracts for sale of real property having no lien other than taxes and assessments prior to the interest of such Trustee; or other property, real, personal or mixed, in such manner and to such extent as prudent men would do under like circumstances. All investments shall be approved and directed in writing by a majority of the Advisory Committee. Cash may be held uninvested at any time, and from time to time, and in such amount as may be deemed advisable.

(b) The Trustee may also purchase, at the direction of the Advisory Committee, insurance for the benefit of the Trust on the lives of the shareholders of the Employers, and on the lives of those Employees of the Employers whose death would result in a reduction of an Employer's profits.

15. *Administration of the Trust Fund.*

(a) *Accounting.*

The Advisory Committee shall keep the books and records of the Trust Fund and shall do all clerical, bookkeeping and accounting work in connection with the management and administration of the Trust Fund. Within 90 days after the close of each Fiscal Year, the Advisory Committee shall prepare financial statements of the Trust Fund and an annual statement showing the Account of each Participant in the Trust Fund. After the close of each Fiscal Year, and at such other times as the Company may require, the Trustee shall render to the Company a report of the Trust Fund, including a statement of transactions for the period and a statement of assets as of the end of the period.

(b) *Trustee to Hold Trust Assets.*

Title to all the assets of the Trust Fund shall be and remain in the Trustee. The Trustee shall have the custody and care of the assets of the Trust Fund.

(c) *Powers of Trustee.*

The Trustee is authorized and empowered:

(i) To purchase bonds, notes, debentures, stocks, including stock of the Company, mortgages, vendor's interest in contracts for sale, life insurance policies for investment purposes and not for the Account of any individual Participant, or property of the kind described in Section 14.

(ii) To pledge or mortgage, assign, lease, contract to lease, sell for cash or on credit, convert, redeem, exchange for other securities or other property in which the Trust may be invested under this Agreement, or otherwise dispose of any securities or other property at any time held by it.

(iii) To settle, compromise, or submit to arbitration any claims, debts or damages due or owing from the Trust, and to commence or defend suits or legal proceedings, and to represent the Trust in all suits or legal proceedings.

(iv) To exercise any conversion privilege or subscription right available in connection with any securities or property at any time held by it, and subject to the provisions of subparagraph 15(c), (vi), to consent to the reorganization, consolidation, merger or readjustment of the finances of any corporation, company, or association, or to the sale, mortgage, pledge or lease of the property of any corporation, company or association, any of the securities of which may at any time be held by it, and to do any act with reference thereto, including the exercise of options, making of agreements or subscriptions, and the payment of expenses, assessments, or subscriptions, which may be deemed to be necessary or advisable in connection therewith and to hold and to retain any securities or other property which it may so acquire.

(v) To borrow money in such amounts and upon such terms and conditions as may be directed by the Advisory Committee.

(vi) To vote any corporate stock belonging to the Trust Fund and to give proxies for the purpose of such voting to other persons, with or without power of substitution; provided however, that any stock of the Company from time to time comprising a portion of the Trust Fund shall be voted in such manner as the Advisory Committee may direct in writing.

(vii) To improve, manage, protect, subdivide, and partition any real estate forming a part of the Trust Fund; to dedicate to the public use and vacate all or any part thereof; to grant options to lease and to lease for any term (including leases for ninety-nine (99) years or for a longer or shorter period of time) although such term extends beyond the period of this Trust, upon such terms and conditions as may be deemed to be proper; to renew, cancel, and amend or extend leases, and consent to the assignment and modification of any lease on any terms which may be deemed to be necessary, proper or advisable.

(viii) To collect the income, rents, issues, profits and increase of the Trust Fund.

(ix) To grant Puts or acquire Calls for stock of the Company.

(x) To employ agents and attorneys and pay their reasonable compensation and expenses. The Trustee shall incur no liability for the acts or defaults of such agents and attorneys selected by it with due care. The Trustee shall be fully protected in acting upon advice of counsel on questions of law, arising in connection with the administration of this Trust.

(xi) To register any securities held by it hereunder in its own name, or in the name of a nominee, and to hold any securities in bearer form.

(xii) To make, execute and deliver as Trustee any and all instruments in writing necessary or proper for the accomplishment of any of the foregoing powers.

(xiii) Subject to the provisions and limitations herein expressly set forth, the Trustee shall have in general the power to do and perform any and all acts and things in relation to the Trust Fund in the same manner and to the extent as an individual might or could do with respect to his own property. No enumeration of specific powers herein shall be construed as a limitation upon the foregoing general powers, nor shall any of the powers conferred upon the Trustee be exhausted by the use thereof, but each shall be continuing. None of the powers granted the Trustee under this Section shall be exercised except upon, and in accordance with, the written directions of the Advisory Committee; and the Advisory Committee is authorized and empowered, in its sole discretion, to give any such directions to the Trustee.

(d) *Expenses of Trust.*

The Trustee shall pay out of the Trust Fund, to the extent not paid by the Employers or the Company, which shall have the privilege of doing so, all reasonable and necessary expenses, taxes, charges, Trustee's fees, administration costs and fees for attorneys and agents incurred in connection with the administration or operation of the Trust.

(e) *Distribution.*

The Trustee, if and as directed by the Advisory Committee, shall make distributions and payments out of the Trust Fund to Participants in such manner, and in such amounts and for such purposes as may be proper under this Trust Agreement.

(f) *Liability for Distributions.*

The Trustee shall be under no obligation whatsoever to determine whether contributions delivered to it hereunder comply with the provisions of this Trust Agreement, and is obligated only to receive and administer the same pursuant to the terms hereof. It shall be the obligation of the Advisory Committee to determine all facts which may be necessary for the proper allocation of Employers' Contributions, and to determine the basis upon which distributions of any kind are to be made, and to notify the Trustee in writing with respect to such distributions. The Trustee is hereby authorized to act solely upon the basis of such notifications and facts received from the Advisory Committee.

(g) *Actions Conclusive.*

Exercise by the Trustee of any discretion, vested either expressly or by implication in it pursuant to this Trust, shall be conclusive and binding upon all persons directly or indirectly affected, wtihout restriction, however, on its right to reconsider and redetermine such actions.

(h) *Bond Not Required.*

No Trustee acting hereunder shall be required to give bond for the faithful performance of its duties hereunder.

(i) *Trustee Relieved from Uniform Accounting Act.*

The Trustee is relieved of all the duties which would otherwise be placed upon it by the Uniform Trustees' Accounting Act and amendments thereto, if any there be, and any similar act.

(j) *Removal.*

The Company may remove the Trustee at any time, and in case of such removal the Company shall appoint a successor Trustee, which must be a bank or trust company organized and existing under the laws of the United States or of the State of New York. Any successor Trustee shall have the same powers and duties as those conferred upon the Trustee named in this Trust Agreement.

(k) *Resignation of Trustee.*

The Trustee may resign this Trust at any time by giving sixty (60) days' notice, in writing, to the Advisory Committee. Upon such resignation becoming effective, the Trustee shall render to the Advisory Committee an account of its administration of this Trust during the period following that covered by its last approved annual accounting, and shall perform all acts necessary to transfer the assets of the Trust to its successor.

16. *Ammendment of the Trust.*

The Company, by action of its Board of Directors, shall have the right at any time, by an instrument in writing, duly executed and acknowledged and delivered to the Trustee, to modify, alter, or amend this instrument in whole or in part; provided, however, that the duties, powers and liabilitites of the Trustee hereunder shall not be substantially increased without its written consent; and provided further, that the amount which at the time of any such modification, alteration or amendment shall appear as a credit to the account of any Participant or any former Participant, shall not be affected thereby; and provided further that no such amendment shall have the effect of revesting in an Employer any part of the principal or income of the Trust.

17. *Termination of Trust.*

An Employer shall not be deemed hereby to have bound itself to make any contributions whatever hereunder in any year, except to the extent provided for in Section 4 hereof, as said section now stands or as the same may hereafter be amended. The continuance of this Trust is not a contractual obligation of the Company, and the right is reserved to the Company by action of its Board of Directors at any time to discontinue the Trust. The discontinuance of this Trust by the Company shall not have the effect of revesting in the Company any part of the Trust Fund.

If this Trust should be terminated, or if contributions should be discontinued, then any amount that shall appear as a credit to the Account of any Participant, or former Participant, shall not be affected thereby; the said amount, including any interest in unallocated funds, shall be fully vested and shall be paid to the said Participant in the manner as is provided for hereinbelow. In the event of the termination of this Trust, said funds may be paid upon the authority of the Advisory Committee, in five (5) equal annual installments or in a lump sum. Said payments shall be made within a reasonable time thereafter with allowances for the Trustee to liquidate that part of the Trust assets that is necessary to accomplish the said payments, and for the Employers to file required information with Internal Revenue Service and receive its determination letter relative to the termination of the Trust; in all events the said lump sum payments and said annual installments shall be made to commence within sixty (60) days after the allowances for the Trustee and the Employers herein have been complied with. It is understood, however, that mere suspension of contributions by the Employer shall not be construed as a discontinuance of such contributions.

Unless sooner terminated as herein provided, this Trust shall continue in full force and effect until the expiration of twenty-one (21) years after the death of the last surviving Employee, whether active or retired, of the Employer, who shall be a Participant in the Trust Fund on the date of this Trust.

18. *Miscellaneous.*

(a) *Successors, etc.*

This Trust Agreement shall be binding upon all Participants, their beneficiaries, heirs, executors and administrators, upon each of the Employers and the Company and upon the Trustee and its successors. In the event of the dissolution, consolidation or merger of the Company, or the sale by the Company of its assets, the resulting successor person or persons, firm or corporation, may continue this Trust by direction from such person or persons or firm, if not a corporation, and if a corporation, by adopting the same by resolution of its Board of Directors and appointing a new Advisory Committee as though all members thereof had resigned, and by executing a proper Supplemental Agreement to the Trust Agreement. If, within ninety (90) days from the effective date of such dissolution, consolidation, merger or sale of assets, such sucessor does not adopt this Trust, as provided herein, this Trust shall automatically be terminated and the Trust Fund disposed of as provided in Section 17 hereof.

(b) *Construction.* The share of each of the Participants in the Trust Fund as represented by the Account of such Participant, shall constitute a separate Trust. If any provision of this Trust Agreement violates any existing or future law against perpetuities or suspension of the power of alienation of title to property, that part of the Trust Fund subject to such provision shall be administered as herein directed for the period permitted by law, and forthwith thereafter such part of the Trust Fund so affected shall be distributed to the Participant or his beneficiary. The validity and effect of this Trust Agreement and the rights and obligations of all parties hereto and of all other persons affected hereby shall be construed and determined in accordance with the laws of the State of New York.

(c) *Right of Employer to Dismiss Employees.*

Neither the action of the Company in establishing this Trust nor any action taken by it or by the Advisory Committee under the provisions hereof, nor any provisions of this Trust shall be construed as giving to any Employee the right to continued employment by an Employer or any right to any payment whatsoever except to the extent of the benefits provided for by this Trust to be paid from the Trust Fund. The Employers expressly reserve their right at any time to dismiss any Employee without any liability for any claim either against the Trust Fund, for any payment whatsoever except to the extent provided for in this Trust, or against any Employer.

(d) *Trust May Be Adopted by a Subsidiary.*

This Trust may at any time during its existence be adopted by a Subsidiary, by proper resolution of the Subsidiary's Board of Directors, and upon written notification to the

Advisory Committee and to the Trustee, which notification shall include therein a statement that the adopting Subsidiary agrees to be bound by all the rules and regulations of the Trust. Upon such notification, the adopting Subsidiary shall become a part hereof as if an original signator hereto.

(e) *Copies.*

A synopsis of this instrument shall be delivered forthwith to every Participant. A similar copy hereof shall be delivered to each new Employee upon his attaining the status of a Participant. An executed copy of this instrument is available for inspection at the office of the Company.

(f) *Acceptance.*

The Trustee, by joining in the execution of this instrument, hereby accepts the foregoing Trust and agrees to carry out the provisions hereof on its part to be performed.

(g) *Effective Date.*

The effective date of this Trust is April 1, 19   , and the first Fiscal Year of the Trust is the year ended March 31, 19

(h) For purposes of determining eligibility (Paragraph 5), allocation of Employer contributions (Paragraph 6(b), and the vested portion of an Account (Paragraph 7(d), years of service shall be the aggregate number of years of service with all Employers.

IN WITNESS WHEREOF, the parties hereto have caused this Trust to be executed by their proper officers thereunto duly authorized as of the   day of   , 19

(SEAL)

EMPLOYER CORPORATION

By

President

By

Secretary

BANK

By

President

FORM OF OUTLINE OF AN EXPLANATION OF AN ESOP TO EMPLOYEES

Each explanation by an employer to employees of the adoption of an ESOP should be carefully drafted to explain accurately in layman's language the circumstances of the adoption of the Plan and its major provisions. An effective means to communicate adoption of an ESOP to employees is distribution of a form of booklet containing a letter from the Company's Chief Executive Officer and appropriate text under headings similar to those set forth below:

1. *Letter of Chief Executive Officer.* This letter is addressed to the employees and may contain, in addition to other information, facts of the adoption and funding of the ESOP.

2. *Purpose of Plan.* The text may refer to accumulation of capital ownership in the Company by the employees as a basic purpose of the plan and may refer to the possible increase in value of the capital ownership as the Company prospers.

3. *What Employee Stock Ownership Plan Means to You.* The text may refer to the opportunity of the employees to share in the success of the Company, and to the increased incentive to employees to do their best work.

4. *Who Is Eligible?* The text should state requirements for eligibility such as full time employees with 12 months service, etc.

5. *Where Does Money Come From?* The text should set forth the method of initial funding, whether by bank loan or cash contributions by the Company, and should indicate that the employees do not contribute.

6. *How Is the Money Repaid to the Bank?* Where a loan from a bank is involved to

fund the ESOP, a repayment schedule may be included, indicating prospective periodic contributions by the Company to repay the loan.

7. *How Are the Company's Shares Allocated to Employees?* The text should indicate how an aggregate number of shares is set aside for employees to be divided among eligible employees.

8. *How Does Setting Aside of Shares for All Eligible Employees Work?* Description of procedures.

9. *How Does Division of Shares Among Eligible Employees Based on Payroll Work?* Description of procedures.

10. *What Is Total Eligible Payroll.* Here describe compensation as defined for purposes of the plan, ie., whether compensation includes overtimes, bonuses, etc.

11. *When Do I Get Stock Allocated to Me?* Here describe method of allocation, normally at the close of each year of the Trust, together with explanation that each employee receives an annual statement from the Trustees.

12. *How Do I Get My Shares of the Company Stock?* Here describe distribution of shares upon retirement, disability, or death.

13. *What Happens If I Leave the Company's Employ Before Retirement?* Here set forth a description of vesting provisions of the Plan, indicating relationship of years of participation to percentage of allocated shares.

14. *Do I Receive Company Stock If I Am Discharged?* Describe receipt of shares vested in accordance with the answer to Question #13, above, provided that the termination was not caused by dismissal for fraud, etc., causing loss of benefits under the Plan.

15. *May Shares Originally Allocated to the Plan Be Increased?* Here indicate the possibility of additional future contributions of stock to the Plan in accordance with decisions of the Board of Directors.

16. *Who Manages the Trust?* Here the text may describe the Trustee.

17. *What Can All of This Mean to Me?* Here the text may include projections, based on assumed levels of compensation, of shares allocated to employees' accounts, and may indicate that the values of such shares will depend upon the prosperity of the Company.

18. *Who Pays the Income Tax?* The text may indicate to employees that income tax is not paid by employees upon the accumulation of capital for the employees until stock is transferred to the employees from the Trust.

19. *Is There a Market for the Company's Stock?* Here describe market, and also indicate whether the Company will have a right of first refusal with respect to stock offered for sale to third parties.

In addition to the foregoing general comments contained in the booklet, the booklet may contain an additional Questions and Answers Sections made up of specific questions such as are set forth below, each with a concise answer in layman's language:

QUESTION AND ANSWER CHECKLIST

(a) *Question:* What is a full-time employee?

     Answer: Those who work more than 20 hours per week and more than 5 months a year.

(b) *Question:* The first step in the annual allocation of shares is determined by the Company's contribution to the Plan. The illustration in this booklet used the annual repayments of the loan as the minimum contribution. Can the contribution be greater?

     Answer: Yes, at the discretion of the Company's Board of Directors.

(c) *Question:* What happens then?

     Answer: Then the annual allocation of shares will be correspondingly greater.

(d) *Question:* Is there a top limit on what the Company can contribute in any one year?

     Answer: Yes, 15% of total covered compensation.

(e) *Question:* If additional shares are sold to the Trust for future allocations, what determines their value?

     Answer: Fair market value in the judgement of the Committee.

(f) *Question:* Can the assets of the Trust be other than Company common stock?

     Answer: Yes. The Committee can direct the Trust to invest in savings accounts, bank certificates of deposit, high-grade short-term securities, or other equity stock, bonds, or investments deemed by the Committee to be desirable.

(g) *Question:* If the assets in the Trust should earn income like dividends or interest, what happens to this income?

     Answer: It will be allocated to you and may be paid at the discretion of the Committee.

(h) *Question:* After an employee has had company stock allocated to his account, and should he leave the Company for whatever reason and cannot draw out his full share, what happens to these shares remaining in the Trust?

     Answer: These shares are called "Forfeitures." They will be reallocated to employees staying with the Company using the same formula as for the annual contribution by the Company.

(i) *Question:* The Trust must have some expenses. Who pays for this?

     Answer: The Company.

(j) *Question:* Who votes the stock until it is distributed to me in the form of a stock certificate?

     Answer: The Trustee in accordance with directions from the Committee.

(k) *Question:* What will my annual statement from the Trust look like?

     Answer: It will contain the following in tabular form:

        (a) Your balances from the preceding year.

        (b) Your share of the Company's annual contribution and forfeitures, if any.

        (c) Your net shares of any income on the investments.

        (d) Your new balances.

(l) *Question:* Who determines if I have been discharged for just cause and must forfeit all my rights to the Plan?

     Answer: The Committee.

(m) *Question:* When I am eligible to draw out my capital accumulations, how can this be done?

     Answer: Several ways are available to you. See Section 15 of the Plan.

(n) *Question:* What if I die and have no designated beneficiary?
    Answer: Distribution will then be made in this order:
        (a) Your spouse.
        (b) Your children.
        (c) Your parents.
        (d) The executor or administrator of your estate.

(o) *Question:* If I designate a beneficiary, may I later change it?
    Answer: Yes, by written notice to the Committee.

In addition to the general explanation and specific questions and answer sections of the booklet distributed to the employees, the booklet should also set out the complete text of the ESOP. In one instance an employer preceded the complete text of the Plan with a one page introduction as the last page of the text of its booklet preceding the text of the Plan, in the following format:

SUMMARY

This Plan is a unique method of providing you and your family with an opportunity to become owners of the Company. There is no cost to you whatever, other than the tax you must eventually pay on your accumulated capital during your employment at the Company. The success of the Plan, however, is dependent upon your efforts to continue making the Company a growing and profitable operation. There are many ways in which you can help the Company grow and thus increase the value of your stock. Just a few examples are: Make sure that our products reach our customers in first class condition so the customer is satisfied and comes back with repeat orders. Reduce waste and inefficiencies in our plants and offices to a bare minimum. Make suggestions to your supervisor as to how the Company can do a better job. Take an active interest in solving problems of the Company—get involved—it's your Company. Plan to stay at Work with the Company as . . .

It Pays to Stay with the Company!

EMPLOYER CORPORATION EMPLOYEE STOCK OWNERSHIP PLAN ACCOUNTING PROCEDURES

The accounting procedures set forth below are hereby established by the Administrative Committee of Employer Corporation Employee Stock Ownership Plan ("Plan"), pursuant to Article _____, Paragraph __, of the Plan. These procedures are designed to provide rules and guidelines for use in recording the various transactions of the Plan and the interests of the Participants in the Trust.

Terms used in these accounting procedures have the same meaning as when used in the Plan. Additional definitions of terms are provided where necessary.

Part I of the procedures sets forth the General Accounting Rules for recording contributions and allocations where there are no financing or other obligations of the Trust involved. The accounting for distributions to Participants for all situations is also covered in Part I.

Part II sets forth rules to cover situations where debt financing is involved or other obligations are incurred by the Trust in connection with the purchase of Company Stock.

The Procedures are subject to amendment from time to time by the Committee in accordance with the authority vested in the Committee under Article _____ of the Plan.

PART I: GENERAL ACCOUNTING RULES

1. Trust Accounts

(a) *Balance Sheet Accounts*—The Trust's balance sheet accounts for Trust assets should include a Company Stock Fund and an Other Investments Fund maintained in dollars and cents. These accounts are designed to record the value of assets (Company Stock, cash and other property) received, held and disbursed by the Trust.

(1) *Company Stock Fund*—The Company Stock Fund will reflect the value of Company Stock acquired by the Trust. In the case of a purchase of Company Stock for cash or other property, such value will be the actual cost of the shares. In the case of a contribution of Company Stock from the Company, such value will be the fair market value of the shares, as determined by the Committee, at the time that the shares are actually issued to the Trust.

(2) *Other Investments Fund*—The Other Investments Fund will reflect the fair market value of any Employer contributions in cash or other property (other than Company Stock) and the fair market value of receipts attributable to assets credited to the Other Investments Fund. As of each Anniversary Date, the Other Investments Fund will be valued at the fair market value of all its assets.

The balances in these Funds are to be adjusted to reflect receipt and disbursement, including distribution, of Trust assets.

(b) *Non-Balance Sheet Accounts*—The Accounts described below are non-balance sheet accounts of the Trust. They are designed to reflect the value of Trust assets prior to allocation to the Accounts of Participants.

(1) *Unallocated Company Stock Account*—This Account, maintained in shares of Company Stock, will be initially credited with all shares of Company Stock received by the Trust. This applies to all shares of Company Stock regardless of how they are acquired by the Trust, whether by contribution from the Company or by purchase from the Company or shareholders (including former Participants). As of each Anniversary Date, shares of Company Stock will be transferred out of this Account and allocated to the Participants' Company Stock Accounts, as described below.

(2) *Unallocated Other Investments Account*—This Account, maintained in dollars and cents, will be initially credited with the fair market value of all cash and other assets received by the Trust. It will be debited with any payments in unallocated cash or other assets from the Other Investments Fund. As of each Anniversary Date, the total balance of this Account will be debited and allocated to Participants' Other Investments Accounts as described below.

2. Participants' Accounts

Records are to be kept separately for the Accounts of Participants under the Plan.

(a) *Company Stock Account*—A Company Stock Account is established for each Participant. It reflects the number of shares of Company Stock which have been allocated to the Participant. The number of shares shall be uniformly recorded in either hundredths or thousandths of a share.

(b) *Other Investments Account*—An Other Investments Account is established for each Participant. It is valued in dollars and cents and reflects the fair market value of cash and other assets of the Trust allocated to each Participant as of each Anniversary Date.

3. Annual Allocations to Participants' Accounts

All Company Stock received by the Trust will initially be credited to the Unallocated Company Stock Accounts. The value of all other assets received by the Trust will be credited to the Unallocated Other Investments Accounts. (The Trust Funds, described in Section 1, reflecting the balance sheet accounts of the Trust, should also reflect these receipts.) As of each Anniversary Date, the amounts of these Accounts will be allocated to Participants' Accounts as follows:

(a) *Employer Contributions*

(1) Employer Contributions in Company Stock are allocated to Participants' Company Stock Accounts in accordance with the allocation formula in Section ___ of the Plan.

(2) Employer Contributions in cash or other property are allocated to Participants' Other Investments Accounts in accordance with the allocation formula in Section ___ of the Plan.

(b) *Forfeitures*

(1) To determine the amount forfeited by a terminated Participant, the following steps should be taken:

(A) Determine the value of the Company Stock in the Participant's Company Stock Account by multiplying the current fair market value per share by the number of shares.

(B) This amount plus the current balances in his Other Investments Account gives the total value of the Participant's Account balances.

(C) To compute the amount of the Forfeiture, multiply the total value of his Account balances by the percentage that is not vested, as determined by the vesting schedule in Section ____ of the Plan.

(D) The Forfeiture should be charged to the Other Investments Account balance to the extent thereof. If the Forfeiture exceeds the Other Investments Account balance, the balance of the Forfeiture will be charged to the Company Stock Account.

(2) The Forfeiture of balances from Participants' Other Investments Accounts is allocated to the Other Investments Accounts of remaining Participants, as described in Section ____ of the Plan.

(3) The Forfeiture of shares of Company Stock from Participants' Company Stock Accounts is allocated to the remaining Participants, as described in Section ____ of the Plan.

(c) *Dividends on Company Stock*

(1) Cash dividends received during a year on shares of Company Stock that have been allocated to Participants' Company Stock Accounts will be credited to the respective Participants' Other Investments Accounts.

(2) Cash dividends received during a year on shares of Company Stock in the Unallocated Company Stock Account will be added to the Trust net income (or loss) and allocated to Participants' Other Investments Accounts as provided in subsection (d) below.

(3) Stock dividends received during a year on shares of Company Stock that have been allocated to Participants' Company Stock Accounts will be credited to the respective Participants' Company Stock Accounts.

(4) Stock dividends received during a year on shares of Company Stock in the Unallocated Company Stock Account will be credited to the Unallocated Company Stock Account and allocated in the same manner as the shares with respect to which they were received.

(5) In the event that cash dividends are distributed to Participants by the Trust (pursuant to Section _____ of the Plan), the amount of the distribution will be debited to the respective Participants' Other Investments Accounts.

(d) *Net Income (or Loss) of the Trust*

(1) As of each Anniversary Date, the net income (or loss) of the Trust will be computed for the Other Investments Fund. Net income (or loss) includes the increase (or decrease) in the fair market value of the assets of the Trust (other than Company Stock), interest income, dividends (other than on allocated Company Stock) and other income (or loss) of the Trust, less any expenses of the Trust that are not paid by the Company. It does not include any interest paid on a loan used by the Trust to purchase Company Stock or under an installment contract for the purchase of Company Stock.

(2) As of each Anniversary Date, the amount of the net income (or loss) will be allocated to the Participants' Other Investments Accounts in proportion to the relative Account balances as of the preceding Anniversary Date (reduced by any distribution of Capital Accumulation during the Plan Year).

4. Allocating Cash Purchases of Company Stock by Trust

The following rules apply where there is no debt incurred for the purchase of Company Stock. Part II of the Manual sets forth rules to cover situations where there are debt obligations (including loans and installment purchases) incurred by the Trust in connection with the purchase of Company Stock.

Shares of Company Stock purchased by the Trust with cash or other property must be allocated to the Participants' Company Stock Accounts. The determination of how to allocate those shares will depend upon the source of the funds used to purchase the Company Stock.

(a) Where purchases are made from current Employer Contributions of cash or other property—

(1) Employer Contributions of cash or other property should be allocated and credited to the Other Investments Accounts of Participants as provided in Section 3(a)(2) above. This allocation should be made as of the particular Anniversary Date prior to recording the purchase of Company Stock irrespective of whether the purchase is made prior to or after the Anniversary Date.

(2) The amount of the purchase price which is paid by the Trust should be debited to the Other Investments Accounts of the Participants in the same proportions as the Employer Contribution was allocated, as described above. This will reduce the Other Investments Accounts of all Participants for the amount of cash or other property disbursed by the Trust.

(3) The number of shares of Company Stock purchased by the Trust should then be credited to the Company Stock Accounts of the Participants in the same proportions as the debit for the payment was allocated to their Other Investments Accounts.

(b) Where purchases are made from amounts previously allocated to Participants' Other Investments Accounts, the Committee will determine how much of the purchase price is to be charged to the Other Investments Accounts of Participants in proportion to the Other Investments Account balances on the preceding Anniversary Date (reduced by the amount of any distribution during the year).

(2) The number of shares of Company Stock purchased by the Trust should be credited to the Company Stock Accounts of the Participants in the same proportions as the debits for the payment were allocated to their Other Investments Accounts.

(c) Where purchases are made partly from a current Employer Contribution and partly from existing assets of the Trust, or where the source for the purchases is unclear, the Committee should account for the purchases on the basis which most nearly reflects the actual origin of the funds.

(d) In all cases, adjustments in the Trust Fund balances should be made to reflect the charges in assets of the Trust as provided in Section 1(a).

5. Accounting for Distributions

(a) The distribution of a Participant's Capital Accumulation *must* be in shares of Company Stock (except for the value of fractional shares), as required by Section ___ of the Plan. Where a Participant's Capital Accumulation includes a balance in his Other Investments Account, such balance must be used to acquire shares of Company Stock for distribution. This generally will be done as a bookkeeping matter within the Trust, as described below.

(b) The Participant's Other Investments Account will be debited for the full amount of the credit balance thereof. This amount will be credited to the Unallocated Other Investments Account.

(c) A number of shares of Company Stock, equal in value to the Participant's Other Investments Account balance, will be credited to said Participant's Company Stock Account and distributed as part of his Capital Accumulation. The value of the shares of Company Stock will be the fair market value, as determined by the Committee, on the Anniversary Date as of which the Capital Accumulation is computed.

(d) The shares credited to the Participant's Company Stock Account will come from one of the following sources:

(1) If there are shares in the Unallocated Company Stock Account, that Account would be debited for the number of shares. In this case, the amount credited to the Unallocated Other Investments Account, pursuant to subsection (b) above, will be allocated to the remaining Participants in the same manner as the shares of Company Stock would have otherwise been allocated.

(2) If there are no shares of Company Stock in the Unallocated Company Stock Account, the shares must come from Company Stock contributed or forfeited that year, prior to allocation of the remainder to other Participants under Section 3(b) above. In this case, the amount credited to the Unallocated Other Investments Account, pursuant to subsection (b) above, will be allocated to the remaining Participants' Accounts as the Company Stock contributed or forfeited would have been allocated.

(3) If sufficient shares of Company Stock are not available from either the Unallocated Company Stock Account or from current Employer Contributions or Forfeitures to credit the Participant's Company Stock Account, as provided in subsection (c) above, the Trust should acquire additional shares from the Company or from

shareholders (including former Participants) to the extent that they are available.

(e) If shares of Company Stock distributed to a Participant (or Beneficiary) are repurchased by the Company in accordance with the terms of the form of enrollment for participation provided for in Section_____of the Plan, the repurchase shall be accounted for as a cash purchase under Section 4, or a financed purchase under Part II, as the case may be.

6. Stock Splits and Capital Reorganizations

Any Company Stock received by the Trust as the result of a stock split or any reorganization or recapitalization of the Company shall be credited to the Account to which the Company Stock affected is credited.

7. Fractional Shares

If a Participant's Capital Accumulation includes a fractional share of Company Stock at the time that a distribution is called for under the Plan, the fair market value of such fractional share, as determined by the Committee, shall be transferred from the Unallocated Other Investments Account to the Participant's Other Investments Account and distributed in cash. The fractional share shall be transferred from the Participant's Company Stock Account to the Unallocated Company Stock Account.

PART II: FINANCED PURCHASE OF COMPANY STOCK

8. In General

The rules contained in this Part cover situations where the Trust purchases shares of Company Stock and the purchase price is paid (i) with the proceeds of a loan to the Trust, (ii) in installments pursuant to a stock purchase or other agreement, or (iii) in any combination thereof. All purchases of Company Stock paid for in this manner shall be referred to as "financed purchases" of Company Stock. The shares of Company Stock will initially be offset by the amount of the debt and the Participants will not have an equity in the shares. Accordingly, while the shares should be credited to the Company Stock Fund, with a corresponding debt in a liability account to record the Trust's liability for financed purchases, the shares are not allocated to the Participants' Accounts at that time. The purpose of this Part II is to set forth rules for the allocation of such shares to the Company Stock Accounts of the Participants as the debt is paid off.

9. Initial Allocation Upon Purchase of Company Stock

(a) Where shares of Company Stock are acquired entirely as a financed purchase, all of the shares shall be credited initially to the Unallocated Company Stock Account.

(b) Where shares of Company Stock are acquired (i) in part with a downpayment out of funds in the Trust (including current Employer Contributions) and (ii) in part as a financed purchase, the total number of shares of Company Stock purchased shall be allocated proportionately between the two categories. The number of shares of Company Stock fully paid for out of existing Trust funds shall be allocated to Company Stock Accounts as provided in Section 4 of Part I (General Accounting Rules). The number of shares acquired as a financed purchase shall be credited initially to the Unallocated Company Stock Accounts.

10. Allocation from Unallocated Company Stock Account

In case of a financed purchase of Company Stock, as the Trust pays a part or all of the debt (principal and interest), a part or all of the Company Stock in the Unallocated Company Stock Account is allocated and credited to the Company Stock Accounts of the Participants. The following rules will apply:

(a) The allocation of Employer Contributions, Forfeitures, and net income (or loss) shall be recorded as of the Anniversary Date as of which they are determined. All other transactions are recorded as of the Anniversary Date after they occur. Thus, Employer Contributions in cash for one year may be actually received by the Trust and used to pay a part of the debt in the following year. In that event, the cash contribution would be allocated to the Participants' Other Investments Accounts as of the Anniversary Date of the first year. The payment on the debt and the allocation of Company Stock to the Participants' Company Stock Accounts would be recorded as of the Anniversary Date of the second year.

(b) As of the Anniversary Date of a year during which payments are made on the debt, the shares which are thereby deemed to be purchased and paid for by the Trust are allocated to Participants' Company Stock Accounts. The number of shares which shall be released from the Unallocated Company Stock Account shall be determined by multiplying the total number of shares acquired in the particular financed purchase by the following fraction:

(1) The numerator is the amount of all debt payments made during that year (including principal *and* interest).

(2) The denominator is the total amount of all payments made and to be made on that entire debt (including principal *and* interest) incurred for that financed purchase.

The product of multiplying this fraction by the number of shares purchased as a financed purchase will be the number of shares of Company Stock to be allocated to the Participants' Company Stock Accounts for the particular year based upon the repayment of debt.

(c) Where the interest rate is fixed, the total interest over the term of the financing is readily determinable. Where the interest rate fluctuates, the foregoing formula shall be followed, except that, in computing the number of shares to be released in connection with payments made following the change in interest rates, all payments made and shares allocated in years prior to the change in interest shall thereafter be excluded from the formula so that:

(1) The numerator will be calculated as before.

(2) The denominator shall exclude payments made prior to the interest rate change and shall be based in part upon a projection of the total interest cost assuming the new interest rate remains constant for the remainder of the repayment period.

(3) The multiplicand shall include only those shares not previously allocated during the terms of prior interest rates.

(d) If additional debt is incurred to meet payments on the original financed purchase, the number of shares which shall be released from the Unallocated Company Stock Account shall be determined by multiplying the unallocated shares remaining from the original financed purchase by the following fraction:

(1) The numerator is the amount of payments made during that year (including principal and interest) less any proceeds of the new debt applied toward payments on the original debt.

(2) The denominator is the total debt payments made that year and to be made (including principal and interest) on the original debt, less any proceeds of the new debt applied toward payments on the original debt, plus the total amount of the payments made and to be made on the new debt.

(e) Any payments made by the Trust under a financed purchase of Company Stock will be debited to the Participants' Other Investments Accounts for each Participants' allocable share of the payment. The debits to the Other Investments Accounts will be allocated among the Participants according to the source of the funds used to make the payment. (See Section 4 of Part I.) Where the source of funds is Employer Contributions, the Other Investments Accounts will be debited in the same proportions as Employer Contributions were allocated to their Accounts initially.

(f) The number of shares of Company Stock released from the Unallocated Company Stock Account, as determined in subsection (b), (c), or (d) above, shall be allocated and credited to the Participants' Company Stock Accounts in the same proportions as their Other Investments Accounts are debited, pursuant to subsection (e) above.

EMPLOYER CORPORATION
Administrative Committee of the
Employees Stock Ownership Plan

By

Authorized Signature

Dated:
September   , 19

Application for Determination for Defined Contribution Plan
For Profit-sharing, Stock Bonus and Money Purchase Plans
(Under sections 401(a), 405(a), 414(i) and 501(a) of the Internal Revenue Code)

This Form is Open to Public Inspection

File in Duplicate

1 (a) Name, address and ZIP code of employer

Telephone number ▶ ( )

(b) Name, address and ZIP code of plan administrator, if other than employer

(c) Administrator's identification number ▶   Telephone number ▶ ( )

2 Employer's identification number

3 Business code number (see instructions)

4 Date incorporated or business commenced

5 Employer's taxable year ends

6 (a) Determination requested for:

(i) ☐ Initial qualification—date plan adopted ▶ .... (ii) ☐ Amendment—date adopted ▶ ....

(b) Were employees who are interested parties given the required notification of the filing of this application? . ☐ Yes ☐ No

7 Type of entity: **(a)** ☐ Corporation **(b)** ☐ Subchapter S corporation **(c)** ☐ Professional service corporation **(d)** ☐ Sole proprietor **(e)** ☐ Partnership **(f)** ☐ Tax exempt organization **(g)** ☐ Other (specify) ▶

8 (a) Name of Plan

(b) Plan number ▶ .... **(c)** Plan year ends ▶ ....

(d) Is this a Keogh (H.R. 10) plan? . . . . ☐ Yes ☐ No

(e) If "Yes," is an owner-employee in the plan? ☐ Yes ☐ No

9 (a) If this is an adoption of a master or prototype plan (other than Keogh), enter name of such plan

(b) Opinion letter serial number

(c) If this is not an adoption of a master or prototype plan, is the plan and trust (or custodial account) agreement patterned after and substantially the same as another plan and trust (or custodial account) agreement which conforms to the participation and vesting standards of the Employee Retirement Income Security Act of 1974 and on which a favorable determination or opinion letter was issued? . . . . ☐ Yes ☐ No

If "Yes," see specific instructions.

10 Type of plan: **(a)** ☐ Profit-sharing **(b)** ☐ Stock bonus **(c)** ☐ Money purchase

11 Effective date of plan | **12** Effective date of amendment | **13** Date plan was communicated to employees ▶ ....

How communicated ▶

	Section and page number	GOVERNMENT USE ONLY
14 (a) Indicate the general eligibility requirements for participation under the plan and indicate the section and page number of plan or trust where each provision is contained:		
(i) ☐ All employees (v) Length of service (number of years) ▶		
(ii) ☐ Hourly rate employee only (vi) Minimum age (specify) ▶		
(iii) ☐ Salaried employee only (vii) Maximum age (specify) ▶		
(iv) ☐ Other job class (specify) ▶ .... (viii) Minimum pay (specify) ▶		
(b) Are the eligibility requirements the same for future employees? . . . ☐ Yes ☐ No		
If "No," explain ▶		
(c) Does the plan recognize service with other employers? . . . . ☐ Yes ☐ No		
If "Yes," explain ▶		

15 Coverage of plan at (give date) ▶ ....

Enter here the number of self-employed individuals ▶

	Number	
(a) Total employed, see specific instructions		
(b) Exclusions under plan (do not count an employee more than once):		
(i) Minimum age or years of service required (specify) ▶		
(ii) Employees on whose behalf retirement benefits were the subject of collective bargaining		
(iii) Nonresident aliens who receive no earned income from United States sources		
(c) Total exclusions, sum of (b)(i) through (iii)		
(d) Balance, line (a) less line (c)		
(e) Ineligible under plan on account of (do not count an employee included in (b)):		
(i) Minimum pay		
(ii) Hourly-paid		
(iii) Other (specify) ▶		
(f) Total ineligible, sum of (e)(i) through (iii)		
(g) Number eligible to participate, (d) less (f)		
(h) Number of employees participating in plan		
(i) Enter percent eligible, (g) divided by (d) . . . . | %		
(j) Enter percent of eligible employees participating, (h) divided by (g) . . . | %		

Under penalties of perjury, I declare that I have examined this application, including accompanying statements, and to the best of my knowledge and belief it is true, correct and complete.

Signature ▶_____ Title ▶_____ Date ▶_____

Signature ▶_____ Title ▶_____ Date ▶_____

179

(Section references are to the Internal Revenue Code)	Yes	No	Section and page number	GOVERNMENT USE ONLY
15 Coverage *(continued)*:				
(k) If percent in (j) is less than 80, see specific instructions.				
(l) Total number of participants, include certain retired and terminated employees, see specific instructions ▶				
16 Employee contributions:				
(a) Are they mandatory?				
If "Yes," specify rate or rates ▶ _____				
(b) Are voluntary contributions limited to 10% of compensation for all qualified plans? . . .				
(c) Are employee contributions nonforfeitable?				
17 Employer contributions:				
(a) Under a profit-sharing or stock bonus plan, are they determined under—				
(i) ☐ A definite formula *(ii)* ☐ An indefinite formula *(iii)* ☐ Both				
(b) Under profit-sharing or stock bonus plans are contributions limited to—				
(i) ☐ Current earnings *(ii)* ☐ Accumulated earnings *(iii)* ☐ Combination				
(c) Money purchase—Enter rate of contribution ▶				
18 Integration:				
Is this plan integrated with Social Security or Railroad Retirement?				
If "Yes," see specific instructions.				
19 Vesting:				
(a) Vesting Schedule—Check the appropriate box to indicate the vesting provisions of the plan:				
(i) ☐ Full and immediate				
(ii) ☐ Full vesting after 10 years of service				
(iii) ☐ 5- to 15-year vesting, i.e., 25% after 5 years of service, 5% additional for each of the next 5 years, then 10% additional for each of the next 5 years				
(iv) ☐ Rule of 45 (see section 411(a)(2)(C))				
(v) ☐ For each year of service, commencing with the 4th such year, vesting not less than 40% after 4 years of service, 5% additional for each of the next 2 years, and 10% additional for each of the next 5 years				
(vi) ☐ 100% vesting within 5 years after contributions are made (class year plans only)				
(vii) ☐ Other (specify) ▶ _____				

(b) If box (a)(v) was checked, check whether you include the following years of service under the vesting provisions of the plan:	Yes	No		
(i) Years of service before age 22				
(ii) Years of service for a period during which the employee declined to contribute to plan requiring employee contributions				
(iii) Years of service during which the employer did not maintain the plan or a predecessor plan				
(iv) Years of service excluded under section 411(a)(6)				
(v) Years of service described in section 411(a)(4)(E)				
(vi) Years of service described in 411(a)(4)(F)				

20 Administration:				
(a) Fund type of entity: *(i)* ☐ Trust *(ii)* ☐ Custodial account *(iii)* ☐ Non-trusteed				
If you checked (i) or (ii), enter date executed ▶ _____				
(b) Enter name and identifying number of fiduciary (trustee or custodian), if any: ▶ _____				
(c) Enter name and identifying number of fund (trust or custodial account), if any: ▶ _____				

	Yes	No		
(d) Does trust agreement prohibit reversion of funds to the employer?				
(e) Specify the limits placed on the purchase of insurance contracts, if any:				
(i) Ordinary life ▶ _____				
(ii) Term insurance ▶ _____				
(iii) Other (specify) ▶ _____				
(f) If the trustees may earmark specific investments, including insurance contracts, are such investments subject to the employee's consent, or purchased ratably where employee consent is not required?				
(g) If Puerto Rican trust, does it qualify for tax exemption under the laws of Puerto Rico? . . .				

	Yes	No	Section and page number	GOVERNMENT USE ONLY

21 Allocations and distributions:

(a) Are contributions allocated on the basis of total compensation? . . . . . .
If "No," see specific instructions.

(b) Enter the maximum amount of employer contribution (or rate of compensation) that may be allocated to a participant ▶ _____ _____

(c) Are trust assets valued at current fair market value? . . . .

(d) Trust assets are valued:
   (i) ☐ Annually   *(ii)* ☐ Semi-annually   *(iii)* ☐ Quarterly
   (iv) ☐ Other (specify) ▶ _____

(e) Trust earnings and losses are allocated on the basis of:
   (i) ☐ Account balances
   (ii) ☐ Other (specify) ▶ _____

(f) Forfeitures are allocated, in case of profit-sharing or stock bonus plan:
   (i) ☐ On basis of total compensation
   (ii) ☐ Other (specify) ▶ _____
   and, in case of money purchase plan:
   (iii) ☐ Reduce employer contributions
   (iv) ☐ Other (specify) ▶ _____

(g) May vested benefits be forfeited because of withdrawal of a participant's contributions or earnings thereon? . . . .

(h) Normal retirement age is ▶ .... State years of service required ▶ ....

(i) Early retirement age is ▶ .... State years of service required ▶ ....

(j) Is the amount distributable at early retirement limited to vested interest? . .

(k) Is employer's consent required for early retirement? . . . .

(l) Other event permitting distribution (specify) ▶ _____
_____

(m) Are distributions permitted prior to termination of employment? . . . . .

(n) Distribution of account balances may be made in:
   (i) ☐ Lump sum   *(ii)* ☐ Annuity contracts
   (iii) ☐ Substantially equal annual installments—not exceeding ▶ .... years
   (iv) ☐ Other (specify) ▶ _____

(o) If distributions are made in installments, are they credited with:
   (i) ☐ Fund earnings
   (ii) ☐ Interest at a rate of ▶ ....% per year
   (iii) ☐ Other (specify) ▶ _____

(p) If insurance contracts are distributed, are the modes of settlement contained in the contracts limited to those provided under the plan? . . . .

(q) Does the plan provide that the payment of benefits, unless the employee elects otherwise, will commence not later than the 60th day after the latest of (1) the close of the plan year in which the participant attains the earlier of age 65 or the normal retirement age specified under the plan, (2) the close of the plan year in which occurs the 10th anniversary of the year in which participant commenced participation or (3) the close of the plan year in which the participant terminates his service with the employer? . . . .

(r) If this is a stock bonus plan, are distributions made in employer stock? . .

(s) In the case of a merger or consolidation with another plan or transfer to another plan, will each participant be entitled to the same or greater benefit as if plan had terminated? . . . .

(t) Are loans to participants in excess of their vested interest permitted? . . .
If "Yes," explain ▶ _____

(u) Does plan prohibit the assignment or alienation of benefits? . . . . . .

(v) Does plan permit divestment for cause? . . . .

22 Termination:

(a) Is there a provision in the plan for terminating the plan and/or trust? . . .

(b) Are the amounts credited to employee accounts nonforfeitable upon termination or partial termination of the plan? . . . .

(c) Upon complete discontinuance of contributions under a profit-sharing or stock bonus plan are the employees' rights under the plan nonforfeitable? . . . . .

23 Miscellaneous:

(a) Has power of attorney been submitted with the application (or previously submitted)? . . . .

(b) Have you completed and attached Schedule A (Form 5301)? . . . .

23 Miscellaneous *(continued)*:	Yes	No	Section and page number	GOVERNMENT USE ONLY
(c) Have you completed and attached Form 5302?				
(d) Is the adopting employer a member of a controlled group of corporations or under common control in the case of partnerships and proprietorships? . . If "Yes," see instructions.				
(e) Is any issue relating to the qualification of this plan or exemption of the trust currently pending before the Internal Revenue Service, the Department of Labor or any court? . . . . If "Yes," attach explanation.				
(f) Other qualified plans—Enter for each other qualified plan you maintain (do not include plans that were established under union-negotiated agreements that involved other employers):				
(i) Name of plan ▶				
(ii) Type of plan ▶				
(iii) Rate of employer contribution, if fixed ▶				
(iv) Monthly benefit, if defined benefit plan ▶				
(v) Number of participants ▶				

24 This section pertains to Keogh (H.R. 10) plans only:	Yes	No		
(a) Do owner-employees have the option to participate?				
(b) May benefits be paid to owner-employees before age 59½, except for disability?				
(c) May excess contributions be made for self-employed individuals?				
(d) Is a definition of earned income provided?				
(e) Are distributions of benefits to owner-employees required to commence not later than age 70½?				
(f) Is any self-employed individual covered under this plan also covered under any other plan as a self-employed individual?				
(g) Does plan prohibit the allocation of forfeitures to self-employed individuals? .				

25 In the case of a request on an initial qualification, have the following documents been included with the application as required by instructions:				
(a) Certified copies of all instruments constituting the plan or joinder agreement? .				
(b) Copy of trust indenture?				
(c) Specimen copy of each type of individual insurance contract?				
(d) Balance sheet of the trust or custodial account?				
(e) Statement of receipts and disbursements of the trust or custodial account? . .				
(f) Evidence that retirement benefits were the subject of good faith bargaining between employee representatives and employer(s)—where that has occurred and is the basis for excluding certain employees, see section 410(b)(2)(A)? .				
(g) Specimen copy of formal announcement containing detailed description to employees?				

26 In the case of a request involving an amendment, after initial qualification, have the following documents been included:				
(a) A certified copy of the amendment(s)?				
(b) Balance sheet and statement of receipts and disbursements of trust or custodial account? . .				
(c) A description of the amendment covering the items changed and an explanation of the provisions before and after the amendment?				
(d) A completely restated plan? *				
(e) A working copy of the plan in which there has been incorporated all of the previous amendments representing the provisions of the plan as currently in effect? *				
(f) Certified copies of all amendments adopted since the date of the last determination letter for which no determination letter has been issued by the Internal Revenue Service? *				
(g) Specimen copy of formal announcement containing detailed description to employees?				

*If plan is being amended for the first time to conform to the participation and vesting standards of the Employee Retirement Income Security Act of 1974, or if the plan has been amended at least three times since the last restated plan was submitted, one of the documents specified under (d) or (e) must be attached.

If more space is needed for any item, attach additional sheets of the same size.

Department of the Treasury
Internal Revenue Service

Instructions for Form 5301

(March 19 __)

Application for Determination for Defined Contribution Plan for Profit-Sharing, Stock Bonus and Money Purchase Plans

(Section References are to the Internal Revenue Code Unless Otherwise Specified)

General Information Regarding Application for and the Issuance of Determination Letters with Respect to Defined Contribution Plans under the Employee Retirement Income Security Act of 1974

An advance determination may be sought from the Internal Revenue Service with respect to the qualification of a defined contribution plan and the exempt status of any related trust.

If you intend to request an advance determination, your request should be submitted as early as possible so that if necessary, the plan may be amended, so as to qualify for its first year of operation. Except as provided in section 401(b), an amendment cannot retroactively qualify a plan for a taxable year prior to the year in which the amendment is adopted. Section 401(b) permits certain retroactive amendments provided such amendments are made within the time prescribed by law for filing the return (including extensions) for the taxable year of the employer in which such plan or amendment was adopted or such later time as the Commissioner of Internal Revenue may designate.

Please follow the instructions carefully in completing the application form and check it over before submitting it to make sure the information provided is accurate and complete in all respects. Incomplete applications will be returned without action. In addition, the Internal Revenue Service may rely on the statements attested to in the application as interpretive of the intent expressed in the language of the plan. Incorrect or misleading information on the application may void any favorable determination letter issued in response to your application.

General Conditions Affecting All Applications and Filing Information

This application must be filed in duplicate; but attach only one copy of each document and statement listed in items 25 and 26. Please complete each item on the application. If an Item does not apply, so indicate with "NA."

If more than one employer maintains a plan, file one application and attach thereto a separate page one of Form 5301 and a separate Form 5302 for each employer who adopted the plan.

A. Who May File.

1. Any employer (including a sole proprietor or a partnership which has adopted an individually designed Keogh (H.R. 10) plan) or plan administrator desiring a determination letter as to initial qualification or amendment of a plan that does not result from collective bargaining. File Form 5303 for collectively-bargained plans.

2. Any plan administrator desiring a determination letter as to initial qualification or amendment of a plan that involves more than one employer (including controlled groups of corporations and employers under common control) but does not result from collective bargaining. In such case, submit a single application.

3. Any employer or plan administrator desiring a determination letter as to compliance with the applicable requirements of a foreign situs trust as relating to the taxability of beneficiaries (section 402(c)) and deductions for employer contributions (section 404(a)(4)).

Note: *Governmental and church plans, etc., to which the participation, vesting and funding standards in Title II of the Employee Retirement Income Security Act do not apply should not use Form 5301. They should use Form 4573.*

This form may not be filed by a sole proprietor or by a partnership which has adopted a Keogh master or prototype plan previously approved by the Internal Revenue Service.

B. What to File.

1. For initial qualification: The application form in duplicate and a copy of the documents and statements listed in item 25.

2. For Amendments: The application form in duplicate and a copy of the documents and statements listed in item 26.

These forms apply to both individually designed plans and joinders to approved master or prototype (other than Keogh) plans.

A separate application must be filed for each defined contribution plan. The term "defined contribution plan" means a plan which provides for an individual account for each participant and for benefits based solely on the amount contributed to the participant's account, and any income, expenses, gains and losses, and any forfeitures of accounts of other participants which may be allocated to such participant's account.

Whether the application is for an initial qualification or for an amendment, attach a completed Form 5302.

3. For plans of controlled groups of corporations or common control employers, submit the documents and statements listed in item 25 or 26 and, in addition, attach a list of the member employers and explain in detail their relationship, the types of plans each member has and the plans common to all member employers.

C. Where to File.

1. A single employer must file with the District Director for the district in which the principal place of business of the employer is located.

2. A parent company and each of its subsidiaries that adopt a single plan must file with the District Director for the district in which the principal place of business of the parent is located, whether or not separate or consolidated income tax returns are filed.

3. An employer adopting a single plan of multiple employers (for example a plan for companies related through common ownership or stockholding, other than parent and subsidiaries) must file with the District Director for the district in which is located the principal place of business of the trustee, or if not trusteed, or if more than one trustee, the principal or usual meeting place of the trustees or plan supervisors.

4. Domestic employers adopting foreign situs trusts should file with the District Director in which the principal place of business of the employer is located.

Foreign employers should file with the Director of International Operations, Benjamin Franklin Station, P.O. Box 896, Washington, D.C. 20044.

D. Signature.—The application must be signed by the plan administrator, proprietor, a partner, or principal officer or trustee authorized to sign.

Specific Instructions

1(a). Enter the name and address of the employer.

1(b) and (c). If a plan administrator, other than the employer, has been appointed, enter the name, address and identification number of such administrator. If none appointed, enter "NA."

3. See pages 3 and 4 for a list of business codes. Select the one that best describes the nature of the employer's business and enter the code number on line 3.

6(a). You must check box (i) or (ii) or both. If the plan or amendment was executed, enter the date signed.

6(b). Section 3001 of the Employee Retirement Income Security Act of 1974 states that the applicant must provide evidence that each employee who qualifies as an interested party (see section 7476(b)(1)) has been notified of the filing of the application. Rules defining "interested parties" and providing for the form of notification are contained in the regulations.

7. If the plan involves more than one employer, check box (g) and enter appropriate explanation, i.e., controlled group of corporations, employers under common control, or uncontrolled group of employers.

8(a). Enter the name you designated for your plan.

8(b). You should assign a three-digit number, beginning with "001" and continuing in numerical sequence, to each plan you adopt. Such numbering will differentiate your plans. Enter your three-digit number here. The number that is assigned to a plan must not be changed or used for any other plan.

8(c). Plan year means calendar, policy or fiscal year on which the records of the plan are kept.

9(c). If you checked "Yes" to question 9(c), attach an exhibit that gives the name of the approved plan, the identifying number of the trust or custodial account and the office that issued the letter. Also show the language differences between the two plans and agreements. Failure to show all the language differences may invalidate any letter issued for this plan.

15. Coverage.—In general, if your plan does not meet the requirements of section 410(b)(1)(A) (70–80% rule), you must submit a schedule using the format below to show that your plan meets the requirements of section 410(b)(1)(B) The question of acceptable classification is a continuing one and must be met in all subsequent years as well. You should review your classification at the time you submit your Form 4848, Annual Employer's Return for Employees' Pension or Profit-Sharing Plans.

1	2		3	4	5	6	7
Group	*Compensation range		Total employees	Statutory exclusions 410(b)(2)	Other exclusions	Employees participating (3 minus sum of 4 and 5)	Participants who are officers or shareholders
	At least	But not more than					
Totals							

*The compensation brackets used must reflect the pay pattern of the employer.

Employees included in collective bargaining.—Section 410(b)(2)(A) provides that a plan may exclude certain employees who are included in a unit of employees covered by an agreement which the Secretary of Labor finds to be a collective bargaining agreement between employee representatives and one or more employers, if there is evidence that retirement benefits were the subject of good faith bargaining between such employee representatives and such employer or employers.

Nonresident aliens.—Section 410(b)(2)(C) provides that a plan may exclude nonresident alien employees who receive no earned income from the employer which constitutes income from sources within the United States.

15(a). Enter the total number of employees as of the date given on line 15. For Keogh plans, include all self-employed individuals. For a controlled group of corporations and for commonly controlled employers (whether or not incorporated), item 15 must be completed as though the controlled group constitutes a single entity.

15(l). The term "participant" includes retirees and other former employees (and the beneficiaries of both) who are receiving benefits under the plan or will at some future date receive benefits under the plan.

16. Employee contributions.—The term "mandatory contributions" means amounts contributed to the plan by the employee which are required as a condition of employment, as a condition of participation in such plan or as a condition of obtaining benefits under the plan attributable to employer contributions.

18. Integration.—If your plan is integrated with Social Security or Railroad Retirement, a computation appropriate to your situation should be submitted to show that your plan meets the integration requirements.

19. Vesting.—A plan to which section 411 applies must provide that each participant has a nonforfeitable right at all times to the portion of his account balance (if any) attributable to his own contributions. Such a plan must also provide a nonforfeitable right to a percentage of the participant's account balance attributable to employer contributions sufficient to satisfy one of the 3 vesting schedules provided by section 411(a)(2) (i.e. 10 year vesting, graduated vesting over 5–15 years, or rule of 45 vesting). Generally, the vesting schedule of a plan is treated as satisfying the vesting element of the nondiscrimination re-

Page 2

184

quirements of section 401(a)(4) if it satisfies the foregoing minimum vesting requirements of section 411. However, in certain cases, additional vesting may be required in order to prevent the turnover of rank-and-file participants from causing prohibited discrimination. Benefits should vest at a rate to assure that rank-and-file employees will appropriately share in the benefits and thus keep the plan from becoming discriminatory in operation. The indicated vesting may be full and immediate, graduated, or deferred, depending upon the facts and circumstances in each case. It may be necessary for us to request additional data in order to determine whether the plan is likely to be discriminatory.

21. Allocations and distributions—*Employer contributions.*—If other than "total compensation" (generally Form W–2 pay) is used as the basis for allocating the employer's contributions, you must show that the allocation formula does not produce discrimination in favor of the prohibited group that is, officers, shareholders and highly compensated employees. As a minimum requirement in establishing the acceptability of the allocation formulas, you must submit with this application a schedule similar in format to the following if there are more than 25 participants in the plan and the plan is not integrated:

1		2	3	4	5
*Brackets based on total compensation		Number of employees in bracket	Total compensation for employees included in compensation bracket	Amount of employer contributions actually allocated to employees included in compensation brackets	Percentage of total (col. 4 divided by col. 3)
At least	But not more than				
Totals					

*The compensation brackets used must reflect the pay pattern of the employer.

Distributions—*Restriction on optional modes.*—Optional modes of distribution must be limited so that if a beneficiary is a person other than the participant's spouse, the present value of the payments to be made to the employee participant shall be more than 50 percent of the present value of the total payments to be made to the participant and his beneficiaries.

In general, if the distribution of benefits is made over the joint life and last survivor expectancy of the participant and his spouse, each periodic payment to the beneficiary shall be no greater than each payment to the participant during his lifetime.

23(d). *Controlled group of corporations.*—If the adopting employer is a member of a controlled group of corporations (see section 414(b)) or of commonly controlled partnerships or proprietorships (see section 414(c)) attach statement showing in detail all members of the group, their relationship to the adopting employer, the types of plans each member has and the plans common to all members.

Additionally, item 15 must be completed as though the controlled group constitutes a single entity.

Codes for Principal Business Activity and Principal Product or Service

These industry titles and definitions are based, in general, on the Enterprise Standard Industrial Classification system developed by the Office of Management and Budget, Executive Office of the President, to classify enterprises by type of activity in which they are engaged. The system follows closely the Standard Industrial Classification used to classify establishments.

AGRICULTURE, FORESTRY, AND FISHING
Code
Farms:
0120 Field crop.
0150 Fruit, tree nut, and vegetable.
0180 Horticultural specialty.
0230 Livestock.
0270 Animal specialty.
Agricultural services and forestry:
0740 Veterinary services.
0750 Animal services, except veterinary.
0780 Landscape and horticultural services.
0790 Other agricultural services.
0800 Forestry.
Fishing, hunting, and trapping:
0930 Commercial fishing, hatcheries and preserves.
0970 Hunting, trapping, and game propagation.

MINING
Metal Mining:
1010 Iron ores.
1070 Copper, lead and zinc, gold and silver ores.
1098 Other metal mining.
1150 Coal mining.
Oil and gas extraction:
1330 Crude petroleum, natural gas, and natural gas liquids.
1380 Oil and gas field services.
Nonmetallic minerals (except fuels) mining:
1430 Dimension, crushed and broken stone; sand and gravel.
1498 Other nonmetallic minerals, except fuels.

Code
CONSTRUCTION
General building contractors and operative builders:
1510 General building contractors.
1531 Operative builders.
Heavy construction contractors:
1611 Highway and street construction.
1620 Heavy construction, except highway.
Special trade contractors:
1711 Plumbing, heating, and air conditioning.
1721 Painting, paper hanging, and decorating.
1731 Electrical work.
1740 Masonry, stonework, and plastering.
1750 Carpentering and flooring.
1761 Roofing and sheet metal work.
1771 Concrete work.
1781 Water well drilling.
1790 Miscellaneous special trade contractors.

MANUFACTURING
Food and kindred products:
2010 Meat products.
2020 Dairy products.
2030 Preserved fruits and vegetables.
2040 Grain mill products.
2050 Bakery products.
2060 Sugar and confectionery products.
2081 Malt liquors and malt.
2088 Alcoholic beverages, except malt liquors and malt.
2089 Bottled soft drinks, and flavorings.
2096 Other food and kindred products.
2100 Tobacco manufacturers.

Code
Textile mill products:
2228 Weaving mills and textile finishing.
2250 Knitting mills.
2293 Other textile mill products.
Apparel and other textile products:
2315 Men's and boys' clothing.
2345 Women's and children's clothing.
2388 Hats, caps, millinery, fur goods, and other apparel and accessories.
2390 Misc. fabricated textile products.
Lumber and wood products, except furniture:
2415 Logging camps and logging contractors, sawmills and planing mills.
2430 Millwork, plywood, and related products.
2498 Other wood products, including wood buildings and mobile homes.
2500 Furniture and fixtures.
Paper and allied products:
2625 Pulp, paper, and board mills.
2699 Other paper products.
Printing, publishing, and allied industries:
2710 Newspapers.
2720 Periodicals.
2735 Books, greeting cards, and misc. publishing.
2799 Commercial and other printing, and printing trade services.
Chemicals and allied products:
2815 Industrial chemicals, plastics materials and synthetics.
2830 Drugs.
2840 Soap, cleaners, and toilet goods.
2850 Paints and allied products.
2898 Agricultural and other chemical products.
Petroleum refining and related industries (including those integrated with extraction):
2910 Petroleum refining (including those integrated with extraction).
2998 Other petroleum and coal products.
Rubber and misc. plastics products:
3050 Rubber products; plastics footwear, hose and belting.
3070 Misc. plastics products.
Leather and leather products:
3140 Footwear, except rubber.
3198 Other leather and leather products.

(Codes continued on page 4) **Page 3**

Code

Stone, clay, glass, and concrete products:
3225 Glass products.
3240 Cement, hydraulic.
3270 Concrete, gypsum, and plaster products.
3298 Other nonmetallic mineral products.

Primary metal industries:
3370 Ferrous metal industries; misc. primary metal products.
3380 Nonferrous metal industries.

Fabricated metal products, except machinery and transportation equipment:
3410 Metal cans and shipping containers.
3428 Cutlery, hand tools, and hardware; screw machine products, bolts, and similar products.
3430 Plumbing and heating, except electric and warm air.
3440 Fabricated structural metal products.
3460 Metal forgings and stampings.
3470 Coating, engraving, and allied services.
3480 Ordnance and accessories, except vehicles and guided missiles.
3490 Misc. fabricated metal products.

Machinery, except electrical:
3520 Farm machinery.
3530 Construction, mining, and materials handling machinery and equipment.
3540 Metalworking machinery.
3550 Special industry machinery, except metalworking machinery.
3560 General industrial machinery.
3570 Office, computing, and accounting machines.
3598 Engines and turbines, service industry machinery, and other machinery, except electrical.

Electrical and electronic machinery, equipment, and supplies:
3630 Household appliances.
3665 Radio, television, and communication equipment.
3670 Electronic components and accessories.
3698 Other electric equipment.

Transportation equipment:
3710 Motor vehicles and equipment.
3725 Aircraft, guided missiles and parts.
3730 Ship and boat building and repairing.
3798 Other transportation equipment.

Measuring and controlling instruments; photographic and medical goods, watches and clocks:
3815 Scientific instruments and measuring devices; watches and clocks.
3845 Optical, medical, and ophthalmic goods.
3860 Photographic equipment and supplies.
3998 Other manufacturing products.

TRANSPORTATION, COMMUNICATION, ELECTRIC, GAS, AND SANITARY SERVICES

Transportation:
4000 Railroad transportation.

Local and interurban passenger transit:
4121 Taxicabs.
4189 Other passenger transportation.

Trucking and warehousing:
4210 Trucking, local and long distance.
4289 Public warehousing and trucking terminals.

Other transportation including transportation services:
4400 Water transportation.
4500 Transportation by air.
4600 Pipe lines, except natural gas.
4722 Passenger transportation arrangement.
4723 Freight transportation arrangement.
4799 Other transportation services.

Communication:
4825 Telephone, telegraph, and other communication services.
4830 Radio and television broadcasting.

Electric, gas, and sanitary services:
4910 Electric services.
4920 Gas production and distribution.
4930 Combination utility services.
4990 Water supply and other sanitary services.

WHOLESALE TRADE

Durable
5010 Motor vehicles and automotive equipment.
5030 Lumber and construction materials.
5050 Metals and minerals, except petroleum and scrap.
5060 Electrical goods.
5070 Hardware, plumbing and heating equipment.
5083 Farm machinery and equipment.
5089 Other machinery, equipment, and supplies.
5098 Other durable goods.

Code

Nondurable
5110 Paper and paper products.
5129 Drugs, chemicals, and allied products.
5130 Apparel, piece goods, and notions.
5140 Groceries and related products, except meats and meat products.
5147 Meats and meat products.
5150 Farm-product raw materials.
5170 Petroleum and petroleum products.
5180 Alcoholic beverages.
5190 Misc. nondurable goods.

RETAIL TRADE

Building materials, hardware, garden supply, and mobile home dealers:
5220 Building materials dealers.
5251 Hardware stores.
5261 Retail nurseries and garden stores.
5271 Mobile home dealers.

General merchandise:
5331 Variety stores.
5398 Other general merchandise stores.

Food stores:
5411 Grocery stores.
5420 Meat and fish markets and freezer provisioners.
5431 Fruit stores and vegetable markets.
5441 Candy, nut, and confectionery stores.
5460 Retail bakeries.
5480 Other food stores.

Automotive dealers and service stations:
5511 New and used car dealers.
5521 Used car dealers.
5531 Auto and home supply stores.
5541 Gasoline service stations.
5580 Boat aircraft and other automotive dealers.

Apparel and accessory stores:
5611 Men's and boys' clothing and furnishings.
5621 Women's ready-to-wear stores.
5631 Women's accessory and specialty stores.
5651 Family clothing stores.
5661 Shoe stores.
5681 Furriers and fur shops.
5698 Other apparel and accessory stores.

Furniture, home furnishings, and equipment stores:
5712 Furniture stores.
5718 Home furnishings, except appliances.
5722 Household appliance stores.
5730 Radio, television, and music stores.

Eating and drinking places:
5812 Eating places.
5813 Drinking places.

Miscellaneous retail stores:
5912 Drug stores and proprietary stores.
5921 Liquor stores.
5931 Used merchandise stores.
5941 Sporting goods stores and bicycle shops.
5942 Book stores.
5943 Stationery stores.
5944 Jewelry stores.
5945 Hobby, toy, and game shops.
5946 Camera and photographic supply stores.
5947 Gift, novelty, and souvenir shops.
5948 Luggage and leather goods stores.
5949 Sewing, needlework, and piece goods stores.
5961 Mail order houses.
5962 Merchandising machine operators.
5963 Direct selling organizations.
5980 Fuel and ice dealers.
5992 Florists.
5993 Cigar stores and stands.
5996 Other miscellaneous retail stores.

FINANCE, INSURANCE, AND REAL ESTATE

Banking:
6030 Mutual savings banks.
6050 Bank holding companies.
6090 Banks, except mutual savings banks and bank holding companies.

Credit agencies other than banks:
6120 Savings and loan associations.
6140 Personal credit institutions.
6150 Business credit institutions.
6199 Other credit agencies.

Security, commodity brokers, dealers, exchanges, and services:
6212 Security underwriting syndicates.
6218 Security brokers and dealers, except underwriting syndicates.
6299 Commodity contracts brokers and dealers; security and commodity exchanges; and allied services.

Insurance:
6355 Life insurance.
6356 Mutual insurance, except life or marine and certain fire or flood insurance companies.
6359 Other insurance companies.
6411 Insurance agents, brokers, and services.

Code

Real Estate:
6511 Real estate operators (except developers) and lessors of buildings.
6516 Lessors of mining, oil, and similar property.
6518 Lessors of railroad property and other real property.
6531 Real estate agents, brokers and managers.
6541 Title abstract offices.
6552 Subdividers and developers, except cemeteries.
6553 Cemetery subdividers and developers.
6599 Other real estate.
6611 Combined real estate, insurance, loans and law offices.

Holding and other investment companies:
6742 Regulated investment companies.
6743 Real estate investment trusts.
6744 Small business investment companies.
6749 Holding and other investment companies, except bank holding companies.

SERVICES

Hotels and other lodging places:
7012 Hotels.
7013 Motels, motor hotels, and tourist courts.
7032 Sporting and recreational camps.
7033 Trailer parks and camp sites.
7089 Other lodging places.

Personal services:
7215 Coin-operated laundries and dry cleaning.
7219 Other laundry, cleaning, and garment services.
7221 Photographic studios, portrait.
7231 Beauty shops.
7241 Barber shops.
7251 Shoe repair and hat cleaning shops.
7261 Funeral services and crematories.
7299 Miscellaneous personal services.

Business services:
7310 Advertising.
7340 Services to buildings.
7370 Computer and data processing services.
7392 Management, consulting, and public relations services.
7394 Equipment rental and leasing.
7398 Other business services.

Automotive repair and services:
7510 Automotive rentals and leasing, without drivers.
7520 Automobile parking.
7531 Automobile top and body repair shops.
7538 General automobile repair shops.
7539 Other automotive repair shops.
7540 Automotive services, except repair.

Miscellaneous repair services:
7622 Radio and TV repair shops.
7628 Electrical repair shops, except radio and TV.
7641 Reupholstery and furniture repair.
7680 Other miscellaneous repair shops.

Motion pictures:
7812 Motion picture production, distribution, and services.
7830 Motion picture theaters.

Amusement and recreation services:
7920 Producers, orchestras, and entertainers.
7932 Billiard and pool establishments.
7933 Bowling alleys.
7980 Other amusement and recreation services.

Medical and health services:
8011 Offices of physicians.
8021 Offices of dentists.
8031 Offices of osteopathic physicians.
8041 Offices of chiropractors.
8042 Offices of optometrists.
8048 Registered and practical nurses.
8050 Nursing and personal care facilities.
8060 Hospitals.
8071 Medical laboratories.
8072 Dental laboratories.
8098 Other medical and health services.

Other services:
8111 Legal services.
8200 Educational services.
8911 Engineering and architectural services.
8932 Certified public accountants.
8933 Other accounting, auditing, and bookkeeping services.
8999 Other services, not elsewhere classified.

TAX-EXEMPT ORGANIZATIONS
9001 Church.
9319 Other tax-exempt organization.
9904 Governmental instrumentality or agency.

U.S. GOVERNMENT PRINTING OFFICE : 19__ —O—559—027

Employee Census

Form 5302
(March 19—)
Department of the Treasury
Internal Revenue Service

▶ Attach to application for determination—defined benefit and defined contribution plans.

Schedule of 25 highest paid participating employees for taxable year ended ▶

(Round off to nearest dollar)

This Form is NOT Open to Public Inspection

Name of employer

Employer identification number

Line no.	Employee's last name and initials (List in order of compensation) (a)	Check		Age (d)	Years of service (e)	Annual Nondeferred Compensation					Defined Benefit	Defined Contribution		
		Officer or shareholder (b)	Percent of voting stock owned (c)			Used in computing benefits or employee's share of contributions (f)	Excluded (g)	Total (h)	Employee contributions under the plan (i)	Amount allocated under each other plan of deferred compensation (j)	Annual benefit expected (k)	Employer contribution allocated (l)	Number of units, if any (m)	Forfeitures reallocated in the year (n)
1														
2														
3														
4														
5														
6														
7														
8														
9														
10														
11														
12														
13														
14														
15														
16														
17														
18														
19														
20														
21														
22														
23														
24														
25														

Totals for above . . . .

Totals for all others (Specify number ▶

Totals for all participants . . . . .

187

General Instructions

(References are to the Internal Revenue Code)

Every employer or plan administrator who files an application for determination with respect to a defined benefit or a defined contribution plan is required to attach thereto this schedule, which must be completed in all details.

Section 6104(a)(1)(B) provides generally that applications, filed with respect to the qualification of a pension, profit-sharing or stock bonus plan, shall be open to public inspection. However, section 6104(a)(1)(C) provides that information concerning the compensation of any participant shall not be opened to public inspection. Consequently, the information contained in this schedule shall not be made available to the public, including plan participants and other employees of the employer who established the plan.

This schedule is to be used by the Internal Revenue Service in its analysis of an application for determination as to whether a plan of deferred compensation qualifies under section 401(a) or 405(a).

If an employer has fewer than 25 employees who are participants in his plan, he should list all the participants. Otherwise, only the 25 highest-paid participants need be listed.

Specific Instructions

In column (a), list the participants in the order of compensation, starting with the highest-paid participant followed by the next highest-paid participant, and so on.

In column (b), enter a check mark or an "X" to indicate that a participant is either an officer or a shareholder. If a participant is neither an officer nor a shareholder, make no entry in this column for such participant.

In column (c), enter only the percentage of voting stock owned by a participant. For example, participant "P" owns 200 shares of voting stock of the employer's 5,000 shares outstanding. His percentage is 4% (200÷5,000). If a participant owns only nonvoting stock of the employer, make no entry in this column.

In column (d), enter the attained age of each participant as of the end of the year for which this schedule applies. For example, if a participant reached his 47th birthday on January 7, 1975, and the schedule covers the calendar year 1975, enter 47 for that participant.

In column (e), enter the number of full years of service of each participant with respect to employment with the employer, and any prior employer if such employment is recognized for plan purposes.

In column (f), enter the amount of each participant's compensation that is recognized for plan purposes in computing the benefit (in case of a defined benefit plan) or in computing the amount of employer contribution that is allocated to the account of each participant (in the case of a defined contribution plan). Do not include any portion of the employer contributions to this or any other qualified plan as compensation for any participant.

In column (g), enter the amount of compensation that is not recognized for purposes of column (f). For example, if a participant received $12,500 compensation for the year, $1,000 of which was a bonus and the plan does not recognize bonuses for plan purposes, enter $11,500 in column (f) and $1,000 in column (g).

In column (h), enter the total amount of compensation for the year for each participant. The amount entered in this column will be the sum of the amounts entered in columns (f) and (g) with respect to each participant. Again, do not enter any amount of employer contributions made to this or any other qualified plan.

In column (i), enter the total amount of mandatory and voluntary contributions made by each participant. If the plan does not provide for employee contributions of any kind, leave blank or enter "NA".

In column (j), enter the portion of the employer's contribution (1) that is attributable to the cost for providing each participant's benefit under all plans other than this plan or (2) that is allocated to each participant's account under all plans other than this plan.

In column (k), enter the amount of benefit each participant may expect to receive at normal retirement age based on current information, assuming no future compensation increases. For example, under a 30% benefit plan, a participant whose benefit is based on annual compensation of $10,000 may expect an annual benefit of $3,000 ($10,000 x 30%) at retirement. In such case enter $3,000.

In column (l), enter the amount of the employer's contribution that is allocated to the account of each participant.

In column (m), enter the number of units, if any, used to determine the amount of the employer contribution that is allocated to each participant.

In column (n), enter the amount of the forfeitures that is allocated to each participant, unless forfeitures are allocated to reduce employer contributions.

FORM OF NOTICE TO INTERESTED PARTIES
OF APPLICATION FOR DETERMINATION

NOTICE TO

[describe class or classes of interested parties]

An Application is to be made to the Internal Revenue Service for an advance determination on the qualification of the following employee retirement plan.

(Name of Plan)	*(Plan I D #)*
....	....
(Name of Applicant)	*(Applicant I D #)*
....	....
(Name of Plan Administrator)	
....	

The application will be submitted to the District Director of the Internal Revenue at *(address of district office)* for an advance determination as to whether or not the plan qualifies under section *(enter 401(a), 403(a), or 405(a))* of the Internal Revenue Code, with respect to *(initial qualification, plan amendment, or plan termination)*.

The employees eligible to participate under the plan are

(describe by class)

....

....

....

The Internal Revenue Service *(enter has or has not)* previously issued a determination letter with respect to the qualification of this plan.

Each person to whom this notice is addressed is entitled to submit, or request the Department of Labor to submit, to the District Director described above a comment on the question of whether the plan meets the requirements for qualification under part I of Subchapter D of Chapter 1 of the Internal Revenue Code of 1954. Two or more such persons may join in a single comment or request. If such a person or persons request the Department of Labor to submit a comment and that department declines to do so in respect of one or more matters raised in the request, the person or persons so requesting may submit a comment to the District Director in respect of the matters on which the Department of Labor declines to comment. A comment submitted to the District Director must be received by him on or before

(date). However, if it is being submitted on a matter on which the Department of Labor was first requested, but declined to comment, the comment must be received by the District Director on or before the later of *(date)* of the 15th day after the day on which the Department of Labor notifies such person or persons that it declines to comment, but in no event later than *(date)*. A request of the Department of Labor to submit a comment must be received by that department on or before *(date)* or, if the person or persons making the request wish to preserve their right to submit a comment to the District Director in the event the Department of Labor declines to comment, on or before *(date)*.

Additional informational material regarding the plan and the procedures to be followed in submitting, or requesting the Department of Labor to submit, a comment, may be obtained at *(place or places reasonably accessible to the interested parties)*.

Index

INDEX